THE

EVERYTHING™

GAMES BOOK

The *EVERYTHING*™ Series:

The Everything™ *Bartender's Book*

The Everything™ *Christmas Book*

The Everything™ *Study Book*

The Everything™ *Wedding Book*

The Everything™ *Baby Names Book*

The Everything™ *Games Book*

THE

EVERYTHING™

GAMES BOOK

Hundreds of Classic Games for All Ages

Tracy Fitzsimmons

and

Pamela Liflander

Adams Media Corporation
HOLBROOK, MASSACHUSETTS

An Everything™ Series book.
The Everything™ Series is a trademark of Adams Media Corporation.

Published by Adams Media Corporation
260 Center Street, Holbrook, MA 02343

ISBN: 1-55850-643-8

Printed in the United States of America.

First Edition
J I H G F E D C B A

Library of Congress Cataloging-in-Publication Data

Fitzsimmons, Tracy.
    The everything games book : hundreds of classic games for all ages : all the games, all the rules, but no sore losers / Tracy Fitzsimmons and Pamela Liflander.
        p.   cm.
    Includes index.
    IBBN 1-55880-643-8 (pbk.)
    1. Games—Rules.   I. Liflander, Pamela.   II. Title.
GV1201.42.F58   1996
790.1'922—dc20   96-26131
                                                                                               CIP

This publication is designed to provide accurate and authoritative information with regard to the subject matter covered. It is sold with the understanding that the publisher is not engaged in rendering legal, accounting, or other professional advice. If legal advice or other expert assistance is required, the services of a competent professional person should be sought.
—From a *Declaration of Principles* jointly adopted by a Committee of the American Bar Association and a Committee of Publishers and Associations

Text illustrations by Barry Littmann.

*This book is available at quantity discounts for bulk purchases.
For information, call 1-800-872-5627 (in Massachusetts, 617-767-8100).*

Visit our home page at http://www.adamsmedia.com

Contents

Part 3: Tile and Dice Games

Part 4: Bar and Basement Games

Part 5: Outdoor Games

Part 6: Indoor Games

Part 7: Party Games

Part 8: Brain Teasers

Acknowledgments

The authors would like to thank the following people for helping to make this book possible: Melanie Mackinaw for generously helping in the research, Javier Amador-Peña for his design work, and David Merengi of Darts and Parts, of Lynn, MA, for his help compiling the dart section of the book.

I'd also like to thank the following people for their support and their knowledge of every game I didn't know how to play myself: Diane and Alan Fitzsimmons (and the rest of my family), Billy Self, Kristen Bergami, Meredith Self, Jen Famolare, Grega (and almost everyone in the Menlo crew), everyone at Adams Media Corporation, and especially Pam Liflander (next time I ask for an idea—forget it!)

Thanks again!
—Tracy

Introduction

Welcome to *The Everything Games Book*! Here you will find a wide selection of the most popular games that your entire family can enjoy together. Not only will you find new and exciting games to play, but you'll have a complete set of easy-to-follow rules and regulations—for literally hundreds of activities—right at your fingertips. Whether you are planning a party or just spending Sundays at home, *The Everything Games Book* provides many activities that your family will love to play.

Most of the games require little additional material. In fact, if you don't have a regulation set of anything that is required here (such as a chess set or a dart board), you can probably create one yourself. A little creativity and ingenuity go a long way, and don't have to cost you a fortune either.

The book is divided into eight distinct sections, which makes finding the right activity simple. Part 1 includes the most classic board games of all time: Checkers, Chinese Checkers, Chess, and Backgammon. While many people already own several of these games, the instruction books are long gone, if they ever existed. Luckily, we've included not only the rules, but secrets on how to beat your opponents, and quick lessons that will help you master each game with confidence.

Card games can provide hours of competitive enjoyment, and Part 2 contains the best card games from around the world. You'll find games for every member of the family, from simple children's games including Go Fish and Crazy Eights, to the very complicated Whist and Euchre. Whether you want to play alone or with a large group, cards are easily adaptable to suit every circumstance. Of the thirty-two chapters in this section, you'll find numerous variations of many of the games: when you do find a game that you like, chances are that there are a host of very similar games that you'll also love to play.

Part 3 focuses on tile and dice games, featuring Dice, Dominoes, and the perennial Asian favorite, Mah Jong. While these games do require specific equipment, once you understand how the games—and the dozens of variations—work, you'll easily see that it's worth a small investment. Tile and dice games are also perfect for early readers, and the rules can be adapted to get even the youngest players involved in learning how to count and match designs.

In Part 4, those games that have moved from the rec room to the bar, and now back again, are highlighted. More and more people are adding dart boards and pool tables to their homes, creating new excitement around these activities. We've provided the complete rules for each of these pastimes, without the technical jargon that makes them even more confusing. The games do require some understanding of the basics of each of these sports, and are not intended to teach you how to hold the cue or throw a dart. However, once you've mastered the basics, you'll be able to play any of the various games listed here.

Part 5 is a complete set of outdoor activities, ranging from sports such as Croquet and Volleyball, to children's relay races and Hopscotch. The wide assortment includes games for every level of physical coordination. But more important, these outdoor games will motivate you to take family time out into the fresh air. Some of the games require specific equipment, while others require little more than a standard rubber ball, or nothing at all.

The indoor games listed in Part 6 are the classic games that you grew up with and surely want to pass down to the younger generations: Jacks, Marbles, and Pickup Sticks. From our research, we've uncovered a groundswell of enthusiasm for these three games, so your kids better know how to play them!

Part 7 features an entire section devoted to children's party games. Whether you are planning a small gathering or inviting the entire fifth grade, you'll find dozens of activities to keep the party moving along. Most of these games require little preparation, and can be adapted to either outdoor or indoor settings. Most important, the clearly defined instructions leave little room for error, which is the last thing you want at a party.

The last section, Part 8, presents a small collection of brain teasers for quieter moments during the day. Many of these games are perfect for long drives, or just spending time together before bedtime. Whenever you can squeeze one of these games in, you'll be glad that you did.

It is our hope that *The Everything Games Book* can help create quality family time, fostering special moments that your loved ones will treasure forever. And if not, at least you'll know how to beat the pants off of them!

—Tracy Fitzsimmons and Pamela Liflander

Part One

Board Games

Board Games

Checkers

Checkers is played by two people, sitting opposite each other, using a board containing sixty-four squares, colored alternately black and white, or any other two colors. The pieces (or men) are comprised of twenty-four flat discs. Each player has twelve pieces of one color, usually either black, red, or white. The board is placed so that a white corner is at the lower left in front of each player. The object is to prevent an opponent from moving in his turn by capturing his twelve pieces, or blocking his remaining pieces.

Figure 1

The game begins when the men are placed on the first three lines of white squares. Their conventional numbers, for the sake of reference, appear in Figure 2. (Throughout this chapter, the upper half of the board is occupied by the twelve black men, and the lower half by their opponents, the white.)

BLACK

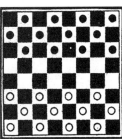

WHITE

Determining the Lead

The player who has chosen to take the black men leads off. This can be decided by a coin toss or any other means mutually agreed upon. The players play alternately, and if A has the lead and the black men in the first game, B will have them in the second game.

Moving

Figure 2

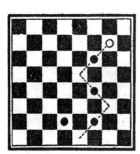

A move consists of pushing a man from the square on which it is situated to another adjacent square, which is unoccupied, along the white diagonal on which the player's man is posted. The men can only move forward, either to the right or the left, one square at a time, until they attain one of the four square positions on the opposite end of the board. When they accomplish this they become kings, and can move either forward or backward, but still only one square at a time.

Suppose Black wishes to move his man placed on square 10. He is entitled to move it to either square 14 or 15. When any one of his men arrives at square 29, 30, 31, or 32, it becomes a king. Similarly, when White moves, he must play along a white diagonal, either to right or left and in the direction approaching squares 1, 2, 3, and 4, on any of which a white man becomes a king.

Capturing

A player can take or "capture" an opponent's man in the direction in which he moves, by leaping over any hostile piece that is on an adjoining square, provided that there is a vacant white square beyond it. The capturing man is placed on the vacant square and the piece taken is removed from the board and held by the captor. If several pieces on a forward diagonal should be exposed by having open squares between them, they may all be taken at one capture, and the capturing man is then placed on the square beyond the last piece taken.

Figure 3

Suppose a white man is placed, as in Figure 3, on square 25. It would be able to capture black men on 22, 14, and 6 in a zigzag line, or on 22, 15, and 8, or on 22, 15, and 7.

Huffing

If a player neglects to take a piece when able, his opponent has three alternatives: (1) He may allow the move to hold good; (2) he may oblige the player in fault to capture the man or men liable to be taken; or (3) he may *huff,* which means he may remove the piece which could have effected the capture but did not, meaning his opponent's man.

In Figure 1, Black has to commence by moving one of the men placed on 9, 10, 11, or 12. Suppose he moves the man from 11 to 15. White replies by moving his piece from 22 to 18. Black can take White by leaping his man from 15 to 22, and removing the captured piece off the board. Should Black not take White but move in another direction, say from 12 to 16, he is liable to be huffed. White may remove the man with which Black should have made the capture as a penalty for not taking a white man off the board.

Instead of huffing, White may, if he thinks it is more to his advantage to do so, leave the offending piece on the board, without exacting any penalty, or he may compel Black to replace the man played to 16, and play from 15 to 22, thereby capturing the white man on 18.

When one party huffs the other, he does not replace the piece his adversary moved in error, but simply removes the man huffed from the board, and then plays his own move. The technical checkers term for this strategy is to *huff and move.*

A player entitled to huff must do so before he moves, or else he forfeits the right to do so during that turn; but if his adversary again neglects to take the man, the opponent can exact the penalty at his next turn.

If a player is able to take a piece in more than one way, he may elect to do so whichever way he pleases, except if he may capture three men in one way and only one man in another.

Kings

When a man belonging to either player arrives at one of the squares farthest from his own end of the board, whether by moving or capturing, he is made a King. The King is marked by having another piece of the same color placed on top of him, which is called *crowning him.* A King can move both forward and backward along the white diagonals. A King can take any number of pieces. However, he is equally liable to be huffed for not taking the correct number of pieces off the board.

The man's turn is finished on reaching one of the extreme squares and being made a king. He must then wait his antagonist's move before moving this piece again, whether to capture his opponent's piece or simply advance his own on the board.

The game is won by whoever can first succeed in capturing or blocking all his adversary's men, so that he has nothing left to move. A draw would occur when each player has a very small and equal force remaining, and neither player can make any decided impression on his antagonist. In such a circumstance, it would need to be obvious that the game might be indefinitely prolonged with the same hopeless chance of natural termination as at the first moment of the pieces being resolved into the position in question.

The Move

To have the move does not mean to be next to move, but that you occupy that position on the board that will eventually enable you to force your adversary into a confined position, and that at the end of the game will secure for yourself the last move. If your men are in a confined state, the move is not only of no use to you, but may occasion the loss of the game.

To know in any particular situation whether you have the move, you must count the men and the squares, and if the number of men are an even number and the squares odd, or the men odd and the squares even, you have the move. If your men and squares are both odd or even your adversary has the move.

There is a second mode: count all the pieces (of both colors) standing on those columns (not diagonals) that have a white square at the bottom, and if the number is odd, and White has to play, he has the move; if the number is even, Black has the move.

In general, there is no advantage to playing first. Whoever goes out first does not have the move, as the men and squares are both even. The second player has the first move, though it can be of no service to him in that early stage of the game. The truth is, that when the combatants continue giving man for man, the move will alternately belong to one and the other. The first player will have it at odd men 11, 9, 7, 5, 3, 1; the second player will have it at even men 12, 10, 8, 6, 4, 2; and therefore some error must be committed, on one side or the other, before the move can be forced out of this groove. So, a player who has the move should avoid exchanging, unless he can force a second exchange, and so recover the move.

The Rules of the Game

1. The choice of men that each player shall take in the opening game is to be decided by tossing a coin or any other means agreed upon. Whoever gains the choice can begin with the black men, or call on his adversary to do so.

2. If a series of games is played, the choice of lead and black men belongs to each player alternately, whether the previous game was won or drawn.

3. A player should not point over the board with his finger, or use any action that may interrupt his opponent's view of the game.

4. At any part of the game it is allowable to readjust the men on their proper squares, provided that the player warns his adversary before doing so. In the absence of such intimation, if a player, whose turn it is to play, touches a piece, he must play it in one direction or other, if possible. If a piece that cannot be moved is touched, there is no penalty.

5. A move or capture of a piece is completed as soon as the hand is withdrawn form the piece played.

6. If a piece is moved so far as to be in any way visible over the angle of the square on which it is resting, that move must be completed notwithstanding that the player so moving it may incur the penalty of being huffed.

7. If a piece is illegally moved, the adversary may require the same piece to make a proper move in either direction he pleases, or may allow the false move to stand good. But if the piece cannot be legally moved in any direction, the adversary has only the option of allowing the false move to stand good.

8. If a player captures one of his own men, the opponent has the option whether the piece capturing in error shall be replaced or allowed to remain where placed in error.

9. If more than one piece can be captured at one move and the player elects to make such a move, he is liable to Rule 12 if he moves his hand from the capturing piece while any of the pieces remain untaken.

10. When a player is in a position from which he can capture on either of two forward diagonals, he may do so whichever way he pleases, without regard to the one capture comprising greater force than the other. For example, if one man is one way or two are another way, a player may capture either the one man or the two at his option.

11. When a player moves a man to the end of the board, which entitles it to be made a king, the adversary is bound to crown it.

12. Each player is obliged to move within a specified time agreed upon by the players before commencing the game. A player who does not move within such time is considered to have lost the game.

13. If a player neglects to take a piece when able, his opponent has three alternatives: either he may allow the move to hold good, or may oblige the player in fault to capture the man or men, or may huff the pieces that could have effected the capture. The necessity for this law is evident, as it is not unusual to sacrifice

The Rules of the Game

two or three men is succession, with the express object of making some decisive and brilliant coup. Were this law different, a player might take the first man so offered, and on the second one being placed, might refuse to capture by quietly standing the huff.

14. If a player entitled to huff has made his election to touch the piece that is liable to be huffed, he is bound to huff, and cannot exact any other penalty.

15. After a player entitled to huff has moved without exercising his right, he cannot remedy the omission unless his adversary should still neglect to take or change the position of the piece concerned, and so render himself liable a second time. It matters not how long a piece has remained; it may at any time either be huffed or the adversary be compelled to take it.

16. When several pieces are taken at one move, they must not be removed from the board until the capturing piece has completed its full move.

17. The act of huffing does not constitute a move, but a huff and a move go together.

18. When at the end of a game a small degree of force remains, the player who has the superiority of force may be required to win the game in a certain number of moves; and if he cannot do so, the game must be abandoned as a draw. A full move in this sense is not complete until both sides have played.

19. When three Kings remain against two, the player with the three may be required to win after not more than forty moves (twenty would be better in our opinion) have been played by each player, the moves to be computed from the point at which notice is given.

20. When two Kings remain against one, the player with the two Kings may similarly be required to win after not more than twenty moves have been played by each player.

21. In no case can these numbers be exceeded, after having been once claimed, and even if one more move would win the game, it must be declared a draw.

22. The rule is to play on the white squares; the exception is to play on the black

The Secrets of the Game

1. At the beginning, it is better to play out your men toward the middle of the board, in the form of a pyramid, than to play into the side squares, because a man at the side can only move in one direction, and consequently loses half his power.

2. Be careful to back up your advanced men, so as not to leave a chance of your opponent making a two-in-one move.

3. Open your game at all times with a plan; this way you will acquire a method in both attack and defense.

4. Play slowly at first and choose an antagonist who will agree to allow you an unconditional time for the consideration of a difficult position rather than one who demands a strict observance of a designated time period.

5. A few judicious exchanges at the opening of the game will greatly simplify its progress; a crowded game is a frequent cause of embarrassment to the beginner. You should, however, vary your tactics accordingly whether you are playing with a player superior or inferior to yourself. If playing with an inferior, keep your game complicated; if with a superior, simplify it as much as possible.

6. Before making a move, look over the board and try to discover your adversary's plan of attack. If you succeed in doing so, you can frequently counteract it, and change his strategy.

7. Never make an attack without a plan, as you will then allow your adversary to take advantage of your lack of planning.

8. When there is only one way of taking a man, take it without hesitation.

9. If you find there is no possibility of saving a piece, live with it, and immediately work to retrieve your position by gaining a move elsewhere.

10. Should your opponent weaken his double or single corner, attack him at this, his weakest point.

11. Avoid scattering your forces; as they get fewer, concentrate them as much as possible.

12. When you have once gained an advantage in the number of your pieces over your opponent, you should increase the proportion by exchanges. As a general rule, many games could not be won without the superior force acting in this manner. Also, in attempting to effect exchanges, you are liable to damage your own position, so be cautious.

13. As it is advantageous for the stronger side to exchange, try to avoid being forced to do so by keeping your Kings in close order, with the side of the board as the base of your operation.

14. Never resort to a risky move unless you realize that you are losing, and you would obtain a decided advantage should your move succeed. When in an equal position with your opponent, wait for an opportunity, and choose a draw rather that make a risky move.

15. When you realize your opponent is aware of the trap you have set for him, give it up at once, and try

The Secrets of the Game

some other attack, unless you can force the position.

16. When fiercely attacked, it is always wiser to exchange, and very frequently even to sacrifice a piece than to attempt to defend a weak position.

17. While moving toward creating a

King, move your men so as to prevent your opponent from pushing his men toward your side of the board.

18. When the force of each player is equal, it is generally a decided advantage to have the move, but not always.

Chinese Checkers

Chinese Checkers can be played with up to six players. If two people are playing, they sit opposite each other, choosing opposite points of the star. If three people are playing, the players sit at every other point. Each player chooses ten marbles of the same color, and places them in the holes in the point of the star in front of them. The object of the game is to be the first player to get ten marbles across the board to the opposite point on the star.

Figure 4

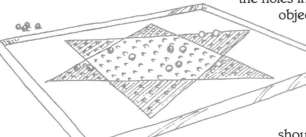

Playing

Players choose among themselves who should go first, and the rest of the players will rotate to the left of the first player. The first player moves a marble one hole in any direction along the lines provided on the board, as long as the hole is empty.

The play can consist of moving to a hole adjacent to the marble's starting point, or by jumping over a marble to the next hole along the line, if there is an empty space beyond the marble. A marble can jump either his own color or any other player's. A play can also be a series of jumps over various marbles, as long as the player follows the lines on the board, and there are empty spaces between marbles for him to land. The marbles that are jumped over are not removed from the board. When the first player is finished moving his marble as far as possible, his turn is over and the player on his left continues, and so on.

Chess

Chess is played by two people, sitting opposite each other, using a board containing sixty-four squares, colored alternately black and white, or any other two colors. Each player has sixteen pieces (or men), all of the same color, but varying in size and shape. The object of the game is to seize the adversary's King.

WE'VE GOT TO STOP MEETING THIS WAY.

The game begins with the men placed on the first two lines of squares. The board must be placed so that each player has a white square at the right-hand corner of the board. The following diagram shows the position of the forces at the commencement of the game.

Figure 5

BLACK

WHITE

Determining the Lead

The players flip a coin, for move and choice of color, though it is usually the rule for the player who has the first move to play with the white men.

The Pieces and Their Movements

The white Queen must always occupy a white square, and the black Queen a black square. The white King, on the contrary, must always occupy a black square and the black King a white one, the Kings and Queens respectively facing each other. The Bishops on each side are posted nearest to the Kings and Queens; next come the Knights, while the Rooks occupy the corner squares.

The King

The King moves only one square at a time in any direction—backward, forward, laterally, and diagonally. Once in the game, however, he has the privilege of moving two squares when castling. He cannot move onto a square next to the one occupied by the hostile King, for the Kings must always be separated from each other by an intervening square. The King cannot move into check, i.e., onto any square that is commanded by a hostile piece or Pawn. He can, however, capture any unprotected piece or Pawn of the enemy on any square adjacent to his own in any direction. When the King is placed in such a position that he cannot avoid capture, he is "checkmated," and the game is lost.

The Queen
The Queen is the most powerful of all the pieces, and can be moved any number of squares in any direction—backward, forward, sideway, or diagonally—on an unobstructed range. When posted on any of the four center squares, she commands twenty-seven out of the sixty-four squares of the board.

The Rook
The Rook is the next most powerful piece. He moves in a straight line, backward, forward, and laterally, but not diagonally.

The Bishop
The Bishop moves diagonally, but only on squares of its own color. For example, the white King's Bishop can never move onto a black square, nor the black King's Bishop onto a white one. On an unobstructed range the Bishop may be moved from a corner square to the opposite corner.

The Knight
The Knight moves one square diagonally and one square straight, and is the only piece that has the privilege of jumping over another piece or Pawn, whether of his own or the opposing force's.

Figure 6

In Figure 6, the black Knight, standing on his King's Bishop's third square, commands eight squares. Were any hostile white man posted on any of these squares he could capture it, removing it from its square and occupying the vacated square himself.

The Pawn

The Pawn moves forward one square at a time, but on his first move may be advanced either one or two squares, at the player's discretion. If, however, he is moved two squares, and a hostile Pawn commands the square over which he leaps, the hostile Pawn has the choice of taking him and intercepting him in his leap, as if he had only moved forward one square. This is called taking *en passant.* The Pawn captures diagonally and in a forward movement only. On reaching the eighth square of any file on which he is advancing, he may be exchanged for a Queen, or any other piece that the player may choose; or he may be refused promotion by his player and remain a Pawn, as before. In such a case he is called a *dummy* Pawn.

Chess Notation

The following are the English notations of chess moves, for the purpose of reading and recording games. Each square is named after the piece that occupies it. For instance, the square on which the King stands is called K sq., or K1, and all the squares are numbered vertically on the whole *file* from 1 to 8. Taking the King and Queen as the center pieces, all the pieces on the right side of the King are called the King's pieces, and the pieces on the left of the Queen are called Queen's pieces, i.e., Queen's Bishop=QB; Queen's Knight=QKt; Queen's Rook=QR. The same rule applies to the black pieces: thus, White's King's square would be Black's King's eight=K8; while Black's King's square would be White King's eight=K8; and so on with all the other squares. (See Figure 7.)

BLACK — *Figure 7*

Q.R.sq. / Q.R.8.	Q.Kt.sq. / Q.Kt.8.	Q.B.sq. / Q.B.8.	Q.sq. / Q.8.	K.sq. / K.8.	K.B.sq. / K.B.8.	K.Kt.s. / K.Kt.8.	K.R.sq. / K.R.8.
Q.R.2. / Q.R.7.	Q.Kt.2. / Q.Kt.7.	Q.B.2. / Q.B.7.	Q.2. / Q.7.	K.2. / K.7.	K.B.2. / K.B.7.	K.Kt.2. / K.Kt.7.	K.R.2. / K.R.7.
Q.R.3. / Q.R.6.	Q.Kt.3. / Q.Kt.6.	Q.B.3. / Q.B.6.	Q.3. / Q.6.	K.3. / K.6.	K.B.3. / K.B.6.	K.Kt.3. / K.Kt.6.	K.R.3. / K.R.6.
Q.R.4. / Q.R.5.	Q.Kt.4. / Q.Kt.5.	Q.B.4. / Q.B.5.	Q.4. / Q.5.	K.4. / K.5.	K.B.4. / K.B.5.	K.Kt.4. / K.Kt.5.	K.R.4. / K.R.5.
Q.R.5. / Q.R.4.	Q.Kt.5. / Q.Kt.4.	Q.B.5. / Q.B.4.	Q.5. / Q.4.	K.5. / K.4.	K.B.5. / K.B.4.	K.Kt.5. / K.Kt.4.	K.R.5. / K.R.4.
Q.R.6. / Q.R.3.	Q.Kt.6. / Q.Kt.3.	Q.B.6. / Q.B.3.	Q.6. / Q.3.	K.6. / K.3.	K.B.6. / K.B.3.	K.Kt.6. / K.Kt.3.	K.R.6. / K.R.3.
Q.R.7. / Q.R.2.	Q.Kt.7. / Q.Kt.2.	Q.B.7. / Q.B.2.	Q.7. / Q.2.	K.7. / K.2.	K.B.7. / K.B.2.	K.Kt.7. / K.Kt.2.	K.R.7. / K.R.2.
Q.R.8. / Q.R.sq.	Q.Kt.8. / Q.Kt.sq.	Q.B.8. / Q.B.sq.	Q.8. / Q.sq.	K.8. / K.sq.	K.B.8. / K.B.sq.	K.Kt.8. / K.Kt.s.	K.R.8. / K.R.sq.

WHITE

The horizontal divisions are called *rows,* and the vertical divisions are called *files.* Other abbreviations used in notation are: *sq.* for square, *ch.* or *(+)* for check, *x* for takes, *dis. ch.* for discovered check, *dble. ch.* for double check, *en pass.* for en passant. *P takes P*, or *P x P*, means Pawn takes Pawn.

Technical Terms

Check and Checkmate—The King is said to be in check when he is attacked by a hostile piece or Pawn, of which warning must be given by the adversary calling, "check." One of three things must then be done: the King must move out of check; or he must take the piece or Pawn that checks him; or, finally, a piece or Pawn must be interposed between the King and the attacking hostile man. If none of these things can be done, the King is *checkmated* and the game is lost.

Figure 8

BLACK

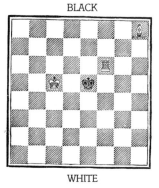

WHITE

Figure 9

BLACK

WHITE

Figure 10

BLACK

WHITE

When check is given by a Knight, the first of the above three courses must be adopted, i.e., the King must move. Several other kinds of check are given in the game. Simple check is when the King is attacked by a single piece or Pawn. Double check occurs when the King is attacked by two pieces at the same time in consequence of a discovered check.

The following diagram illustrates a discovered check. White, having to play, can give discovered check from the Bishop by moving his Rook on fourteen different squares. (See Figure 8.)

Perpetual check occurs when the position is such that the attacked King cannot escape from one check without rendering himself constantly liable to another. Perpetual check constitutes not a winning, but a drawn game, and may be resorted to, when possible, to save a losing player from defeat. (See Figure 9.)

In the above position Black draws the game by establishing a perpetual check, thus: Black is threatened with checkmate by Q to R 8, or Q to Kt 7. But, it being Black's move, he would play Kt to Kt 6: chi.; White *must* play K to R2; Black again returns to his old position, and as there is nothing to prevent his repeatedly making these two moves. Therefore, the game is drawn.

Stalemate—A stalemate occurs when the King, though not in check, *cannot move without going into check,* and when no other piece or Pawn can be moved. The game is then drawn. Stalemate necessarily occurs only at the end of a game, when the King on one side stands alone or without any available pieces to move.

In figure 10, Black, having to move, is stalemated, his King being unable to move on any square out of check from the Pawns, and being unable to capture the Pawn next him.

Smothered Mate, or Philidor's Legacy—when the King is so hemmed in that he cannot move out of check of a hostile Knight. It occasionally happens that this mate can be effected by heroically sacrificing the Queen.

En Prise—French, meaning "exposed to capture." When a piece or Pawn is attacked by a hostile man, it is said to be *en prise*—i.e., in danger of being captured.

J'Adoube—French, meaning, "I adjust or replace," to be used when a player touches a piece or Pawn to adjust it in the center of the square it occupies, without intending to move it.

Forced Move—When a player can only make one move on the board, it is called a forced move.

Minor Pieces—The Knights and Bishops are so termed to distinguish them from the Queens and Rooks.

The Exchange—Winning or losing a Rook for a minor piece is called winning or losing the exchange.

Gambit—This term is derived from an Italian word meaning "to trip up in wrestling," and is used in Chess in those openings in which the first player purposely sacrifices a Pawn for the attack. The Pawn sacrificed is called the *gambit Pawn.*

Doubled Pawn—When two Pawns are on the same file they are called *doubled Pawns.*

Isolated Pawn—A Pawn standing alone without the support of other Pawns is called an *isolated Pawn.*

Passed Pawn—A Pawn is labeled *passed* when the enemy has no Pawns either in front or on the adjacent files right or left to obstruct its march to *queen.*

Drawn Game—When neither player can checkmate his opponent, the result is a drawn game. Drawn games are brought about (1) by stalemate; (2) by perpetual check; (3) when both players persist in repeating the same moves; (4) when there is not sufficient force to give checkmate, as a King and two Knights only, or a King and Bishop; (5) when the forces on each side are equal, or nearly so, as Queen versus Queen, Rook versus Rook, etc.; (6) when a player, having sufficient force, as, for instance, a Knight and a Bishop, is unable to effect checkmate in fifty moves.

To Take En Passant—The Pawn has the privilege, on his *first* move, of advancing two squares. If, in thus advancing, he passes a square occupied by one of the enemy's Pawns that has advanced to a fifth square, he is liable to be taken by the said Pawn, which may intercept him in his passage or leap, as if he had only moved one square.

But, if taken *en passant,* he must be taken at once on the move. He cannot be thus captured at any subsequent stage of the game. Only pawns—not pieces—can be taken *en passant.*

False Move—Any illegal move, such as moving a Knight like a Bishop, or castling when the King is in check or has been already moved, is called a false move.

Relative Value of the Pieces

In the middle of the game the Queen is usually better than two Rooks; but in the end two Rooks are stronger than the Queen.

Sometimes the Queen may be advantageously exchanged for three minor pieces, but as a rule three minor pieces are not preferable to the Queen.

A Rook and two Pawns are usually better than two minor pieces; but a Bishop and Knight are better than a Rook and Pawn and far superior to a single Rook.

Two Bishops and a Knight are better than two Knights and a Bishop.

Two Bishops are stronger than two Knights; two Bishops can easily force checkmate, whereas two Knights can never do so.

Generally speaking, the Bishop is always better than the Knight, but the real relative value of these two pieces depends on their position. A Bishop and a Knight are each worth more than three Pawns.

In average positions the Queen should win against (1) a Rook, (2) Rook and Pawn, (3) two Knights, (4) two Bishops, (5) a Bishop and Knight (6) a Bishop or Knight; but in certain exceptional situations the weaker force can draw the game.

A Rook and Knight can only win against a Rook in very rare instances; in fact, in ninety-nine cases out of a hundred Rook and Knight versus Rook is a legitimately drawn game.

A Rook can usually win against a Bishop or Knight when there are an equal number of Pawns on each side, though in the end the Rook against Bishop is generally a draw.

Rook versus Knight is also usually a drawn game, unless the Knight can be prevented from approaching his King.

The Rules of the Game

1. The board must be so placed during play that each combatant has a white square in his right-hand corner. If, during the progress of a game, either player discovers that the board has been improperly placed, he may insist on its being adjusted.

The Rules of the Game

2. If, at any time in the course of the game, it is found that the men were not properly placed, or that one or more of them were omitted at the beginning, the game in question must be annulled. If at any time it is discovered that a man has been dropped off the board, and moves have been made during its absence, such moves shall be retracted and the man restored. If the players cannot agree as to the square on which it should be replaced, the game must be annulled.

3. The right of making the first move and (if either player require it) of choosing the color, which shall be retained throughout the sitting, must be decided by flipping a coin. In any series of games between the same players at one sitting, each shall have the first move alternately in all the games, whether won or drawn. In an annulled game, the player who had the first move in that game shall move first in the next.

4. If a player makes the first move in a game when it is not his turn to do so, the game must be annulled if the error has been noticed before both players have completed the fourth move. After four moves on each side have been made, the game must be played out as it stands.

5. If, in the course of a game, a player moves a man when it is not his turn to play, he must retract the move, and after his adversary has moved must play the same man if it can be played legally.

6. A player must never touch any of the men except when it is his turn to play, or except when he touches a man for the purpose of adjusting it; in the latter case he must inform his opponent before touching the piece. A player who touches with his hand (except accidentally) one of his own men when it is his turn to play, must move it, if it can be legally moved, unless, before touching it, he says, "I adjust," as above; and a player who touches one of his adversary's men, under the same conditions, must take it if he can legally do so. If, in either case, the move cannot be legally made, the offender must move his King; but in the event of the King having no legal move, there shall be no penalty.

   If a player holds a man in his hand when he can't decide which square to play it, his adversary may require him to replace it until he has decided its destination; that man, however, must be moved.

   If a player, when it is his turn to play, touches with his hand (except accidentally or in castling) more than one of his own men, he must play any one of them, legally movable, that his opponent selects. If he touches two or more of the adversary's men, he must capture whichever of them his antagonist chooses, provided it can be legally taken. If it happens that none of the men so touched can be moved or captured, the offender must move his King; but if the King cannot be legally moved, there shall be no penalty.

7. If a player makes a false move—that is, either by playing a man of his own to a square to which it cannot be legally moved, or by capturing an adverse man by a move that cannot be legally made—he must, at the choice of his opponent, and according to the case, either move his own man legally, capture the man legally, or move any other man legally movable.

The Rules of the Game

If, in the course of a game, an illegality is discovered (not involving a King being in check), and the move on which it was committed has been replied to, and not more than four moves on each side have been made subsequently, all these latter moves, including that on which the legality was committed, must be retracted. If more than four moves on each side have been made, the game must be played out as it stands.

8. A player must audibly say, "Check," when he makes a move that puts the hostile King in check. The mere announcement of check shall have no significance if check is not actually occurring. If check is occurring, but not announced, and the adversary makes a move that blocks the check, the move must stand.

   If check occurs and is announced, and the adversary neglects to block it, he shall not have the option of capturing the checking piece or of covering, but must "move his King" out of check; but if the King has no legal move, there shall be no penalty.

   If, in the course of the game, a King has been left in check for one or more moves on either side, all the moves subsequent to that on which the check was given must be retracted. Should these not be remembered, the game must be annulled.

9. A player is not bound to enforce a penalty. A penalty can only be enforced by a player before he has touched a man in reply. Should he touch a man in reply in consequence of a false or illegal move of his opponent, or a false cry of check, he shall not be compelled to move that man, and his right to enforce a penalty shall remain. When a King is moved as a penalty, it cannot castle on that move.

10. Once in the game, if neither King nor Rook have been previously moved, the King has the privilege of moving two squares in conjunction with either of the Rooks. This operation is referred to as *castling*. If the space between the King and Rook is unoccupied, the King moves two squares to the right or left, and the Rook is placed on the next square that was originally occupied by the King. The King must not be in check, nor can he alight upon or pass over a square threatened by a hostile piece or Pawn.

    In castling, the player shall move King and Rook simultaneously, or shall touch the King first. If he touches the Rook first, he must not let go of it before having touched the King; or his opponent may claim the move of the Rook as a complete move.

11. A player may call upon his opponent to draw the game, or to mate him within fifty moves on each side, whenever his opponent persists in repeating a particular check, or series of checks, or the same line of play, or whenever he has a King alone on the board, or one of the following occurs against an equal or superior force:

The Rules of the Game

King and Queen,
King and Rook,
King and Bishop,
King and Knight,

or against King and Queen:

King and two Bishops,
King and two Knights,
King, Bishop, and Knight,

and in all analogous cases; and whenever one player considers that his opponent can force the game, or that neither side can win it, he has the right of submitting the case to the umpire or bystanders, who shall decide whether it is one for the fifty-move counting. Should he not be mated within the fifty moves, he may claim that the game shall proceed.

For example: White has a King and Queen against Black's King and Rook. Black claims to count fifty moves. At the forty-ninth move, White, by a blunder, loses his Queen. Black can claim that the game proceed, and White in his turn may claim the fifty-move counting.

12. Should a player be left with no other move than to take a Pawn in passing, he shall be bound to play that move.

13. When a Pawn has reached the eighth square, the player has the option of selecting a piece, except a King, whether such piece has been previously lost or not, whose name and powers it shall then assume, or of deciding that it shall remain a Pawn. This is called either *queening a Pawn,* or a *Pawn queens.* Thus one player may have two or more Queens, Rooks, Knights, or Bishops on the board at the same time. A player can often win a game by claiming a Knight or a Rook, whereas he would lose by claiming a Queen.

14. If a player abandons the game, discontinues his moves, voluntarily resigns, upsets the board, or refuses to abide by these laws, he must be considered to have lost the game.

15. The umpire shall have authority to decide any question that may arise in the course of a game, but must never interfere except when asked. He must always apply the laws as expressed, and not assume the power of modifying them or of deviating from them in particular cases, according to his own judgment. When a question is submitted to the umpire, or to bystanders, by both players, the umpire's decision shall be final.

The Secrets of the Game

1. Never take back a move.
2. Accept odds only from players vastly superior to yourself.
3. Bring out your pieces as rapidly as possible; in other words, develop your game with the least possible delay.
4. When you have a Knight or Bishop strongly posted either in the center of the board or in your enemy's entrenchments, try to hold that position until the end of the game or until your opponent is driven to a liquidation of pieces favorable to you. In general, avoid relinquishing similarly strong positions.
5. It is a good idea to castle on the King's side early in the game.
6. After castling on the King's side, beware of uselessly pushing your King's Rook's Pawn to one square to prevent your King's Knight from being pinned by the hostile Queen's Bishop. Such a precaution is often a mere waste of time, and often results in your being exposed to a terrible attack.
7. Be wary of allowing your adversary to post either of his Knights at his King's Bishop's fifth square after you have castled on the King's side. Either capture or dislodge such an intruder.
8. Try to post one of your Knights at your King's Bishop's fifth square, and, if possible, maintain him there. This is the most threatening position he can occupy after your opponent has castled on King's side, especially if he has pushed his King's Rook's Pawn one square.
9. When you have played your Queen's Knight to Queen's Bishop's third, if you cannot post him at Queen's fifth square, bring him round by way of K 2 (or Q sq.) to KKt 3 and B5 (or K3 and B5).
10. When you find that you have made a bad move, try to avoid the consequences and to retrieve your position on your next turn.

A Preliminary Game

The game of Chess is so full of intricacies, requiring not only thorough method, but also the exercise of foresight, that an example of a simple game, thoroughly explained at every step, is necessary to gain better insight. You can follow the moves using Figure 5 as a starting point. All the plays are numbered. In formal matches, the defending player always takes Black:

White	Black
1 P—K4	1 P—K4
2 Kt—KB 3	

This is a good move, bringing out a piece and attacking at once Black's undefended King's Pawn.

	2 Kt—QB 3

Black defends his Pawn.

3 B—B4	

White attacks Black's KBP, with the idea of bringing another piece to bear on it, as it could not be taken at this time since it is defended by the King. Remember, a Bishop is worth at least three Pawns.

	3 B—B4

4 P—Q3	

This move liberates the Queen's Bishop.

	4 P—Q3
5 Kt—QB 3	5 Kt—KB 3

6 Castles   6 Castles
7 B—KKt 5

Here White pins the black Knight, which cannot be moved without losing the Queen.

	7 P—KR 3

Black tries to drive away this troublesome Bishop.

8 B x Kt	8 Q x B

Black retakes with Queen in order to avoid a doubled Pawn on KBP file, and the attack of Q—Q2 threatened by White.

9 Kt—Q5	9 Q—Kt 3
10 Kt x QBP	10 B—KR 6

Black leaves the Rook open to be taken, and menacing immediate checkmate.

11 Kt—KR 4

White instead stops the mate and attacks the Queen.

	11 Q—B 3
12 Kt x R	12 Q x Kt
13 P x B	13 Q x KRP
14 Kt—B7	

White is overanxious to save his piece.

	14 Kt—Q5

15 P—KB 3

White is vainly trying to prevent the danger.

	15 Kt x KBP

Black discovers that he is in double check. The white King is now checked both by Bishop and knight, and must move into the corner square.

16 K—R sq.	16 Q x RP checkmate

Backgammon

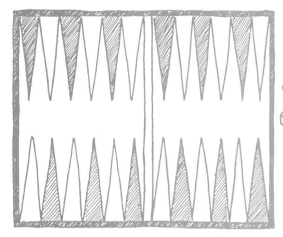

Backgammon is played by two people, sitting opposite each other. The borders of the board should be raised, and across the middle of the board, there should be a raised bar, separating the board into two tables, called *inner* (or home) and *outer* tables.

The object of the game is for each player to bring his men around and into his own inner table. This is accomplished by throws of the dice.

Each player has fifteen pieces (or men), which are small, flat disks. The tables are marked with twenty-four points, colored alternately white and black, or any other two colors. The points should be long enough to hold five men, about half of the fifth man projecting beyond the point. Between the points in White's tables and those in Black's tables is a space on which the dice are thrown.

Each point has a name: The one to the extreme left in White's inner table is called White's Ace point; the next, White's Deuce point; the others in order, White's Three, Four, Five, and Six points. The Ace point in White's outer table is called his Bar point. The points on Black's table are similarly named.

Figure 11

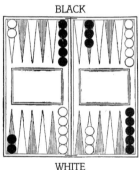

BLACK

WHITE

Throwing

Each player is provided with a box and two dice, and pieces are moved around the board depending on the number of spots that are faced up when the dice are thrown.

At the start, each player takes his dice-box and shakes one die in it, two fingers being placed over the open end of the box to prevent the die from being shaken out.

After shaking, the die is thrown on the board. The player who throws the higher number has the first play. He may either adopt the two numbers just thrown, or he may take up the dice and throw them again.

Playing

After throwing the dice, the caster should call out the numbers rolled. If he throws a Four and a Two, he calls "Four Two" (the higher number always being called first), and proceeds to move any of his men a number of points corresponding to the numbers thrown.

The march of men is from the opponent's inner table to his outer table, then to the caster's outer table, and lastly to his own home table.

The White and Black men are moved in opposite directions.

The move may be divided by two men: One man may be moved the entire value of the throw, or two men may move, each one moving one of the numbers thrown. Thus, White might play Four Two by carrying one man from the Six point of Black's outer table to his own six point; or he might play one man from the Deuce point of his outer table to his Four point, and another man from his Six point to his Four point.

When men are played in the latter example, so as to occupy a previously blank point with two men, it is called making a point. If White plays in this way, the man who played the Four will remain on a point by himself. This is called *leaving a blot.*

If two equal numbers are thrown (called doubles), the caster plays double what he throws. For example, if he throws two Aces, he plays four Aces instead of two.

The players throw and play alternately throughout the game.

Limitations in Playing

The only limitations to the play are that neither player can play (A) beyond his own home table, nor (B) onto any point occupied by two or more of his adversary's men. If White throws Five Ace in his opening move, he cannot play a Five in Black's inner table, nor an Ace from Black's outer table to his own inner table, because the points are already occupied by Black. He could play Five Ace from Black's inner table by playing the Ace first and then the Five, but not by playing the Five first. In this position the play is not affected, as the caster is at liberty to play first whichever number he chooses. Any part of a throw that cannot be played is lost, but the caster must play the whole throw if he can.

Hitting Blots

If the caster plays a man to a point that is occupied by a single adverse man, he is said to *hit a blot.* The man hit is taken off the table and placed on the bar, and has to be played into the adversary's inner table at the next throw. This is called entering. If an Ace is thrown, the man is entered on the Ace point, and so on for other numbers. Of course he cannot be entered on any point that is occupied by two or more adverse men. If the points corresponding to both the numbers thrown are occupied, the player who has a man up cannot re-enter the game. A player is not permitted to play any other man while he has a man to enter; consequently, in the case above, he would lose his turn.

It sometimes happens that one player has a man up, and that his adversary has his home table made up, that is, each point is occupied by two or more men. In this case it is obvious that the player who is up cannot enter; and as it is useless for him to throw, his opponent continues throwing and playing until he opens a point on his home table.

Two or more blots may be taken up at once, or in successive throws. It is not compulsory to hit a Blot if the throw can be played without doing so.

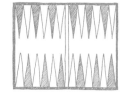

Bearing

The game proceeds as described until one player has carried all his men into his home table. He then has the privilege of taking his men off the board, or of bearing them. If every point on his home table is made up and he throws Four Three, he can take off one man from his Four point and one from his Three point. Or, if he prefers, he may move a Four from his Six or Five point, and a Three from his Six, Five, or Four point; or he may move one and bear the other. If he cannot move any part of the throw, he must bear it. For example, if he has no man on his Six or Five points, he must bear the four.

If he throws a number that is higher than any point on which he has a man, he must bear the man from the highest occupied point. For example, if he has no man on his Six point and throws a Six, he must bear from his Five point or, if that is unoccupied, from his Four point, and so on. And, of course, in the reverse case, if he throws an Ace, and his Ace point is unoccupied, he must move another man toward the Ace point.

Doubles similarly entitle the caster to bear or play four men.

If, after a player has commenced bearing his men, he should be hit on a blot, he must enter on his opponent's inner table, and he cannot bear any more men until the one taken up has been played back again into his own home table.

The player who first bears all his men wins the game.

The game counts as a single win or hit if the adversary has borne any of his men; a double game or gammon if the adversary has not removed any of his men; and a triple or quadruple game (according to agreement) or backgammon, if at the time the winner bears his last man the adversary (not having borne a man) has a man up, or one in the winner's inner table. Should a player, having borne a man, be taken up, he can only lose a hit, even if he fails to enter the man before the adversary bears all his.

When a series of games is played, the winner of a hit has the first throw in the succeeding game; but if a gammon or backgammon is won, the players each throw a single die to determining the first throw of the next game.

The Rules of the Game

1. The game shall be played with fifteen men on either side.
2. The players shall determine by agreement who shall command the inner and the outer table.
3. The white men are arranged as follows: Two on the Ace point of the inner table most remote from the player; five on the Six point of the outer table most remote from the player; three on the Deuce point of the outer table nearest the player; and five on the Six point of the inner table nearest the player. The Black men, in like numbers, shall occupy the points immediately opposite.
4. If a player begins to play with less than his proper number of men on the board, he cannot afterward claim to place the man or men he has omitted.
5. If, at the outset of the game, any of the men shall be placed incorrectly, either player may rectify the error before he has played; but after he has once played, he is not entitled to require such rectification. After both players have played, no rectification shall be made, save by mutual consent.
6. The dice must be thrown into one or the other of the tables.
7. If either die jump from one table into the other, or off the board, the cast is void, and the caster shall throw both dice again.
8. If either die rests, wholly or partially, on the other die, on the bar or frame of the board, on any of the men, or in any manner other than with its underside in complete contact with the surface of the table into which it is thrown, the cast is void, and the caster shall throw both dice again.
9. The caster must call his throw before playing it.
10. If a die is touched while in the act of falling from the box, or while still in motion on the board, the player not in fault shall be entitled to name the number that shall be played for that die.
11. If a die, even at rest, is touched before the caster has called his throw, and the throw be disputed, the player not in fault shall be entitled to name the number that shall be played for that die.
12. Should the caster call his throw incorrectly, he must abide by the call, unless he shall have perceived and corrected the mistake before the dice are touched by either player.
13. If the caster, after throwing, touches one of his own men, unless for the purpose of adjusting it, he must play such man, if it is possible to do so. If he has moved a man to any point and let go of it, it shall remain on such point.
14. If a wrong number of points is played, the adversary may require the rectification of the error before he has again thrown; but after he has thrown, the move shall stand, unless altered by mutual consent.
15. The total amount of a throw must be played, if it is possible to do so. If there are alternative modes of play, one only of which will enable the whole throw to be played, such alternative shall be adopted.

The Rules of the Game

16. If either player bears off a man or men before he has brought the whole of his men into his home table, the man or men so borne shall be placed on the bar, and re-entered in the adversary's table.
17. A hit shall entitle the winner to a single stake; a gammon to double, and a backgammon to triple the amount of the stake.

The Secrets of the Game

1. A leading principle of Backgammon play is to *make points* whenever you can, especially in or close to your home table. A second general principle is to avoid the leaving of blots, particularly where they are likely to be hit by the adversary. This latter principle is, however, subject to many qualifications. The advantages of spreading your men, in readiness to make points, may more than counterbalance the risk, and in certain critical conditions of the game it is sometimes even desirable to be hit, as it enables you to make a start from your adversary's home table, and so get the opportunity in turn of taking him up.

2. At the opening of the game, the men on both sides are in a uniform position, and it is consequently possible to give specific rules as to the best method of playing any throw that may occur.

   Aces—(The best possible throw at starting.) Play two men on your Bar point, and two on your Five point. This leaves a blot on the Deuce point in your outer table, but this is a small disadvantage as compared with the gain of at once securing four points side by side.

   Deuce Ace—For a hit, play the Deuce from the five men in your adversary's outer table, and the Ace from the Ace point in his inner table. For a gammon, play the Ace from the Six to the Five point in your own table.

   Deuces—For a hit, play two men from the Six to the Four point in your own table, and the other two men from the Ace to the Three point in your opponent's inner table. For a gammon, play the second pair from the five men in his outer table.

   Three Ace—Make your Five point.

   Three Deuce—The approved play is to carry two men from the five in your adversary's outer table

to the Four and Five points in your own outer table. This, of course, makes two blots. To avoid this, some, for a hit, play one man from the same point to the Deuce point in the outer table, but the bolder play is to be preferred.

Double Three—There are three ways of playing this throw. Some players make the Bar point. The more usual play is, for a hit, to play two men to the Five point in the player's own, and the other two to the Four point in the adversary's table. For a gammon, play the last two men from the Six to the Three point in your own table.

Four Ace—Play the Four from the five men in your opponent's outer table, and the Ace from his Ace point.

Four Deuce—Make your Four point.

Four Three—Play two men from the five in your adversary's outer table.

Double Four—Play two men from the Ace to the Five point in the adversary's inner table, and two from the five in his outer table. For a gammon, play two men only, from the point last mentioned to the Five point in your own table.

Five Ace—Play the Five from the five men in your adversary's outer table, and the Ace from the Ace point in his inner table. For a gammon, play the Ace from the Six to the Five point in your own table.

Five Two—Play both men from the five in your adversary's outer table.

Five Three—Make your Three point.

Five Four—Move one man from your adversary's Ace point to the Three point in his outer table.

Double Five—Carry two men from the five in the adversary's outer table, and make your Three point.

Six Ace—Make your Bar point.

Six Deuce—Move a man from the five in your adversary's outer table to the Five point in your own table.

Six Three, Six Five—Carry one man from your adversary's Ace point as far as the throw will permit.

Six Four—Make your Deuce point.

Sixes—Place two men on your adversary's Bar point and two on your own.

Of the foregoing throws, double Ace is reckoned the best, and double Six next best. Double Three comes third, followed by Three Ace and Six Ace.

Any throw in which the higher of the two numbers is *two in advance of the other* (as Five Three, Three Ace) is also good, as it enables you to make a point in your table.

3. In order to play Backgammon well, it is necessary to understand the probabilities of roles on two dice.

For example, you have to leave a blot; therefore, it should be left where there is the least probability of its being hit. To find the chance of being hit on an Ace; consider this: the number of ways in which two dice can be thrown is 36; of these,

The Secrets of the Game

25 will not contain an Ace, 11 will contain an Ace. Consequently, ithe odds are 25 to 11 against being hit on an Ace.

The following table gives the odds against being hit on any number within the reach of single or double dice:

It is 25 to 11 or about 9 to 4 against being hit on 1
It is 24 to 12 or 2 to 1 against being hit on 2
It is 23 to 13 or about 3 to 2 against being hit on 3
It is 22 to 14 or 7 to 5 against being hit on 4
It is 21 to 15 or 7 to 5 against being hit on 5
It is 20 to 16 or 9-1/2 to 8-1/2 against being hit on 6
It is 30 to 6 or 5 to 1 against being hit on 7
It is 31 to 5 or 5 to 1 against being hit on 8
It is 32 to 4 or about 6 to 1 against being hit on 9
It is 33 to 3 or 11 to 1 against being hit on 10
It is 34 to 2 or 17 to 1 against being hit on 11
It is 35 to 1 against being hit on 12

The table proves that if a blot must be left within the reach of a single die (i.e., on any number from 1 to 6), the nearer it is left to an adverse man the less probability there is of being hit; also, that it is long odds against being hit with double dice, and that, on any number from 7 to 11, the farther off the blot is the less chance there is of it being hit.

However, this table assumes that there is only one adverse man within range. Of course, the chances of being hit are much greater if several points within range are occupied. On the other hand, if any intervening points are held by men belonging to the player who leaves the blot, the chance of being hit will be less in proportion. Thus, a blot may be hit with Eight in five ways; but if the Fourth point is blocked, the blot can only be hit in four ways, and so on.

4. At the beginning of the game you should endeavor to secure your Five point, or your adversary's Five point, or both. The next best point to hold is your Bar point, and next to that your Four point.

5. If you can secure all these points, and your adversary's inner table is not favorably made up, you should open your Bar point, in hopes of compelling the opponent to run out of your home table with a Six and to leave two blots. You should also spread your men in the outer tables, i.e., not crowd a number of men on one point. This will give you a good chance of hitting the blots on your Bar point and Ace point.

6. Should you hit both these men, and your adversary have a blot in his inner table, you ought not to make up your home table, but leave a blot there in hopes of the adverse man being obliged to enter on it. You then have a chance of hitting a third

The Secrets of the Game

man, which will give you considerable odds in favor of winning a gammon. Otherwise, if you have only two adverse men up, the odds are against your gammoning your opponent.

7. If, in trying to gain your own or your adversary's Five point, you leave a blot and are hit, and your adversary is more forward in the game than you (see Secret No. 8), you should play another man on your Five or Bar point, or in your adversary's home table. If this man is not hit, you may then make a point and get as good a game as your opponent. If the man is hit, you must play a back game, i.e., allow your adversary to take up as many men as he likes, and then, in entering the men taken up, you should endeavor to hold your adversary's Ace and Three points or Ace and Deuce points, and if possible, keep three men on his Ace point, so that if you hit a blot from there, you still keep the Ace point guarded.

8. To determine which player is winning at any time in the game, count how many points you require to carry all your men to your Six point. Add to this six for every man on your Six point, five for every man on your Five point, and so on; and then make the same calculation for your adversary's men.

9. Whenever you have two of your opponent's men up, and have made two or more points in your home table, spread out your other men to increase the chance of making

another point in your home table, and of hitting the man your opponent enters. If your game is equal to or better than his, take up the man as soon as he enters, except if you are playing for a hit only and you can play the throw so as to make points that obstruct his running out, which gives you a better chance for the hit.

10. Always take up a man if the blot you leave can only be hit with double dice, except when playing for a hit only, and if you have two of your opponent's men in your home table and you seem to be winning.

11. In entering a man that it is to your adversary's advantage to hit, leave the blot on the lowest point you can, e.g., Ace point in preference to Deuce point, and so on; because, if he hits you, it crowds his game, by compelling him to play on his low points.

12. Avoid carrying many men on to the low points in your own tables, as these men are out of play and the board is left open for your adversary.

13. In carrying the men home, carry the most distant man to your adversary's Bar point, next to the Six point in your outer table, and lastly to your own Six point. By following this rule, you will carry the men home in the fewest number of throws. When all are home but two, and you can play one of them on to an unoccupied point in your home table, you should do so if you can put it within the power of a high throw to save a gammon.

Board Games

The Secrets of the Game

14. When your adversary is bearing his men, and you have two men on a low point in his table and several men in the outer table, it is advisable to leave a blot in his table, because it prevents his bearing his men to the greatest advantage, and gives you the chance of hitting him if he leaves a blot. But if, on calculation, you find that you can probably save the gammon by bringing both your men out of his inner table, do not wait for a blot.

To make this calculation, try to determine how many throws it will take to bring all your men home and bear one (a throw averaging seven points), and in how many throws he can bear all his men (on the assumption that he will bear two men at each throw). Doubles need not be considered, as this chance is equal for both players.

VaRiATiONS

Russian Backgammon

Though played on the same board with the same number of men, and the moves are governed by throws of the dice in the same manner, Russian Backgammon is very different from the more traditional game. Instead of placing the men on the various points before commencing the game, the men are entered by throws of the die, both players entering into the *same table,* which may be at the left hand of either player; and both move in the same direction around the board to the opposite table. For example, if the entering table is White's home (see Figure 11), the moves would be through White's outer and Black's outer tables to Black's home.

The first entry is determined by each player throwing two dice; the highest throw commences and may be adopted for that entry, or another throw made.

The men are placed on the points of the entering table according to the numbers of the dice thrown, one man only for each number, except in the case of doubles.

When either player has his men all entered, he may commence moving them toward the opposite table or home; but no move can be made by a player until all his men are entered.

The player who first bears all his men from the board wins. As in regular Backgammon, it may be a hit gammon, or backgammon.

The same rules apply as in the preceding game, with regard to bearing the men after they are brought home, and also to men hit, which must be sent back to the entering table and re-entered as at the commencement of the game.

Blots occurring in the entering table, while entering the men, are under the same rules as after the moves commence. So, if one player throws Six Deuce, he enters one man on each of those points; the other, throwing Six Ace, would take up the Six, placing his own man on that point, and enter one on the Ace point.

What makes this Russian Backgammon interesting is that the player who throws doubles is entitled not only to four moves of the number thrown, but also to four moves of the number on the opposite side of the dice, and another throw of the dice in addition. For example, if a player threw two Sixes on his first move, he would place four men on the Six point and four on the Ace point, and throw again. If then he throw two Deuces, he would place four on the Deuce point, the remaining three on the Five point, and move one man five points on its course home, having still another throw left. In such a case as this, the adversary would have only two points open on which to enter his men and, most likely, before he succeeded in getting them all entered, the first player would have his men removed from the entering table, and well advanced on the board.

In order for a player to take the four additional moves by his doubles, he must be able first to complete those of the number thrown; he will not be allowed another throw unless he can move all the points to which he is entitled. For example, if he throws Threes doubles, he must first move his four Three points; then he will have the right to move four Four points. If he succeeds in this, he may throw again. If he cannot complete any part of his turn, he forefeits the right to throw again.

As both players move in the same direction, it would be reasonable to assume that he who entered the board first and gains the start in the movement toward home must have a decided advantage over his adversary. But this apparent advantage is deceptive, because he who is in the rear has the chance of hitting blots, and thus retarding his opponent's game.

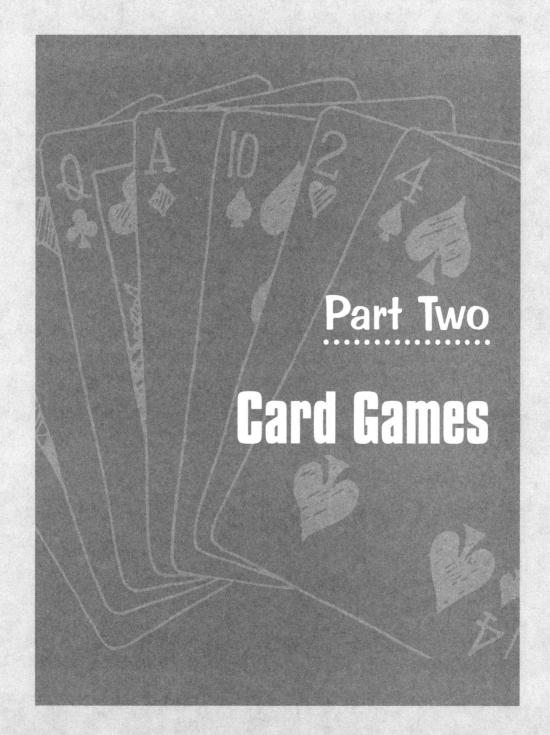

Part Two

Card Games

Card Games

All-Fours

The game of All-Fours, sometimes called *Old Sledge* and *Seven-Up,* is played with a full pack of fifty-two cards, which rank as in Whist—the Ace being the highest and the Deuce the lowest. The game can be played with either two, three, or four players. There are also slight variations to All-Fours, which are included in this chapter as well: All-Fives, Auction Pitch, California Jack, and Pedro Sancho. The object of the game is to score seven points first.

Dealing

The players cut for the chance to deal, and the person who draws the highest card becomes the dealer. The dealer then gives six cards to each player, three at a time, and turns up the next card when he has finished dealing. The turned-up card is the trump.

Begging

The nondealer then looks at his hand, and determines whether he will hold it for play, or *beg.* If he is satisfied with his hand, he says, "I stand;" but if he is not satisfied with his cards, he says, "I beg," in which case the dealer must choose to either grant his adversary one point, saying, "Take one," or give each player three more cards from the pack, and then turn up the next card, for trump. If, the new trump turned up is of the same suit as the first, the dealer must go on, giving each player three more cards and turning up the next, until a change of suit for trump takes place.

Playing the Hand

After these preliminaries have been settled, the *eldest* hand (the player to the left of the dealer) leads a card, and the dealer plays a card to it; these two cards constitute a trick. The player who plays the highest card of the suit led, or trump, wins the trick, and has the next lead. The play proceeds in this way until all the tricks are played. Each player must follow suit, if he can, unless he chooses to trump.

Scoring

The following is a list of points that may be scored, in order of their precedence:

High—The highest trump out; the holder scores one point.

Low—The lowest trump out; the original holder scores one point, even if it is taken by his adversary.

Jack—The Jack of trumps. The winner of the trick containing it scores one point. When the Jack is turned up for trump it counts one point for the dealer, and in that case takes precedence over every other point in the score.

Game—The greatest number of points that, in the tricks gained, can be shown by a player. The following are worth—

Each Ace	*four* toward game
Each King	*three* toward game
Each Queen	*two* toward game
Each Jack	*one* toward game
Each Ten	*ten* toward game

The other cards do not count toward scoring points; it may happen that a deal may be played without either party having any cards worth a score, if no one is holding picture cards or Tens.

When the players hold equal numbers—ties—the eldest hand scores the point for game.

One card may count all fours; for example, the eldest hand holds only the Jack of the trump suit, and stands his game; if the dealer has neither trump, Ten, Ace, nor picture card, it will follow that the Jack will be both high, low, Jack, and game.

The game consists of seven points, and the player who scores that number first, wins the game.

All-Fours for Four Players

The parties usually decide who shall be partners by cutting the cards, the two highest and the two lowest being partners. Each player sits opposite his partner. The first deal is decided by cutting the cards, the highest cut having the deal, but afterward the turns are taken by each player in rotation.

The dealer and the player on his left are the only players permitted to look at their cards prior to the player deciding on how he will play out his hand. The other parties must not raise their cards if the player begs until the dealer announces whether he will *give one* or run the cards for another trump.

The Rules of the Game

1. The deal is determined by cutting the cards, and the player cutting the highest card deals. In cutting, the Ace is the highest card, and ties cut again. (In the four-handed game, the two highest play against the two lowest.)
2. Less than four cards is not a cut, and the player cutting must leave at least four cards at the bottom of the pack.
3. If a card is exposed, a new cut may be demanded.
4. The dealer must give each player six cards, three cards at a time. If four are playing the dealer begins with the player to his left, and continues in rotation.
5. If the dealer deals without having the cards properly cut, or if a card is faced incorrectly in the pack, or if the dealer in any way exposes any of his adversary's cards, or if he gives out to any player too few or too many cards, there must be a fresh deal. The cards are reshuffled and recut, and the dealer deals again. If the dealer exposes any of his own cards, the deal stands good.
6. After the first hand the players deal alternately, if only two play. If more than two play, the players deal in rotation to the left. When playing for money, the players cut for deal at the commencement of each game.
7. Points are scored in the following order of precedence: *high; low; Jack;* and, *game.*
8. Each Jack turned up by the dealer counts one point for him in the game, unless a misdeal should occur *before* the Jack is turned. The dealer is not excluded from scoring the point if he turns over a Jack and a misdeal should occur afterward, even though it be in the same hand, or if he turns over a Jack and the cards run out by reason of the same suit being turned.
9. Should there be a tie for *game,* the nondealer scores the point. If three or more are playing and there is a tie, the eldest hand scores the point.

The Rules of the Game

10. If a player begs, it is at the option of the dealer to give him one point or run the cards for a new trump. When playing three-handed, if the dealer gives one player new cards, he must give both.

11. No player may beg more than once in each hand. However, there is nothing to prevent the dealer and the eldest hand from *bunching the cards*, i.e., having a fresh deal, after the latter has begged, and the cards have been run by the former, provided they mutually agree to do so. If the new trump is unsatisfactory to both, they may agree to run them again instead of bunching; but a suit cannot become trump that has once been turned down during the deal. This, is more a matter of agreement than of actual law.

12. Should the same suit be turned until the cards run out, then the cards must be bunched and dealt again.

13. When playing the four-handed game, the dealer and the player on his left only are permitted to look at their cards previous to the latter deciding upon his hand. The other parties must not raise their cards in case he begs, until the dealer announces whether he will give one, or run the cards to another trump.

14. Each player must follow suit, if he can, unless he chooses to trump. If a player can follow suit (or trump) but fails to, he becomes liable to the following penalty:

     A. If the player making the revoke plays Jack and game, he cannot score either point, but his adversary may add both points to his score.

     B. If the player making the revoke plays either Jack or Game when both points are out, he cannot score the point, but his adversary may add two points to his score.

     C. If both Jack and Game are out and the revoking player holds a Jack but does not play it, his adversary may score two points.

     D. If a Jack is not out, the adversary scores one point for the revoke.

15. A revoke is established as soon as the trick in which it occurs is turned and quitted, or a card has been led for the next trick.

VARIATIONS

All-Fives

This game is played with an entire pack of cards in the same way as All-Fours. It may be played by four persons, either as partners or singly. Instead of playing to seven points, the goal is to reach sixty-one points, which is marked on a cribbage board. For the Ace of trumps the holder marks four points when he plays it; for King of trumps, five; for Queen, two; for Jack, one; for the Five of trumps, five; and for the Ten of trumps, ten. If the Jack, Ten, or Five are taken in play by superior cards, the points belonging to them are scored by the winner. In counting for game, the Five of trumps is reckoned as five, and all the other Aces, Kings, Queens, Jacks, and Tens are counted as in All-Fours. A trump after a trick is not compulsory unless all players previously agree. The first card played by the nondealer is the trump. The rest of the rules are the same as in All-Fours.

Auction Pitch

This variation of All-Fours is also known as *Commercial Pitch*. Auction Pitch is played with a full pack of fifty-two cards, which rank as in Whist, and by any number of persons, from four to eight.

Dealing

The deal is determined by cutting the cards; the player cutting the highest card deals. Ace is high. Ties are cut over.

After the deal has been determined and the cards have been shuffled and cut by the player to the right of the dealer, the dealer delivers six cards to each player, three at a time, in rotation, beginning with the player to his left. No trump is turned. After the first hand has been played, the deal passes in rotation to the left.

Selling the Pitch

After the cards have been dealt, the *eldest hand* (the player to the left of the dealer) proceeds to sell the privilege of pitching the trump. Each player in turn has the right to make only one bid. The bidding proceeds in rotation, beginning with the player to the left of the eldest hand. The eldest hand has the last say, and may either sell to the highest bidder or decline to sell, and pitch the trump himself.

If the seller declines to entertain the highest bid and pitches the trump himself, he is entitled, if successful, to score all the points he can make; but if he fails to make as many points as the highest number offered, he must be set back just that number of points, and he cannot score anything he may have made during the play of that hand.

A player whose bid has been accepted may score not only the number of points he bid, if he makes them, but also any points he may make in excess thereof.

If a player buys the privilege of pitching the trump and fails to make or save the necessary number of points, he must be set back the number of points he bid, and cannot score anything he may have made during the play of that hand.

The seller, when he accepts a bid, scores the points at once, before a card is led.

If no bid is made, the seller must pitch the trump himself.

Scoring

The game is ten points. All points a player may make are deducted from his score. All points a player may be set back are added to his score. The player whose score is first reduced to nothing wins the game.

The points are ranked and scored in the following order:

High (the highest trump out); *low* (the lowest trump out), *Jack* (the Jack of trumps); *Game* (same as in All-Fours). In the event of a tie in counting game, that point is not scored by either party.

Playing the Hand

After it has been determined who is to pitch the trump, the player having that privilege must lead a card of the suit he decides will be trump. Each player, beginning with the player to the left of the leader, plays a card to the lead. When all the players have played to the lead, that constitutes a trick.

The highest card of the suit led wins the trick, and the winner of the trick has the next lead.

After the first trick it is not compulsory to lead a trump, and a player may lead a card of any suit he chooses.

Each player must follow suit if he can, unless he choose to trump. If he has no card of the suit led, he is not compelled to trump, but may play a card of any suit he chooses.

The playing proceeds in this way until all the cards held by each of the players are played out. After the hand is played, the scores are made, and a new deal ensues; this is continued until someone wins the game.

If a player makes a revoke, he is excluded from scoring any points he may have made in the play of the hand; and, in addition, the revoking player must be set back the highest number of points that was bid (in that hand) for the privilege of pitching the trump.

Any loss an innocent player may have sustained by reason of the revoke, if claimed, must be corrected, provided the same can be clearly demonstrated by subsequent examination of the tricks.

The game is governed by the same rules as in All-Fours.

California Jack

This game is also related to All-Fours. It is usually played by two or four people, with a full pack of fifty-two cards, which rank as in Whist. The deal is determined by cutting the cards; the player cutting the highest card deals.

Ace is high, and ties are cut over. After the deal has been determined and the cards cut by the player to the right of the dealer, the dealer delivers six cards to each player, three at a time, in rotation, beginning with the player to his left.

After the cards have been dealt, the dealer turns the remainder of the pack (the stock) face upward upon the table. The exposed card determines the trump suit. The exposed card is then taken by the dealer and slipped into the stock, as near the center as possible, and the stock remains face up. Sometimes the dealer, instead of placing the trump card in the center of the stock, reshuffles the stock and then turns it face upward again. This is done to prevent any possible indication of where the trump card lies.

The eldest hand (the player to the left of the dealer) now leads any card he chooses, and each player, beginning with the player to the left of the leader, plays a card to the lead.

When all the players have played to the lead, that constitutes a trick. The highest card of the suit led wins the trick, and the winner of the trick has the next lead.

Each player must follow suit if he holds a card of the suit led. If he does not have any cards of the suit led, he is not compelled to trump, but may play a card of any suit he chooses.

After each trick is played, the dealer gives one card to each player, face up, beginning with the winner of the trick. Each player will thus continue to hold six cards in hand until the stock is exhausted.

The game is usually ten points, and the points score in the following order of precedence: High, the Ace of trumps; low, the Deuce of trumps; Jack, the Jack of trumps; and game (same as in All-Fours). High is the only sure point. Low, Jack, and game are each scored by the player who takes or saves them in play.

The penalty for revoking is the same as in All-Fours.

Pedro Sancho

This game is derived directly from Auction Pitch. Any number of persons may play, but six or eight make the best game. Pedro Sancho is played with a full pack of fifty-two cards, which rank as in Whist.

The primary object for each player is, of course, to make points for his own score; but if he finds that he is not able to succeed in that, he can try to set back the player who is gaining the most points to make his bid good.

Therefore, it is a good policy, when a player holds points that he finds he cannot make, to play them, if possible, into the hands of the one whose score is lowest. It is even better to let these points go to the bidder, if his score is low, than to aid in his defeat by permitting them to fall into the hands of another player whose score already stands high.

Dealing

The deal is determined by giving a card to each player, and the player receiving the highest card deals. Ties are dealt over. After the cards have been shuffled and cut by the player to the right of the dealer, the dealer delivers six cards to each player, three at a time, beginning with the player to the left of the dealer. No trump is turned.

Rank and Value of the Points

The following is a list of points that may be scored, in order of their precedence:

> *High*—The highest trump out; the holder scores one point.
> *Low*—The lowest trump out; the holder scores one point.
> *Jack*—The Jack of trumps; the holder scores one point.
> *Game*—The Ten of trumps; the holder scores one point.
> *Pedro*—The Five of trumps; the holder scores five points.
> *Sancho*—The Nine of trumps; the holder scores nine points.

High counts for the player who holds it.
Low is not a sure point as in All-Fours, but counts for the player who wins it. Low may be taken by any trump.
Jack may be taken with any higher trump.
Game may be taken with any trump higher than the Ten.
Pedro may be taken with any trump higher than the Five.
Sancho may be taken with any trump higher than the Nine.

Bidding to Make the Trump

After the deal has been completed, the dealer proceeds to sell the privilege of making the trump. The player to the left of the dealer has the first bid, and the bidding goes in regular rotation to the left. The bids may pass around the board one or more times, until all the players are satisfied. For instance, after all the players have bid or refused the first time, they may again bid or supersede their former bids; and this may be repeated until the highest bid that can be obtained has been made, and accepted or rejected by the dealer.

If no player makes a bid the dealer leads the trump.

Playing the Hand

Either the player who purchases the right to make the trump, or the dealer, if he refuses to accept the points bid for that privilege, must now lead a card of the trump suit. The other players, beginning with the player to the left of the leader, must each play a card to the lead, and follow suit if they can. The highest card of the suit led takes the trick, and the winner of the trick has the next lead, but after the first trick has been played, it is not compulsory to lead trump. If a player cannot follow suit, he may trump the trick, or play any card he pleases. Each player must follow suit if he can, unless he choose to trump.

The Revoke

If a player makes a revoke, he is excluded from scoring any points he may have made in the play of the hand; in addition, the revoking player must be set back the highest number of points that was bid (in that hand) for the privilege of pitching the trump.

Any loss an innocent player may have sustained by reason of the revoke, if claimed, must be corrected, provided that it can be clearly demonstrated by subsequent examination of the tricks.

Misdeal

The laws of All-Fours regulating exposed cards and misdeals apply with equal force to Pedro Sancho, with one exception: when a fresh deal occurs for any cause, the player to the left of the dealer has the deal.

Scoring

The game is usually fifty points. Each player begins the game with a score of fifty points. All the points any player may make are deducted from his score as soon as possible after the hand is played out.

If a player buys the privilege of making the trump, and succeeds in taking or saving the number of points bid, he not only deducts from his score the number bid, but all points he may make in excess thereof. If he fails to make or take the necessary number of points, he is set back the whole number of points he bid, and they are added to his score.

When the dealer sells the privilege of making the trump, he is entitled to deduct from his score all the points he may make, provided he make or take as many points as are offered by the highest bidder. But if the dealer fails to make or save as many points as the highest number offered, he must be set back that number of points, and they are added to his score.

If a player is set back he is not permitted to count anything in that hand. That is, he cannot deduct from his score any points he may have taken or saved during the play of the hand.

The points score in the following order of precedence:

High, Low, Jack, Game, Pedro, and *Sancho.* For example, if two players have already reduced their score to two, and one of them has made High, Game, Pedro, and Sancho, the other could go out before him with Low and Jack.

Variations of Pedro Sancho

1. Sometimes it is agreed to play with one Joker. This makes the pack consist of fifty-three cards. The Joker when taken or saved scores fifteen points, and is always a trump, no matter what suit is made trump. The Joker may be taken with any trump, but although the lowest trump, it does not score for Low. The Joker is called *Dom,* and in rank or order of precedence follows Sancho. When *Dom* is permitted in the game, thirty-three points may be scored in the play of one hand. The game thus played consists of 100 points, and is called *Dom Pedro.*

2. Sancho is sometimes omitted, when only nine points can be made in the play of one hand. The game thus played consists of twenty-one points, and is known as *Pedro.*

3. When four play, the four Threes may be discarded from the pack, and twelve cards dealt to each player, so that all the cards are in play. For eight players, six cards to each will produce the same result. When less than four play, nine or twelve cards may be dealt to each, as agreed upon, to increase the chances of counting cards being out.

I'LL JUST BE A MINUTE

Boston

Boston is played by four people with two full packs of fifty-two cards, which rank as in Whist—the Ace being the highest and the Deuce the lowest. One pack is used for the deal, and the other is used to determine the trump.

Value of the Chips

The chips employed in playing Boston are usually white and red. The chips may represent any value, but one red chip must be equivalent to ten white chips.

Shuffling and Dealing

After the deal has been determined and the cards of one pack properly shuffled and cut, the dealer distributes the whole pack, beginning with the player at his left, and continuing in the same direction, giving every player four, then four again, and lastly five each, so that each player is holding thirteen cards. The cards are only shuffled once, at the beginning of the game; after that, instead of being shuffled, they are simply cut. Each player has the privilege of cutting once, but the dealer must cut last. After the first deal, each player takes the deal in rotation, beginning with the player to the left of the dealer.

Determination of Trump

While one pack is being dealt, the player opposite the dealer must cut the other pack and turn up the top card for trump. The suit turned up is called *First Preference;* the suit the same color as First Preference, whether red or black, is called *Second Preference,* and the other two are called *common suits.* For example, if Clubs are turned up as First Preference, then Spades will be Second Preference and Hearts and Diamonds will be common suits.

Bidding

After the cards have been dealt and the trump determined, the eldest hand (the player to the left of the dealer) has the first say. If his hand is not good, he can pass, and the next player to his left can do the same, and so on in rotation. If, however, the eldest hand considers his cards good enough to make five tricks, he says, "I play Boston." The next player can outbid him or pass; the other two players in turn have the opportunity to bid higher or pass.

If the eldest hand bid Boston he may do so in any suit; but if a player following him also bid Boston, it is understood that the second player must play Boston *in color,* that is, with either of the suits the same color as trump. Should a third player or the dealer also bid Boston, he must play it *in trump,* i.e., first preference.

When a player makes a bid and another player bids over him, the first has the privilege of increasing his bid to whatever he may think he can achieve. Each higher declaration that is made outranks the lower.

If a player bid six or more tricks, any player following and also bidding the same number must play in color or in trump precisely the same as in the bid of Boston.

If the eldest hand passes, the second or third hand or the dealer may proceed as the eldest hand.

If all except one player pass, he, having bid Boston, may play it in any trump of his choice.

If all players pass, the cards must be thrown in, and dealt by the player to the left of the former dealer, and each player must deposit a red chip in the pool that goes to the winner of the next bid.

When a player passes his hand, he cannot come in for the second round of bids, but must relinquish his right to bid until the next deal, unless he choose to play a *Misère*.

When a Misère is bid and played, there is no trump during that hand; and when the player bidding a Misère is forced to take a trick, his hand is *played out,* and after settlement is made, a new deal begins. There are four varieties of Misère explained in the Technical Terms section.

If a player is successful in achieving all or more than he undertakes, he wins and must be paid according to Figure 12 on page 47. If he fails to accomplish what he engages to do, he must pay in proportion to the tricks he falls short of completing in his bid. For example, if he bids Boston and only takes four tricks, he is said to be *put in* for one trick, and forfeits eleven white chips to each of the other three players; if he is *put in* for two tricks, he pays twenty-one white chips to each.

Playing the Hand

The eldest hand leads. Each player plays a card to the lead, and must follow suit if he can. If he cannot follow suit, then he may play any trump or card he chooses. The highest card of the suit led wins the trick unless it is trumped. The winner of the trick has the next lead, and so on.

When any player makes a bid, the others all play against him, and endeavor to put him in for as many tricks as possible. It is hardly necessary to say that the players opposing the Misère all scheme to force the bidder to take a trick, and that the play is entirely reversed from what it would be if Boston or more were bid.

Rank and Order of the Bids

The following is a list of the different bids in their order of precedence:

1. Boston, Common Suit
2. Boston, Second Preference, five tricks
3. Boston, First Preference
4. Six tricks
5. Seven tricks
6. Petit Misère (*Little Misery*)
7. Eight tricks
8. Nine tricks
9. Grand Misère (*Grand Misery*)
10. Ten tricks
11. Eleven tricks

12. Petit Misère Ouverte (*Little Misery Exposed on the Table*)
13. Twelve tricks
14. Grand Misère Ouverte (*Grand Misery Exposed on the Table*)
15. Thirteen tricks, *Grand Slam*

Table of Payments

Figure 12 shows the number of white chips to be paid to any player making a successful bid. For example, suppose that a player has bid Boston, and takes five tricks. In order to find the number of white checks each player must pay him, look at the number 5 in the column of figures at the left of the table, representing the number of tricks bid; then find the number 5 in the row of figures at the top of the table, which represent the tricks taken by the player, and under it will be found 12, showing that each player must pay the winner 12 white chips.

In Table II, the column of figures at the left of the table show the number of tricks bid by the unsuccessful player, and the top row shows the number of tricks he is *put in for.* To ascertain what the bidder must pay each of the other players, first find the number he has bid and follow to the right, and under the number of tricks he is put in for, you will find the number of white chips he is compelled to pay each of the other three players. For example, suppose a player bids Boston (five tricks), and is put in for one trick, we first find the number 5 in the column to the left; and under the number 1, in the top row, we find 11, showing that he must pay each of the other players 11 *white* chips.

Figure 12

Tricks bid, and to be taken by the Player.	Tricks taken by the player making the bid.									
		5.	6.	7.	8.	9.	10.	11.	12.	13.
.... 5...........	....	12	12	13	13	14	14	14	15	15
.... 6...........	....		15	16	16	17	18	19	20	20
.... 7...........	....			18	20	21	22	23	24	26
.... 8...........	....				23	24	26	28	29	31
.... 9...........	....					32	34	36	39	41
...........10...........	....						42	45	48	52
...........11...........	....							63	68	72
...........12...........	....								106	114
...........13...........	....									166

What the Four Misères Win or Lose

Petit Misère: Over 7 tricks, wins or loses 20 white chips.

Grand Misère: Over 7 tricks, wins or loses 40 white chips

Petit Misère Ouverte: Over 11 tricks, wins or loses 80 white chips

Grand Misère Ouverte: Over 12 tricks, wins or loses 160 white chips

Tricks bid by the Player.	Tricks which the player is " put in for."												
	1.	2.	3.	4.	5.	6.	7.	8.	9.	10.	11.	12.	13.
... . 5	11	21	31	41	50	....	....	....	....	....	....	....	....
.... 6...........	15	24	35	45	55	66	....	....	....	....	....	....	....
.... 7...........	19	29	40	50	60	72	82	....	....	....	....	....	....
.... 8...........	23	34	46	56	67	78	89	110	....	....	....	....	....
.... 9...........	33	44	57	68	80	92	103	115	127	....	....	....	....
...........10...........	44	56	70	82	94	107	119	132	145	157	....	....	....
...........11...........	67	80	95	109	123	138	151	165	180	194	208	....	....
...........12...........	113	130	148	165	182	200	217	234	252	270	286	304	....
...........13...........	177	198	222	241	262	284	305	326	348	369	390	412	433

Technical Terms Used in Boston

Boston—A bid of five tricks.

First Preference—Trump the same suit as the card turned up on the pack.

Second Preference—The same color, but not the same suit as the card turned up on the pack.

Common Suit—Either suit of a color different from the card turned up on the pack.

Petit Misère—To lose the whole twelve tricks after having discarded a card that is not to be shown. This is sometimes called *Little Misery*. When any of the different Misères are bid, there is no trump during that hand.

Grand Misère—To lose every trick without discarding a card. Sometimes called *Great Misery*.

Petit Misère Ouverte—To discard a single card, expose your hand, and lose the twelve tricks.

Grand Misère Ouverte—To lose every trick, without discarding, after having exposed your hand.

Grand Slam—A bid to win every trick.

Eldest Hand—The first player to the left of the dealer.

In Color—Same color as trump.

I Keep—An expression which signifies that a player will play *in color*.

I Keep Over You—Signifies that the player using that expression will play *in trump*.

Put in—When a player fails to take as many tricks as he bids, he is said to be *put in*. If he bid Boston but only takes four tricks, he is put in for one trick.

Revoke—Playing a different suit from the card led, though it is in the player's power to follow suit.

The Pool

At the beginning of the first deal, each player deposits a red chip in the pool. Any player who makes a bid of seven tricks or more in value and succeeds in his bid takes the pool, in addition to his regular receipts from the other players.

Any player who bids less than seven and is obliged by his opponents to play out the hand and succeeds in making the amount of his bid, takes the pool, in addition to his regular receipts from the other players.

If, before playing to the second trick, the opponents of one who bid less than seven tricks, say, in turn, "I pay;" the hand is played no further, the bidder is paid, and the pool remains on the table. All the players opposed to the bidder must agree to this, otherwise, the hand must be played to its conclusion.

Any player who makes a *pool bid,* i.e. one of seven tricks or more in value, must play his hand out, unless his opponents agree to pay him before playing to the second trick; and if he fails is obliged to double the pool, and in addition he must pay the other players in accordance with the schedule. The same rule applies to a hand that is played out on less than a pool bid, and fails.

When all the players pass without making a bid, the cards are gathered in sequence for a new deal, and each player contributes another red check to the pool.

The pool is usually limited to a fixed number—say, four or five hundred white chips, and when it has reached this limit and is subsequently doubled, the amount is set aside for the next pool. When a pool starts with the limit in it, the amount cannot be increased except by the addition of the usual four red chips deposited at each deal.

Any error affecting the amount in the pool must be corrected before the eldest hand has either bid or passed.

The Rules of the Game

1. The deal is determined by cutting the cards; the player cutting the lowest card is the first dealer. All ties are cut over, and at least four cards must be picked up from the pack to constitute a valid cut.
2. At the beginning of the game, the pack to be dealt may be shuffled by any of the players, the dealer being entitled to shuffle last, but in all subsequent deals, the pack is only cut, not shuffled.
3. The deal is performed by delivering to each player *four* cards at a time for *two* rounds, and *five* cards on the last round, beginning with the player on the dealer's left hand, thus giving each player thirteen cards.
4. The dealer is not at liberty to touch the cards on the table to determine how he has disposed of them, but he may count those undealt to see how many remain in his hand.
5. If the dealer deals without having the cards properly cut; or if he in any way exposes any of the adversaries' cards; or if he give to either player too few or too many cards, there must be a fresh deal, and the dealer must deposit a red chip in the pool. The cards are recut, and the dealer deals again. If, however, the pack is faulty; or one or more cards are faced in the pack; or either of the other players touch their cards or in any way interrupt the dealer, the dealer deals again without penalty. If the dealer exposes any of his own cards, the deal stands good.

The Rules of the Game

6. The trump is determined when the cards are being distributed by the dealer, the player immediately opposite to him cuts a second pack, and turns up the top card, which is trump, and is called *first preference*.

7. The deal passes to the left, and the pack used for the deal and the other pack must be alternately used for that purpose.

8. Any player dealing out of turn, or with the wrong pack, may be stopped before the deal is completed; if he is not stopped the game must proceed as if no mistake had been made.

9. The eldest hand has the first privilege of bidding or passing, after which the other players bid or pass in turn.

10. When a player passes his hand, he cannot afterward, during that deal, come in and bid, but must relinquish that privilege until the next deal, unless he chooses to play a Misère.

11. When the eldest hand makes a bid of five or more tricks, and another player bids the same number of tricks, the eldest hand may bid over him, or abandon his bid (in which case the younger hand must play his bid in color).

12. When a player has made a bid, and all the other players pass, the party so bidding may name any suit he chooses for trump.

13. If all the players pass, the cards must be bunched, and a new deal ensues, and each player must deposit a *red* chip in the pool, which goes to the winner of the next bid.

14. A player having the highest bid must declare the suit he plays in as soon as the bidding ceases.

15. When the playing begins, the eldest hand always leads.

16. If either of the players opposed to the bidder leads out of turn, and it is discovered before the bidder has played to it, the latter may either treat it and the cards played to it as exposed cards, or he may call a lead of any suit from the player whose proper turn it was to lead. If the error is not discovered until after the bidder has played to it, the lead stands good, and the winner of the trick has the next lead.

17. If a player is called to lead a suit, the card led out of turn and those which may have been played to it are not considered as exposed cards, and may be taken up.

18. If the bidder led out of turn he may be corrected before the player to his left has played to it, otherwise the lead stands good.

19. If a player bid Petit Misère or Petit Misère Ouverte, and a player opposed to him should lead a card before his partner, or either of them, have discarded, the bidder may call a lead of any suit, or demand that the opposing players each play their highest or lowest card of the suit led.

20. If any of the players opposed to the bidder play out of turn to a card led, the bidder may demand that the player or players whose proper turn it was to play, shall play the highest or lowest card of the suit led, or win or lose the trick.

21. If a player who has rendered himself liable to have the highest or lowest card of a suit called or is called upon to win or lose the trick and fails to play as desired, or if when called upon to lead one suit leads another while having in his hand one or more cards of the suit demanded, he and the players associated with him incur the penalty of a revoke.

22. If a player called upon to lead a suit has none of it, the penalty is paid.

23. In no case can a player be compelled to play a card that would oblige him to revoke.

24. All cards exposed by either of the players opposed to the bidder are liable to be called and must be left on the table face up; a card is not exposed when dropped on the floor, or elsewhere below the table.

25. Any card detached from the hand, i.e. taken out of the hand but not dropped, may be called if it can be named, and must be placed upon the table face up.

26. The call of a card may be repeated at every trick, until such card has been played.

27. No cards exposed by the player making a bid can be called.

28. If when making the discard for Petit Misère or Petit Misère Ouverte, either of the partners opposed to the bidder should expose a card; the bidder wins his bid and the pool, if any, without playing out the hand.

29. When a player holding one or more cards of the suit led plays a card of a different suit, he makes a revoke.

30. A revoke is established if the trick in which it occurs is turned and quitted, i.e., the hand removed from the trick after it has been turned face downward on the table—or if the revoking player (or his partner, if the revoking player is not the bidder), whether in his right turn or otherwise, leads or plays to the following trick.

31. The players opposed to the bidder may ask a partner whether or not he has a card of the suit that he has renounced; should the question be asked before the trick is turned, subsequent turning and quitting does not establish the revoke, and the error may be corrected, unless the answer is *no,* or unless the revoking player or his partner have led or played to the following trick.

32. If a player opposed to the bidder discovers his mistake in time to save a revoke, the bidder may call the card played in error, or may require the revoking player to play his highest or lowest card to that trick in which he had renounced. If the highest or lowest card is called, the card played in error is not treated as an exposed card.

33. If a revoke is claimed and the accused player or his partner mix the cards before they have been sufficiently examined by the opposing player or players, the revoke is established.

34. At the end of a hand, those that claimed a revoke may search all the tricks.

35. A revoke cannot be claimed after the cards have been cut for the following deal.

36. When a revoke has been made by the bidder, if it is discovered *before* the hand

is played out, he is put in for at least one trick, or just as many as he is short of accomplishing his bid. In addition to this he must deposit four red chips in the pool, which go to the winner of the next bid.

37. When a revoke is made by any player opposed to the bidder, the revoker and his partner must pay the bidder the amount of his bid, whether the latter would have been successful or not, and also for all overtricks; and, in addition, the player who actually made the revoke must deposit four red chips in the pool, which go to the winner of the next bid.

38. When a revoke occurs the hand must be played to a conclusion.

39. Any player may demand to see the last trick turned. Under no circumstances can more than eight cards be seen during the play of the hand, including the four cards on the table that have not been turned and quitted, and the last trick turned.

40. Anyone may demand, during the play of a trick or after the four cards are played, and before, they are touched for the purpose of gathering them together, that the cards be placed before their respective players. When a bid has been made, the bidder and the player opposite to him are the only persons who have a right to gather up the cards and arrange the tricks.

41. If anyone opposed to the bidder should call attention to the trick—either by saying that it is his, or by naming his card, or without being required so to do, by drawing it toward him—the bidder may require that opponent's partner to play the highest or lowest of the suit then led, or to win or lose the trick.

42. If anyone opposed to the bidder plays two cards to the same trick, and the error is not discovered until he has played to the next; or if he discards two cards in Petit Misère, or Petit Misère Ouverte, or if from any other cause he plays with less than the proper number of cards, his side must pay the bidder for his bid, and also for all overtricks. If the error is committed by the bidder, he is put in for at least one trick, or just as many as he is short of completing his bid.

43. If any player has more than the proper number of cards it is a misdeal, and a new deal ensues.

VaRiATiONS

Variations

Misère Partout

This variety is sometimes played when all the players pass without making a bid. There is no trump, and each player endeavors to take as few tricks as possible. The player who takes the greatest number of tricks pays the others ten white chips for every trick he has taken in excess of the tricks held by each respectively.

The player who captures the fewest number of tricks does not take the pool, which remains for the next hand.

When Misère Partout is played no penalty can be exacted for a lead out of turn, but the erroneous lead must be corrected unless the player next to the one who makes the lead out of turn has played to the trick; when this is done the lead stands good.

No exposed cards can be called, but, a player making a revoke pays five red chips to each of the other players, and the player who plays with less than thirteen cards is subject to the same penalty.

French Boston

French Boston is played with four people with a full pack of fifty-two cards, which rank as in Whist. You will need four baskets or trays of different colors, one for each player, each containing five red chips, which represent one hundred points each; twenty white chips, which represent fifty; and twenty black chips, which represent five. The object of the game is for a player to name the trump, playing either alone against the other three, or with a partner.

Dealing

When the deal has been determined by cutting, the dealer delivers thirteen cards to each player, in the same manner as in regular Boston. The cards are shuffled only once, at the beginning of the game. In all subsequent deals the cards are simply cut. Each player has the privilege of cutting the pack once, but the dealer must cut last. Previous to dealing, the dealer deposits one white chip in the pool.

Announcements or Bids

The naming of the trump is given to the player who bids to accomplish the most. The player who makes the highest bid is entitled, if successful, to the

contents of the pool, and a certain number of chips from each of the players; but if he is unsuccessful, he must pay into the pool and to each of the other players a certain number of chips.

The bids rank as follows, beginning with the lowest:

1. *Simple Boston* is when a player binds himself to a certain suit, which he designates, to win five tricks; or, if he can find a partner to sustain him, to win three additional, or eight tricks in all. Whenever a player announces a certain number of levees, it must be understood that, should he need the assistance of a partner, he and his partner must win three tricks more than the levees announced in order to take the pool. In all cases losses and gains must be equally shared between the two.

2. *Six Levees* is to win six tricks, upon the same condition with regard to trumps as above-mentioned, i.e., six alone, or independent, or nine—three extra—with a partner.

3. *Little Misère* is to not win any tricks at all. Before commencing to play this bid, each player must discard any single card he may choose from his hand, and play with the remaining twelve.

4. *Seven Levees* is to win seven tricks upon the same conditions as regular Boston.

5. *Picolissimo* is to discard one card, as in Little Misère, and to win only one trick.

6. *Eight Levees* is to win eight tricks upon the same conditions as regular Boston.

7. *Grand Misère* is to not win a single trick, without discarding any card.

8. *Nine Levees* is to win nine tricks upon the same conditions as regular Boston.

9. *Little Misère on the Table* is played like Little Misère, only that the player must spread his hand upon the table, exposing it to the other three players.

10. *Ten Levees* is to win ten tricks upon the same conditions as regular Boston.

11. *Grand Misère on the Table* is played like Grand Misère, only that the player must spread his hand upon the table, as in *Little Misère on the Table.*

12. *Eleven Levees* is to name a trump, and win, eleven tricks unassisted.

13. *Twelve Levees* is to win twelve tricks as above.

14. *Chelem,* or *Grand Boston,* is an announcement of the whole thirteen tricks.

15. *Chelem,* or *Grand Boston, on the Table,* is an announcement of the whole thirteen tricks, but with the player spreading out his cards face up on the table.

In each of the announcements (excepting, of course, numbers 3, 5, 7, 9, and 11, in which there is no trump suit), the designated trump suits rank and take precedence as follows: Diamonds, Hearts, Clubs, and lowest of all, Spades.

Bidding

After the preliminaries of cutting and dealing have been concluded, the eldest hand proceeds to make his bid, or pass; the succeeding players have the opportunity of overbidding or passing. If the eldest hand thinks he can get five tricks with Clubs for trump, he declares, "Five in Clubs." But if the second player undertakes to make five tricks with Diamonds for trump, he supersedes the first, and may in his turn be superseded by the third engaging to get six or seven levees, or play Little Misère. The fourth hand, or dealer, may also supersede the third hand by declaring Picolissimo, or eight levees, or any of the other chances lower down on the table. In short, whoever undertakes to do more than the other players has the preference.

When a player has once declined bidding he cannot afterward do so in that hand; but if he makes a bid and it is exceeded by some other subsequent bid, he may, in his regular turn, increase his first bid if he chooses.

If all players pass without declaring, then the hand must be played, and he who takes the least number of tricks wins the pool. In this hand there is no trump.

The player, whose announcement proves to be the highest, provided he bids either one, two, four, six, eight, or ten, can call for a partner. Any other player who wishes to aid the caller in winning the announced number of tricks plus three tricks, may join him and share in profit or loss. The right of answering goes in rotation to the left of the caller.

Playing the Hand

After the preliminaries of bidding have been concluded, the eldest hand leads any card he chooses. The next player to his left plays a card to it, and so on in rotation until each player has played a card to the lead; the four cards thus played constitute a trick.

Suit must be followed. If suit cannot be followed, trumping is optional.

The highest card of the suit led (unless the same is trumped), wins the trick. Trumps win all other suits. When any of the Misères or

Figure 13

PAYMENTS OF BOSTON DE FONTAINEBLEAU.		Clubs or Spades.	Hearts.	Diamonds.
1.	Five Levees.	10	20	30
	With two by honors.	20	30	40
	With four by honors.	30	40	50
	For each trick more, add.	5	5	5
2.	Six Levees.	30	40	50
	With two by honors.	40	50	60
	With four by honors.	50	60	70
	For each trick more, add.	5	5	5
3.	Little Misère, no trumps	75		
4.	Seven Levees.	50	60	70
	With two by honors.	60	70	80
	With four by honors.	70	86	90
	For each trick more, add.	5	5	5
5.	Picolissimo, no trump.	100		
6.	Eight Levees.	70	80	90
	With two by honors.	80	90	100
	With four by honors.	90	100	110
	For each trick more, add.	5	5	5
7.	Grand Misère, no trump.	150		
8.	Nine Levees.	90	100	110
	With two by honors.	100	110	120
	With four by honors.	110	120	130
	For each trick more, add.	5	5	5
9.	Little Misère on the table, no trump.	200		
10.	Ten Levees.	110	120	130
	With two by honors.	120	130	140
	With four by honors.	130	140	150
	For each trick more, add.	5	5	5
11.	Grand Misère on the table, no trump.	250		
12.	Eleven Levees.	130	140	150
	With two by honors.	140	150	160
	With four by honors.	150	160	170
	For each trick more, add.	5	5	5
13.	Twelve Levees.	150	160	170
	With two by honors.	160	170	180
	With four by honors.	170	180	190
	For one trick more, add.	5	5	5
14.	Chelem, or Grand Boston.	400	450	500
	With two by honors.	410	460	510
	With four by honors.	420	470	520
15.	Chelem on the table.	600	700	800
	With two by honors.	610	710	810
	With four by honors.	620	720	820

Picolissimo are bid and played, there is no trump suit. When all the cards of the hand are played out, the payments are made.

Table of Payments

Figure 13 shows what payments for losses or gains must be made for all the different bid that can be made.

Honors

The Ace, King, Queen, and Jack of trumps are honors. When the four honors are held they count one trick each, and the successful bidder receives payment for each. Any three honors count for two tricks (two by honors), but less than three do not count. Honors cannot be counted in as tricks bid for.

If the player announces five levees in Hearts and makes an additional two, this would be seven; he would then receive thirty chips from each player. The laws that govern this game are the same as those of Boston.

Calabrasella

Calabrasella is one of the few games that is really interesting for three players. The game is played with a pack of forty cards: the Tens, Nines, and Eights are removed from a complete deck.

Dealing

The players cut for the deal; the lowest card wins the deal. The player to the dealer's right cuts the deck. The dealer reunites the deck and distributes the cards two at a time to each player, starting at his left, until each player has twelve cards. Four cards (called the *stock*) remain. These are placed face own in the middle of the table.

Order of the Cards

The cards rank in the following order from lowest to highest: Three, Two, Ace, King, Queen, Jack, Seven, Six, Five, Four. Their value in scoring is different from their rank in play.

Declaring to Play

The deal being completed, the eldest hand (player to the dealer's left) looks at his hand and declares whether he will play along or not, saying, "I play," or, "I pass." If he passes, the next player has the option; and if the second player also passes, the dealer has the option. If all three pass, the hand is discarded and the deal goes to the eldest hand.

If a player declares to play his hand, the other two become allies and play against him. The single player is entitled, before he plays, to strengthen his hand by exchanging cards with other players or the stock:

1. The single player may ask the other players for a Three in the suit he chooses. The player holding that card must surrender it, receiving a card in exchange from the single player's hand. If no one is holding that specific Three (if it remains in the stock), no other card can be demanded. If the single player happens to hold all the Threes, he may then ask for a specific Two.
2. The single player then declares how many cards he will exchange for cards in the stock. He must exchange at least one, and of course, cannot exchange more than four. He discards from his hand the number he desires to exchange, and places them face down on the table. He then turns the stock face up, and selects from it the number required to supply the places of the discarded cards.

   The other players have a right to see the stock when turned up; but they must not look at the cards discarded by the single player.

   The cards discarded, together with those not taken from the stock (if any), form a second stock, called the *discard*. The discard remains face down, and belongs to the winner of the last trick.

Playing

The eldest hand (whether single player or not) has the first lead. Each player plays one card in turn, the dealer playing last: the three cards played constitute a trick. The highest card of the suit led wins the trick (refer back to the order of the cards on this page). There are no trumps. The players are bound to follow suit if able, but if not, may play any card. A player is not bound to take a trick. The winner of one trick leads to the next, and so on, until all the twelve tricks are played out.

The single player makes a pile of all the tricks he takes, and the allies make a pile of theirs, each trick being turned face down. The winner of the last trick takes the discard and adds it to his heap.

Scoring

When all the cards are played out, each side counts the points in their respective piles. The points accrue as follows:

Ace counts	3	Each King counts	1
Three counts	1	Queen counts	1
Two counts	1	Jack counts	1
The winner of the last trick counts			3

The total number of possible points is thirty-five; but the number reckoned is the difference between the respective scores. For example: If the single player has twenty points and the allies fifteen, the former wins five points from each of the allies. On the other hand, if the single player has fifteen points and the allies twenty, the single player loses five points to each of the allies. Each hand is a complete game in itself.

The Rules of the Game

1. The players cut for deal; the lowest card deals.
2. Each player deals in turn, the order of dealing going to the left.
3. There is no misdeal. If there is any irregularity in dealing, on discovery, there must be a fresh deal, even though the hand has been played out.
4. The allies have a right to count the discard face down, and if they find that it contains too few cards they have the option of requiring the single player to make up the difference from his hand, or of ending the game. If the discard is found to contain too many cards, the single player has to suffer the loss of his first available trick.
5. If the single player asks for a Two, when he has not all the Threes dealt him, his opponents have the option of ending the game.
6. If a card is asked for and is not surrendered, and it is not in the stock, the single player may again require its surrender, and may alter his discard, notwithstanding that he has seen the stock.
7. A round is finished when the deal returns to the original dealer.
8. If the single player exposes a card there is no penalty.
9. If the single player plays out of turn there is no penalty. The card led in error must be taken back, and the right player must lead. If the second player has played to such lead he must also take back his card; but if all three players have played, the trick is complete, and the hand proceeds as though no error had been committed.
10. If either of the allies exposes a card, the single player may call it (except as provided in Rule #9). The call may be repeated at every trick until the exposed card is played.
11. If either of the allies leads out of turn, and the error is discovered before the trick is complete, the single player may call a suit from the right leader (or, if it is his own lead, may call a suit the first time he loses the lead), or he may refrain from calling a suit, and treat the card led in error as an exposed card. If a suit is called and the leader has none of it, he may play any card he pleases, and no further penalty can be demanded.
12. When the single player leads, it is unfair for the third player to play before the second.
13. If a player does not follow suit when able, the opponents may take nine points from the score of the side offending and add them to their own.
14. When a trick is complete it must be turned over and put aside. No one has a right to see it again during the play of the hand.

1. With average cards the eldest hand should elect to play.
2. Discarding more than two cards is not recommended: Chances are that two of the cards in the stock will be of little value.
3. Remember that the Ace, which is the highest scoring card, is not the highest in play. Try to use Aces in your own tricks, and to entrap the Aces of your opponents.
4. When it is obvious that your ally has won, or will win the trick, you should generally throw a low-numbered card to it.
5. Try to remember how many cards of each suit have been thrown out.
6. The last trick is by far the most important. It is worth three points in itself, is generally rich in good cards, and takes the discard and all points in it. It is therefore a good idea to reserve good cards in order to secure the last trick. This is called *playing back*. If, however, you can ensure eighteen points by playing any trick, it is not a good idea to hold the card back for the sake of the last trick.

Casino

Casino is played by two players, with a pack of fifty-two cards. The object of the game is to win by pairing and building.

Dealing

The players cut for deal. The dealer gives four cards to each player, and lays out four other cards face up on the table. The cards are dealt two or four at a time; the eldest hand first, the laid-out cards next, the dealer last. After the cards are all played, four more cards are similarly dealt to each player, but none laid out; and this is repeated until all the cards have been dealt.

Playing

After the deal is completed the eldest hand plays first. The object in Casino is to capture as many cards as possible, and this is done in four different ways: pairing, combining, building, and calling. One card *must* be played from the hand at each turn. If a card is played, and it cannot be used for pairing, or to take a combination, or to form a build or call, that card must remain on the table.

Pairing—This consists of capturing one or more cards from the table by matching it with a similar card played from the hand. For example, a King held in the hand will take all the Kings that are on the table. The card played and all the cards it captures become the property of the player.

Combining—A player may group together two or more cards that are on the table and add their value together. For example, a Two and a Six on the table can be combined to form an eight, and taken off the table by an Eight the player holds in his hand. Two or more combinations may be made at the same time, provided that each combination produces a similar numerical result (using the above example, if there is more than one possible combination to reach Eight).

Building—A player lays a card from his hand upon a card or cards on the table, which can then only be captured in his next turn by a card worth the total number of points. Suppose there is a Five on the table, and a player has a Seven and a Two in his hand; when it is his turn, he may lay his Two upon the Five, and say, "Seven." When his next turn comes, he can capture the build with his Seven, unless his adversary has already done so, or has raised the build.

A player cannot raise his own build; but his opponent can, if he holds the card needed to redeem it. Thus, as in the previous instance, A has *built* a seven; he cannot raise his build by playing a Three upon it to make a ten, but his opponent, B, can. B can play a Two upon A's build, and says, "Nine"; A, if he has an Ace and a Ten, can then play his Ace on the nine-build, and say "Ten," and then nothing but a Ten would capture it.

A player may make another build, or may pair or combine other cards, or capture his adversary's build, before taking his first build.

Calling, or *Duplicating*—This consists of grouping together similar cards, builds, or combinations, and then *calling* their denomination. Once a call is made, the cards, builds, or combinations cannot be interfered with; they can only be captured by a card of the denomination *called.* Suppose a player has two Nines in his hand, and there is a Nine (or a build or a combination of nine) on the table; instead of pairing it or taking it, he can play one of the Nines from his hand upon it and say, "Nines," and then only another Nine will capture it.

A Sweep—If a player can capture all the cards on the board with one play it is called a *sweep,* and counts one point for the player who makes it.

When a player makes a sweep he turns the *sweep-card* (the card that takes the sweep) face up. This is done to keep tally of the number of sweeps made by each player. If the opposing player makes a sweep, these two sweeps cancel each other, and the players turn the canceled sweep-cards down. Only the difference in the number of sweeps is scored; thus, if A makes three sweeps and B makes two, A deducts B's two sweeps from his own three and scores the difference, one.

Last-cards—After all the cards have been dealt, and the hands finally played out, all cards that remain upon the table belong to the player who took the last trick.

Points Value and Scoring

The following are the points that may be scored:

Great Casino—The Ten of Diamonds	2 points
Little Casino—The Two of Spades	1 point
The Majority of Cards	3 points
The Majority of Spades	1 point
Each Ace	1 point
Each Sweep	1 point

The points gained by each party are counted at the end of the deal, and whoever has the greatest number of points wins the game. Casino is sometimes played for a fixed number of points. If both players make the same number of points, the game is drawn.

The Rules of the Game

1. The deal is determined by cutting the cards, and the player cutting the lowest card must deal. Ties are cut over. In cutting, Ace is low.
2. Each player has a right to shuffle. The dealer has the right of shuffling last.
3. If, in cutting to the dealer, or in reuniting the separated packets, a card is exposed, or if there is any confusion of the cards, there must be a fresh cut.
4. The dealer must deal the cards either two or four at a time; first to his adversary, next for the layout, and lastly to himself. The laid-out cards are dealt face up. After the first four cards are played, four more cards must be similarly dealt to each player, but none laid out; this is repeated until the pack is exhausted.
5. If the dealer deals without having the pack cut, or if he shuffles the pack after it has been cut with his consent, there must be a fresh deal, provided the opposing side claims it before any cards are turned up on the table. In this case the cards must be reshuffled and recut, and the dealer must deal again.
6. If a card is face up in the deck or if the dealer, while dealing, exposes any of his adversary's cards prior to turning up any of the cards in the layout, there must be a fresh deal, provided the opposing player demands it. If a card is exposed after any portion of the layout has been turned up, the opposing player may keep it or reject it; if he rejects it, the dealer must place the rejected card in the middle of the stock, and deal a fresh card. If the dealer exposes a card in the last round, he should take the exposed card, and allow his adversary to draw one card from his hand in exchange.
7. If the dealer deals too many or too few cards, it is a misdeal, and the dealer forfeits the game.
8. If a player makes a build and holds no card of the proper denomination to take it in, the opposing player may take back in his hand all the cards he has played

The Rules of the Game

since the error was made; and, after separating the cards composing the improper build, may use them as any other cards on the table, in every way the cards will permit, playing again and again, if he can, before his opponent is allowed to resume the play.

9. If a player makes a build, his adversary cannot raise the build by adding any card to the table. The denomination of a build cannot be changed except by a card played from the hand.

10. If a player makes a build and his opponent declines to add to it, the first player may not alter his build with his next turn. He may, however, make another build, or he may pair or combine any other cards, or capture an opponent's build, before taking up his first build.

11. When a card is played for the purpose of building or calling, the player must declare the denomination of the proposed build or call so that his opponent understands; if he fails to do so, his opponent may separate the cards, and employ them in any lawful way he may deem to his advantage.

12. If a player picks up a card or cards that do not belong to the combination, the delinquent player must restore to the layout not only the card or cards thus improperly taken up, but also all the cards that rightly composed the combination.

13. Tricks that have been taken must not be examined throughout the game.

Twenty-One-Point Casino

Casino is often played for a fixed number of points. In this variation, the first player who succeeds in scoring twenty-one points wins the game. No one point takes any precedence over another; the points are scored as soon as made, and a player wins the game the moment he has accrued twenty-one points.

When playing Casino for a given number of points, sweeps are scored as soon as made, and are not turned down as in the single deal game.

If a player claims to have won the game and cannot show the requisite points, the hand is ended and he loses the game.

The deal passes in rotation throughout the game.

Three- and Four-Handed Casino

These games are identical to Twenty-One-Point Casino. The dealer delivers the cards to each player in rotation, beginning with the player to his left. The player who first scores the number of points agreed upon wins the game.

Commerce

Commerce is played with a pack of fifty-two cards. Any number of people can play.

Determination of Deal

One player shuffles the pack, and after having it cut by the player to his right, deals one card face up to each player, beginning with the player to his left. The lowest card has the deal.

Dealing

The dealer must deal face down, two at a time and then three at a time, to each player in rotation, beginning with the player to his left. When each player holds five cards, the dealer places five cards face up on the table.

Playing

The player to the left of the dealer may exchange up to five cards for those on the table, placing his discarded cards face up on the table with those he leaves; or, if content with his hand, he may pass. The next player to the left may similarly exchange cards or pass, and so on. A player having once passed cannot exchange again. The exchanging goes around twice, after which the hands are shown, and the two players with the lowest hands retire from the game.

Another round then ensues, and the player to the left of the previous dealer deals. The second round proceeds precisely as the first, the retired players being excluded, and again the two showing the lowest hands retire from the game.

The rounds continue to be played in this manner, retiring two players at a time, until only two players remain. Of these two, the player who shows the highest hand wins the game. The winner receives a chip from each of the other players. In case of an absolute tie, the winner is decided by cutting the cards; the player cutting the lowest card loses.

In case the game is played with an odd number of players, the two lowest hands retire after each round, until only three players remain; at the end of the round played by the three players only one (the lowest hand) retires, leaving two competitors for the final round.

With a single pack of cards, up to nine people can play; if two packs of cards are used, up to nineteen people can play. When playing with two decks, you might want to remove some of the lower cards, so that you can deal out most of the remaining cards. When the active players are reduced to less than ten, the use of a single pack should be resumed.

When the party is small in number, you can retire only one player (the lowest hand), instead of two after each show of hands. If there are many players, three may be retired at a time.

Rank of the Hands

The hands rank in the following order of precedence, beginning with the highest:

1. Straight Flush
2. Fours
3. Full
4. Flush
5. Straight
6. Triplets
7. Two Pair
8. One Pair

Retired Players

After each show of hands, and until the cards have been cut for the succeeding round, general conversation is free and unlimited; but the moment the cards are dealt, and until the hands are again shown, conversation is forbidden between those playing (the *ins*) and those not playing (the *outs*). A retired player or *out* may make as many remarks as he pleases to try to trap an *in*; but if an *in* replies, the *in* and the *out* must immediately exchange their positions in the game; the *in* must give up his cards, plus a chip, to the *out,* and retire from the game until he succeeds in trapping some other active player.

VaRiATiONS

Commerce with Three Cards

This game is played with a pack of fifty-two cards. The deal is determined in the same way as regular Commerce.

The dealer gives three cards, one at a time to each player in rotation, commencing with the player to his left, and turns up three more in the center of the table.

The player to the left of the dealer may exchange one of his cards for one on the table, placing his discarded card with the two he leaves, or he may pass. The next player to the left may similarly exchange a card or he may pass, and so on. A player having once passed cannot exchange again. The exchanging continues until two of the players are satisfied with their hands, when each of the succeeding players are allowed to exchange only one more card, after which the hands are shown. The best hand wins, and the winner receives a chip from each of the other players. In case of a tie between the two best hands, each receives a chip from the other players.

After any one of the players is satisfied with his hand he signifies this by rapping on the table. After a player raps the other players are allowed to exchange once more only; the hands are then shown and the best wins. The value of the hands is as follows, commencing with the highest:

1. *Tricon*—Three cards of the same denomination. Three Aces is the best, and next three Kings, Queens, Jacks, or Tens, etc., down to three Twos, which is the lowest.
2. *Sequence*—Three cards in unbroken succession of rank; Ace, King, Queen being the highest sequence; down to Three, Two, Ace, which is the lowest.
3. *Flush*—Three cards of the same suit; the flush containing the best point wins.
4. *Pair*—Two cards of the same denomination, and a third card that does not make a tricon. If pairs are equal the highest remaining card wins.
5. *Point*—The greatest number of pips on the cards held. Ace counting eleven, court cards ten each, and the others according to their pips.

Trade and Barter Commerce

Commerce is also played without turning up any cards. When this plan is adopted, each player contributes a sum of chips agreed upon to the pool. The players in turn then trade by giving the dealer a card and chip and receiving a card from the top of the pack; the rejected card, which must not be exposed, is placed at the bottom of the pack. The players can also barter, that is, exchange a card from the hand dealt with the player to the left, for which no payment is made. The player to the left must not refuse to barter unless he stands content on the hand dealt. The players in turn must either trade, barter, or stand. When a player stands, no other player can trade or barter; the hands are shown, and the best hand wins the pool.

The chips given to the dealer in trading are kept by him, and are not added to the pool; but the dealer has to pay a chip to the winner.

If the dealer holds a tricon, sequence, flush, or pair, and does not win the pool, he has to pay a chip to every player. Sometimes it is agreed that the dealer only pays those players who hold better hands than himself.

Concentration

Concentration is played by two or more people, with a deck of fifty-two cards.

Playing

The players cut for the chance to go first. All of the cards are placed face down and spread out on a table, in neat rows. The first player turns any two cards over, and tries to remember which cards he turned. The second player (to the left of the first player) and all subsequent players follow in order, trying to locate a pair of matching cards. The first player to succeed removes the cards from the table, and takes another turn.

The game is over when all of the cards have been removed from the table. The player who makes the most matches wins, regardless of the value of the cards.

Coon Can

Coon Can is played by two people, with a pack of forty cards—the Eights, Nines, and Tens are removed from a complete pack. The cards rank in the following order: Ace, Two, Three, Four, Five, Six, Seven, Jack, Queen, and King.

Dealing

The players cut for deal; the highest card deals. After the cards have been properly shuffled and cut, the dealer deals three cards to each player, beginning with the eldest hand (the player to the left of the dealer), then three again, and lastly four cards, thus giving each player ten cards. The cards remaining undealt (called the stock) are then placed face down on the table.

Playing

The object of the game is for each player to form runs of Fours, Threes, and Sequences with the assistance of cards drawn from the stock, or taken from the discard pile. By placing such combinations on the table, the players unload their original ten cards, and one card more. The winner is the player who can get rid of his cards first.

The Sequences may be formed with Ace, Two, Three, etc., or with Five, Six, Seven, Jack, etc., of the same suit. The Ace is not in sequence with the King and Queen.

The play begins when the eldest hand draws one card from the top of the stock and, with the assistance of that card, tries to form any Threes or Fours, or a Sequence. If he has any of these combinations, he places them on the table and then discards from his hand one card. If he does not use the card that he drew, he places it, face up, by the side of the stock in the discard pile.

If the dealer can use the discarded card to form any combination, he takes it in hand and similarly places the combination on the table, and discards a card from his hand. If he cannot use the discard, he draws a card from the stock to try to form combinations. The play proceeds in this manner until one of the players succeeds in combining all his ten cards and one card more, eleven in all.

If neither of the players succeeds, the game is a draw. The losing player deals, but when a draw occurs the eldest hand deals.

Crazy Eights

This game is usually played by two to four players, but any number can play. When more than four play it is best to use two complete decks of fifty-two cards.

Dealing

One player shuffles the deck and, after having it cut by the player to his right, deals one card face up to each player, beginning with the player to his left. The lowest card has the deal. The dealer then deals one card to each player at a time, until all the cards are dealt.

Playing

The players arrange their cards in order of suits. The eldest hand (the player to the left of the dealer) puts down a card, face up, on the table. The next player must put down a card from his hand that matches either the pip or the suit of the first card. If the player cannot make a match, he can choose to either skip his turn, or throw down an Eight. Eights are wild, and the player can announce a change of suit to whatever he has the most of in his hand, regardless of what suit the Eight he has thrown has. The game continues in rotation. The game is won by the first player to get rid of all of his cards.

Cribbage

Cribbage is entirely different from any other card game. It is usually played by two people, with a full pack of fifty-two cards, with five cards to a player. Sixty-one points constitute game. These points are scored on a Cribbage board (see Figure 14), which consists of two linear divisions, one division for each player's independent score. Each division contains sixty holes; and at one end, between the divisions, is another hole, called the *game-hole.* Each division is marked off in subdivisions of five points each.

Figure 14

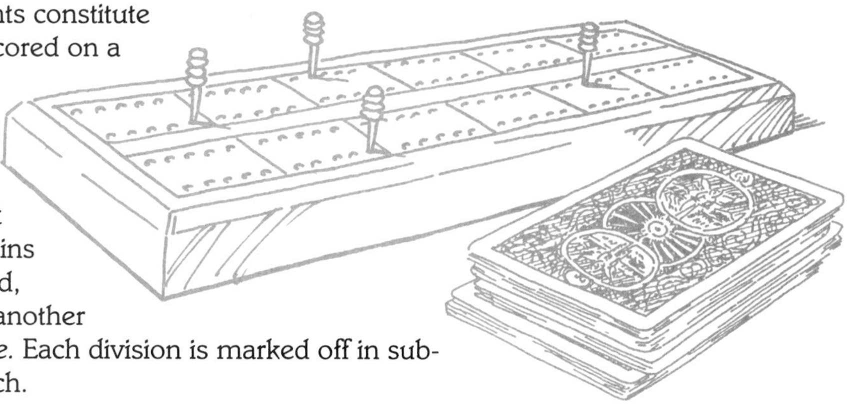

The players begin the game in the outside row on the side of the game hole. The pegs will travel along the outside edge, pass across the top, then down the inside row to game. Each player will use two pegs for scoring.

Dealing

The players cut for the deal; the low card deals. The pack is shuffled, and the nondealer cuts it. The dealer reunites the deck and gives five cards to each player, one at a time, beginning with his adversary. The undealt portion of the pack is placed face down, between the game-hole end of the board and the edge of the table. The nondealer is entitled to mark three holes, called *three for last* while his adversary is dealing.

Laying Out for Crib

The deal being completed, the players proceed to look at their hands and to *lay out for crib*. Each has to put out two cards. The players, having decided which two cards they want to discard, place the cards face down in a pile on the table, by the side of the board nearest to the dealer. The four cards laid out are called the *crib*.

Cutting for the Start

After the crib is laid out, the nondealer cuts the pack and the dealer turns up the top card of the bottom pile. The card turned up is called the *start*. If the start is a Jack the dealer marks two (called *two for his heels*) on his side of the board.

Playing

The hands are now played. The nondealer plays any card from his hand he sees fit, placing it face up on the table by the side of the board nearest to himself, and calls out the number at which it is valued. The King, Queen, Jack, and Ten (called *tenth cards*) are valued at ten each, the other cards at the number of pips on them. The dealer then plays any card he chooses, placing it face up by his side of the board, and calls out the value of his card added to the value of the card first played. The nondealer next plays another card, and then the dealer, and so on, as long as any cards remain in hand, or until a card cannot be played without passing the number thirty-one. When it happens that a player cannot play without passing thirty-one, he says, "Go." His adversary then, if he has a card that can be played without passing thirty-one (called *coming in*) is entitled to play it. When there is a *go*, or when thirty-one is reached, the remainder of the cards in hand are not played.

Counts and Combinations in Play

The players are entitled to score for certain combinations of cards as follows: pairs, fifteen, sequences, the go, and thirty-one.

Pairs—If, when a card is played, the next card played pairs it (for instance, if a four is played to a four), the player pairing is entitled to mark two points on the cribbage board.

Pair Royal—If, after a pair has been played, the card next played is also of the same denomination, a *pair royal* is made, which entitles that player to mark six points.

Double Pair Royal—If, after a *pair royal* has been played, the card next played is again of the same kind, it constitutes a *double pair royal* that entitles the player to a score of twelve points, in addition to the pair already scored by him.

Tenth cards only pair with tenth cards of the same denomination. Thus, Kings pair with Kings, but Kings do not pair with Queens, although they are both considered tenth cards.

Fifteen—If a player reaches exactly fifteen by adding the pips of all the played cards, he is entitled to mark two points.

Sequences—The sequence of the cards is King, Queen, Jack, Ten, Nine, Eight, Seven, Six, Five, Four, Three, Two, Ace. The Ace is not in sequence with the King and Queen. If any three cards are played in sequence order, the player of the third card is entitled to mark three (called a *run* of three). If a fourth card is similarly played, that player is entitled to a run of four; if a fifth card is similarly played, a run of five accrues, and so on. If there is a break in the sequence, and in the subsequent play the break is filled up without the intervention of a card out of sequence order, the player completing the sequence is entitled to a score of one for each card forming the sequence.

It is not necessary for the cards forming a sequence to be played in order. For example, A plays a Four; B a Two; A a Five. B can then come in with a Three, and mark a run of four with Two, Three, Four, Five. After the Three is played, A can come in with an Ace or a Six, making a run of five, or with a Four, making a run of four. But if any card not in sequence intervenes, the run is stopped. Thus, if Four, Two, Five, and Five are played in this order, a Three or a Six will not come in, as the second Five, which intervened, disrupted the run.

The Go—The player who gets closest to thirty-one is entitled to mark one, for the *last card, go,* or *end hole.* If a player reaches thirty-one exactly, he marks two instead of one.

For instance: two tenth cards and a Four are played, making twenty-four. If the next player has no card in hand under an Eight, he cannot come in, and his adversary marks a go. If, however, the adversary has a Seven, he may play that and score two for thirty-one; or, if he has a Four he may play it and mark two for the pair, and, if his adversary has no card that will come in (i.e., no card under a Four remaining in his hand), the last player marks again one for the go.

Compound Score—More than one mark can be obtained at the same time. In the last case given, a pair and a go are scored together. A pair and a thirty-one, or a pair and a fifteen, may occur—scoring four; or a sequence and a fifteen, and so on.

Showing

As soon as a go or thirty-one is reached, the players show their hands and try to create certain combinations within their own hands. The non-dealer has the *first show*. He places his hand face up on the table, marking points for whatever he is holding, making use of the start as though it were a part of his hand, but without mixing it with his cards. The dealer does the same with his hand. He then shows the crib, and has the opportunity to use that with the remainder of his hand, and mark any points made with it and the start.

The points counted in hand or crib may be made by fifteens, by pairs, or pairs royal, by sequences, by flushes, or by *his nob*.

Fifteens in hand or crib are counted by adding together all the different cards (including the start), the pips of which will make exactly fifteen, without counting the same set of cards twice. In reckoning fifteens, tenth cards are valued at ten each. Each separate fifteen that can be made with a different combination is worth two. For example: a player holding, either with or without the start, a tenth card and a five, reckons two (called *fifteen-two*). If he has another five, he combines this also with the tenth card and reckons two more, or *fifteen-four;* or if his other cards were a Four and an Ace, he would similarly reckon another fifteen.

Suppose a player holds two tenth cards with a Five, and a Five is turned up, he reckons fifteen-eight, the combination being as follows:

Ten of Clubs	Ten of Spades	Ten of Clubs	Ten of Spades
Five of Clubs	Five of Spades	Five of Spades	Five of Clubs

Pairs are reckoned on the same principle. In the above example the total score would be twelve: eight for the fifteens, and four for the two pairs. To take a less easy example, a hand consisting of four fives would score twenty (twelve for the double pair royal and eight for the fifteens), as under:

Five of Spades	Five of Spades	Five of Spades	Five of Hearts
Five of Hearts	Five of Hearts	Five of Clubs	Five of Clubs
Five of Clubs	Five of Diamonds	Five of Diamonds	Five of Diamonds

Sequences of three or more cards are counted the same way as in the regular, with one addition. If one card of a sequence can be substituted for another of the same kind, the sequence is counted twice. For example, a Seven, Eight, and two Nines give two sequences of seven, eight, nine, by substituting one Nine for the other, in addition to the fifteen and the pair, making the total ten.

A *flush* is counted by a player whose entire hand consists of cards of the same suit. The flush counts three; if the start is of the same suit as the hand, the flush counts four. For example, a player has Three, Four, Five of the same suit, and a Six is turned up. The hand counts fifteen-two; four for sequence, six; and three for the flush, nine. If the start is also of the same suit, the hand reckons ten. No flush can be counted in crib, unless the start is of the same suit as the crib, when the flush reckons five. *His Nob*—If a player holds a Jack in hand or crib of the suit turned up, he counts *one for his nob.*

When the hands and crib are all counted, the deal is at an end. The cards are put together and shuffled, and a fresh deal begins. The player who was the nondealer in the first hand now deals, and so on, alternately, until the game is won.

Scoring

The points made during the hand accrue in the following order: two for his heels; points during the play of the hand; the nondealer's show; the dealer's show; and the crib show. Each player marks the points to which he is entitled as soon as they accrue by placing a peg in the hole on the board corresponding to the number to which he is entitled. For the first score on each side, only one peg is used; for the second score, the second peg (called the *foremost peg)* is placed in front of the first. At the next score the *hindmost* peg is moved in front of the other, and becomes in turn the foremost peg.

When a player arrives at the top, he proceeds to mark *down the board,* on the inner row of holes on his side of the board. The player who first scores sixty-one places his foremost peg in the game-hole and wins the game. If a player wins the game before his adversary has scored thirty-one points, he wins a double.

The Rules of the Game

1. In cutting for the deal, the player cutting must leave sufficient cards for the player cutting last to make a legal cut. He who cuts last must not leave less than four cards in the remainder of the pack.
2. The player who cuts the lowest card deals. The Ace is lowest, the King highest.
3. If, in cutting for the deal, a player exposes more than one card, his adversary may treat whichever of the exposed cards he chooses as the one cut.
4. If, in cutting, or reuniting the separated packets, the dealer exposes a card or if there is any confusion of the cards, there must be a fresh cut.
5. There must be a fresh cut for the deal after each game.
6. Each player has a right to shuffle the cards. The dealer has the right to shuffle last. The players deal alternately throughout the game.
7. The dealer must deal the cards one at a time to each player, beginning with his adversary. If he deals two together, he may rectify the error, provided he can do so by moving one card only; otherwise, there must be a fresh deal, and the non-dealer marks two holes.
8. If the dealer exposes any of his own cards, there is no penalty. If he exposes one of his adversary's, the adversary marks two holes, and has the option of a fresh deal, prior to looking at his hand. If a card is exposed through the nondealer's fault, the dealer marks two, and has the option of dealing again.
9. If there is a faced card in the pack, there must be a fresh deal.
10. If the dealer gives out too many cards, the nondealer marks two holes, and a fresh deal ensues; but, in such case, the nondealer must discover the error before he takes up his cards, or he cannot claim the two, though there must still be a new deal.
11. If the dealer gives out too few cards, the nondealer marks two holes, and has the option, after looking at his hand, of a fresh deal, or of allowing the imperfect hand to be completed from the top of the pack.
12. If a player deals out of turn, and the error is discovered before the start is turned up, the deal in error is void, and the right dealer deals.
13. If either player lays out with too few cards in hand, he must play out the hand with less than the right number of cards.
14. The dealer may insist on his adversary laying out first.
15. If a player takes back into his hand a card he has laid out, his adversary marks two holes, and has the option of a fresh deal.
16. The crib must not be touched during the play of the hand.
17. If the dealer turns up more than one card, the nondealer may choose which of the exposed cards shall be the start.

The Rules of the Game

18. If a jack is turned up, and the dealer plays his first card without scoring his heels, he forfeits the score.

19. If a player plays with too many cards in hand, his adversary marks two holes, and has the option of a fresh deal. If he elects to stand the deal, he has the right of drawing the surplus cards from the offender's hand, and of looking at them, and the option of playing the hand again, or not.

20. If a player plays with too few cards, there is no penalty.

21. If a card that will come in is played, it cannot be taken up again. If a card that will not come in is played, no penalty attaches to the exposure.

22. If two cards are played together, the card counted is deemed to be the one played, and the other must be taken back into the player's hand.

23. If a player neglects to play when he has a card that will come in, his opponent may require it to be played, or may mark two holes.

24. There is no penalty for miscounting during the play.

25. When reckoning a hand or crib, the cards must be shown and must remain exposed until the opponent is satisfied with the claims of combinations.

26. If a player mixes his hand with the crib or with the pack before his claim is properly made, he forfeits any score the hand or crib may contain.

27. If a player scores more points than he is entitled to, the adversary may correct the score and add the same number to his own score. This rule applies even if a player places his peg in the game-hole.

28. There is no penalty for scoring too few points. A player is not bound to assist his adversary in making out his score.

29. If a player touches his opponent's pegs except to put back an overscore, or if he touches his own pegs except when he has a score to make, his adversary marks two holes.

30. If a player displaces his foremost peg, he must put it behind the other. If he displaces both his pegs, his adversary is entitled to place the hindmost peg where he believes it should go, and the other peg must then be put behind it.

31. A lurch (or double game), cannot be claimed, unless by previous agreement.

32. The three for last may be scored at any time during the game, but not after the opponent has scored sixty-one.

The Secrets of the Game

1. In laying out for crib, keep in mind whether or not you are the dealer. When you are the dealer, you should lay out cards that are likely to score in crib; when you are not the dealer, you should do the reverse. It is more important to lay out bad cards for the adversary's crib (called *balking the crib),* than to keep the cards in hand that will give you the greatest score. The crib and start together consist of five cards, the hand and start of only four cards. The largest number of points that can be made out of four cards is twelve, but with five cards, there are many hands that score from twelve to twenty-nine. Therefore, you should put out for the opponent's crib the most unlikely scoring cards. If your adversary is a good player, he will prefer the interest of his crib to that of his hand, and put out cards that are likely to make long scores in combination with three others. This is an additional reason for balking his crib.

2. The least likely card to consider in crib is a King, as that card can only score in sequence one way. For a similar reason, an Ace is a good balk. The best balking cards for the opponent's crib are King, with Ten, Nine, Eight, Seven, Six, or Ace (King and Nine being the best); or Queen, with any of these except the Ten. If

you are unable to lay out any such combination, discard cards that are not in sequence.

3. The best cards to lay out for your own crib (and, therefore, those to be avoided for your adversary's) are Fives, Five and Six, Five and a tenth card, Three and Two, Seven and Eight, Four and Ace, Nine and Six, or pairs, particularly low pairs. If you are unable to lay out any of these, discard cards as close as possible. It is generally good to retain a sequence in hand, because if a card similar to any one of the cards held is turned up, you can earn at least eight points. Pairs royal are also good cards to keep.

4. The layout is affected by the state of the score. Toward the end of the game, if you have cards that in all probability will take you out, that is more important than balking the opponent's crib.

5. In playing out your hand, the card first chosen should be the one that presents the least chance of an adverse score. Aces, Twos, Threes, or Fours, are the best cards to lead, as it would be hard to get to fifteen with them, and the only chance of a score is by pairing them. The pair, however, is very likely to be declined, as it is common to begin with a card of which you hold a duplicate (except with two Fives), so

The Secrets of the Game

that you may make a pair royal.

6. When leading from a sequence, first play the highest or lowest instead of the middle card.

7. If the adversary plays a card close to the one led, it is frequently because he desires you to make a run of three, as he might have a fourth card to come in.

8. If the adversary plays a card that you can pair or make fifteen of, choose the latter. At the same time you must not forget, if a Seven or Eight is led and you make fifteen, that you give the opponent a chance of coming in with a Six or a Nine.

9. Avoid making eleven with a Four because, if the Four is paired, the adversary gains four holes. The rule applies to all similar combinations. For example, twelve made with a Three, twenty-seven made with a Four, or twenty-eight with a Three. Avoid making the number twenty-one in play, as the next tenth card will come in for two points.

10. When playing the cards, the state of the score should constantly be considered. When you are leading, try to keep the advantage by refusing pairs or by declining to make fifteen with close cards. Playing in this way is called *playing off*. On the other hand, if you are behind in the game, you can run more risks by pairing (risking a pair royal), by making fif-

teen with close cards, or by playing close cards when, if your adversary makes a small run, you have a card that will come in and give you a larger one. Playing in this way is called *playing on*.

11. In order to determine whether you should play on or play off, keep in mind that the average points in the play of the hand are two for the dealer, and one-and-a-half for the nondealer; that the average points in hand are more than four and less than five; and that the average points in crib are five. Each player then needs to make six in hand and play throughout the game, and seventeen-and-a-half in two deals. If the players score this average, they are said to be at home. If your adversary is about seven holes behind you, you are said to be safe at home. When you are at home you should play off; when your adversary is safe at home you should play on.

12. The dealer's chance of making the game-hole is greater than that of the nondealer.

13. In reckoning the hand and crib, first search your cards for fifteens, then for pairs, then for sequences, then for a flush, and lastly, for his nob.

VaRiATiONS

Six-Card Cribbage

Six-Card Cribbage is more popular than the five-card game. It is played on the same board and follows most of the rules of the more traditional five-card version.

The dealer gives six cards to his adversary and himself. Each player lays out two of these for crib, retaining four in his hand. The nondealer is not allowed any points at the beginning.

The main difference between the games is that in the five-card game, the object is to get thirty-one and then abandon the remaining cards; in the six-card game, all the cards are played out. There are more points made in the play while, at five cards, the game is often decided by the loss or gain of one point.

At Six-Card Cribbage, the last card played scores a point (but not if the last card played makes thirty-one). The hands and crib are scored the same as the five-card game. The winner is the player who first reaches sixty-one.

Playing Last Cards

If one party exhausts his hand and his adversary still has two cards, the remaining cards are to be played to their full advantage. For instance, C has played out his four cards and D, having two left (an Eight and Seven), calls fifteen as he throws them down, and marks three points—two for the fifteen, and one for the last card.

Four-Handed Cribbage

The game of Four-Handed Cribbage is played by four people, playing as partners—each sitting opposite to his partner. Sixty-one points constitute a game, but it is usual to go around the board twice, making the game 122 points.

Before you begin, decide which two players will manage the board. The others are not allowed to touch the board or pegs. The laws that govern Five-Card Cribbage are applicable here.

The deal and crib pass round the table in rotation to the left. Before dealing, the cards must be cut by the player to the right of the dealer. The dealer gives to each player in rotation one card at a time, beginning with the player to his left, until all have received five cards. The remainder of the pack is placed at the dealer's left hand. Each person then lays out one card for the crib. The left-hand adversary must discard first, and the players continue around the table, with the dealer laying out last.

When all have laid out for the crib, the pack is cut for the start-card. This cut is made by the player to the left of the dealer. So, the dealer's right-hand adversary cuts before dealing, but his left-hand adversary cuts for the start-card.

Having cut the start-card, the player to the left of the dealer leads off first, the next player to the left following, and so on around the table, untill all of the cards are played out. Should any player be unable to come in under thirty-one, he declares it to be a go, and the right of play moves to his left-hand neighbor.

When the hand is played out, the different amounts are pegged, the crib being taken last. Whoever led off must score first, and so on around to the dealer.

Division Loo

Division Loo can be played by any number of people, but five or seven make the best game. It is played with a pack of fifty-two cards, which rank as in Whist.

Dealing

Before dealing, the dealer deposits *three* chips into the pool, the value of which has previously been agreed upon. It is necessary to make the pool a number that can be exactly divided by three. The chips deposited by the dealer are called a *single.*

After the cards are shuffled and cut, the dealer proceeds to deal three cards, one at a time to each player, beginning at the eldest hand (the player to the left of the dealer), and going round to the left; he also deals an extra hand, called a *Dummy,* to the center of the table, and turns up the next card for trump.

In the first deal, or whenever a single occurs, a *bold stand* is played. A bold stand compels every player to play his hand; but the eldest hand has the sole privilege of immediately exchanging the hand that was dealt to him for the dummy. A bold stand can only occur at the first deal; or when three players declare to play, and each take a trick; or when only two play, and one takes two tricks and the other one trick. Sometimes it is agreed to omit bold stand, and at the first deal, or whenever a single occurs, each player deposits three chips in the pool , and the dealer six chips.

After the deal has been completed each player looks at his cards, and declares whether he will play his hand or pass. If he plays, he says,

"I play"; if he resigns, he says, "I pass," and his interest in that pool ceases, unless he elects to exchange his hand for the dummy. The first player to declare has the first right of taking dummy, and if he declines, the next player has that privilege, and so on; but whoever takes the dummy must play it.

No player is permitted to look at his hand before it is his turn to declare. Once he declares, he is compelled to adhere to his decision. When a player resigns his hand he gives it to the dealer, who places it in the stock.

Sometimes it is agreed that when only one declares to play and the dummy remains on the table, the dealer has the option of taking it and playing for the good of the pool. When this variation is played, the dealer must declare, before taking the dummy, whether he plays for himself or the pool, otherwise he is assumed to be playing for himself.

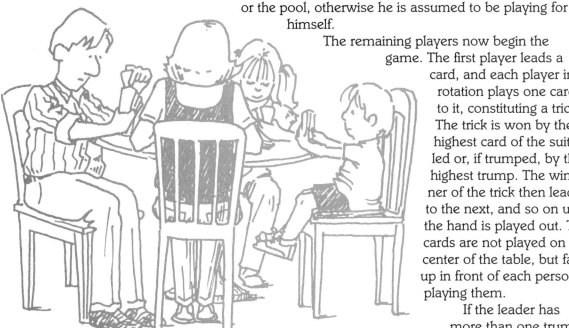

The remaining players now begin the game. The first player leads a card, and each player in rotation plays one card to it, constituting a trick. The trick is won by the highest card of the suit led or, if trumped, by the highest trump. The winner of the trick then leads to the next, and so on until the hand is played out. The cards are not played on the center of the table, but face up in front of each person playing them.

If the leader has more than one trump, he must lead the highest, unless his trumps are in sequence; but if he does not hold two or more trumps, he may lead with whichever card he chooses. The other players, in rotation, must follow suit. Holding none of the suit led, they must head the trick with a trump. If a player is unable to follow suit or trump, he may play any card he chooses.

The winner of the first trick must lead a trump, and if he holds two trumps, he must lead the higher of the two. If the leader holds the ace of trumps (or the King if the Ace is turned up), he must lead it whether he has another trump or not. It is sometimes agreed that when there are more than two players, the leader is not obliged to play his highest trump unless it is the Ace (or King if the Ace is turned up).

After the hand is played to its conclusion, the winner or winners of the tricks divide the amount in the pool, one-third for each trick. If a player wins one trick he gets one-third of the pool, if he wins two tricks he takes two-thirds of the pool, and if he wins all the tricks, he captures the whole pool.

If a player declares to play and fails to take a trick, he must contribute three chips to the next pool. When none of the players who declared to play owe chips to the pool, a bold stand occurs. After the pool has been divided and the new payments are made, the dealer deposits three chips into the pool, and the game proceeds as before.

Sometimes Club-law is introduced, in which case every one must play when a Club happens to be turned trump. When Club-law is played, there is no dummy.

The Rules of the Game

1. The deal is determined by dealing a card, face up, to each player, beginning at the left of the person dealing the cards. The player holding the lowest card deals.
2. The player to the dealer's right cuts the cards. At least four cards must be cut, and at least four must be left in the lower packet.
3. When cutting to the dealer, if a card is exposed, there must be a fresh cut.
4. If, in reuniting the separated cards the dealer exposes a card, you must recut.
5. Each player has the right to shuffle, and it is the dealer's right to shuffle last.
6. The dealer must give to each player one card at a time, beginning with the player to his left, and at the end of each round he must deal one card to the dummy prior to beginning the next round. In this order, the dealer must deliver three cards to each player, and three to dumby.
7. After completing the deal, the dealer must turn up the next card for trumps.
8. If a card is faced in the pack and it is discovered before the deal is completed, there must be a fresh deal.
9. If the dealer deals without having the pack cut; or shuffles the pack after it has been cut with his consent; or deals out of order, he forfeits a single (three chips) to the pool. This penalty goes to the present pool. The cards are reshuffled and recut, and he deals again.

The Rules of the Game

10. After the first deal, each player takes the deal in rotation, beginning with the player to the left of the dealer. The game should not be abandoned until the deal has returned to the original dealer.

11. If a player deals out of turn, and is not stopped before the trump card is turned, the deal stands good.

12. Each player must declare whether he will play or not, in rotation, beginning with the player to the dealer's left.

13. If a player looks at his cards before it is his turn to declare to play, he forfeits a single to the pool. This penalty goes to the present pool.

14. If a player exposes a card before declaring to play or declares to play before his turn, he forfeits a single to the pool. This penalty goes to the present pool.

15. If a player takes the dummy, and no one plays against him, he takes the pool. If no one declares to play, the dealer takes the pool.

16. If a player, having declared to play, exposes a card before it is his turn to play; or plays a card out of turn; or before all have declared; or exposes a card while playing so as to be named by any other declared player, he must leave in the pool any tricks he may make, and, in addition, forfeit twelve chips. If he fails to take a trick he must pay into the pool, up to the limit (if any) in lieu of penalty. These tricks and forfeitures go to the next pool.

17. If a player holds the Ace of trumps and does not lead it, or if he holds King (Ace being turned up) and does not lead it, he must leave in the pool any tricks he may make, and forfeit twelve chips. This forfeiture and the tricks go to the next pool.

18. If a player does not lead the higher of two trumps, unless his trumps are sequence cards, that is, cards of equal value; or does not head the trick when able, or revokes; or holding a trump does not lead trump after trick, he must leave in the pool any tricks he may make, and forfeit twelve chips. This forfeiture and the tricks go to the next pool.

19. When a revoke or any error in play occurs, the cards must be taken up and the hand replayed, if so desired by any player except the offender.

20. If a deck is discovered to be incorrect, the deal in which the discovery is made is void. All preceding deals stand good.

Écarté

Écarté is played by two people with a pack of 32 cards—the Sixes, Fives, Fours, Threes, and Twos are removed from a complete pack. The object of the game is to win three tricks, then to achieve *vole* by winning all five.

Dealing

The dealer gives five cards to each player. The cards are not dealt singly, but two at a time to each, and then by three at a time to each.

The eleventh card, now the top of the pack, is turned up for trump. Should it happen to be a King, the dealer marks one; otherwise the turn-up is of no value; it merely indicates the trump suit for that deal. The remainder of the pack after the trump card is turned up is called the *stock*. The stock should be placed to the dealer's left.

Discarding

The players now look at their hands. Should the nondealer be satisfied with his cards, he may at once proceed to play them. But if he considers it to his advantage to exchange any or all of them, he proposes, saying, "I propose," or, "Cards."

If the nondealer proposes, the dealer has the option of accepting or refusing. If he accepts he may change any or all of his opponent's cards, and he signifies his intention of doing so by saying, "I accept," or, "How many?" But if the dealer is satisfied with his hand he refuses to give cards, saying, "I refuse," or, "Play." If the nondealer plays without proposing, the dealer must also play without exchanging any cards.

When a proposal is accepted, the nondealer separates from his hand the number of cards he desires to exchange, and places them face down on the table to his right, at the same time naming the number discarded. The dealer also puts out his discard, and places it to his right, keeping it separate from his adversary's discard. The trump card is put aside, and the cards required by the nondealer to restore the number in hand to five again are given him from the top of the stock. The dealer then helps himself to the number he has discarded.

If the nondealer is still dissatisfied, he may propose a second time, saying, "Again," and the dealer may accept or refuse as before; and so on until the nondealer has a hand that he wishes to play, or until the dealer refuses.

Marking the King

After the discard (or, if there is no discard, after the deal), the nondealer, if he holds the King of trumps in his hand, should announce it, saying, "I

have the King," or, "King," and mark one. He must announce the King before playing a card, unless the card first played is the King, when he may announce it at any time before the dealer plays to it.

If the dealer has the King of trumps in his hand, he similarly announces it, and marks one. If it is the card he first plays, he may announce it at any time before he plays a second card.

Playing

The nondealer leads any card he chooses. His adversary plays a card to it; the two cards thus played constitute a *trick*.

The second player must not *renounce* if he holds a card of the suit led, i.e., he is bound to follow suit, if able, and he must win the trick if he can. The highest card of the suit led wins the trick. The cards rank in the following order, beginning with the highest: King, Queen, Jack, Ace, Ten, Nine, Eight, Seven. Trumps win other suits. Failing the suit led, the second player, if he has a trump, must win the trick by trumping. The winner of the trick leads to the next, and so on until the hand is played out.

Scoring

The score accrues from turning up or holding the King, and from winning the majority of tricks. The player who wins three tricks out of the five gains the *point* and scores one. If he wins all five tricks he gains the *vole,* and scores two. Winning four tricks is no better than winning three.

If the nondealer plays without proposing and fails to make three tricks, his adversary scores two, just the same as though he had won a vole. Similarly, if the dealer refuses cards and fails to win three tricks, his adversary scores two. The player who first obtains five points wins the game.

The rule for playing without proposing and for refusing only applies to the first proposal or refusal in each hand. Playing without proposing a second time, or refusing a second proposal, does not entail any penalty.

The Rules of the Game

1. Each player has a right to shuffle the deck. The dealer has the right to shuffle last.
2. The pack must not be shuffled below the table, nor in such a manner as to expose the faces of the cards, nor during the play of the hand.
3. A cut must consist of at least two cards.
4. A player exposing more than one card when cutting for the deal must cut again.
5. The player who cuts the highest card deals, and has the choice of cards and seats.
6. The cut for the deal holds good even if the deck is incorrect.
7. The dealer must give five cards to his adversary and five to himself, two at a time to each, and then by three at a time to each.
8. If the dealer gives more or less than five cards to his adversary, or to himself, or does not adhere to the order of distribution, and the error is discovered before the trump card is turned, the nondealer, before he looks at his hand, may require the dealer to rectify the error, or may claim a fresh deal.
9. The hands having been dealt, the dealer must turn up for trumps the top card of those remaining.
10. If the dealer turns up more than one card, the nondealer, before he looks at his hand, may choose which of the exposed cards shall be the trump, or may claim a fresh deal. If the nondealer has looked at his hand, there must be a fresh deal.
11. If, before the trump card is turned up, a faced card is discovered in the pack, there must be a fresh deal.
12. If the dealer exposes any of his own cards, the deal stands good. If he exposes any of his adversary's cards, the nondealer, before he looks at his hand, may claim a fresh deal.
13. If a player deals out of his turn, and the error is discovered before the trump card is turned up, the deal is void.
14. If either player has more than five cards, he may claim a fresh deal. Should the nondealer not claim a fresh deal, he discards the superfluous cards, and the dealer is not entitled to see them.
15. If either player has less than five cards, he may have his hand completed from the stock, or may claim a fresh deal.
16. If a fresh deal is not claimed when the wrong number of cards are dealt, the dealer cannot mark the King turned up.
17. If the nondealer plays without taking cards and it is then discovered that he has more or less than five cards, there must be a fresh deal.
18. If the dealer plays without taking cards and it is then discovered that he has more or less than five cards, his adversary may claim a fresh deal.
19. If a King is turned up, the dealer is entitled to mark it at any time before the trump card of the next deal is turned up.
20. If either player holds the King of trumps, he must announce it before playing his first card, or he loses the right to mark it. It is not sufficient to mark the King held in hand without announcing it.

The Rules of the Game

21. If the King is the first card led, it may be announced at any time prior to being played. If the King is first played by the dealer, he may announce it at any time before he plays again.

22. If a player not holding the King announces it, and fails to declare his error before he has played a card, the adversary may correct the score and has the option of requiring the hands to be played over again. If the offender wins the point, he marks nothing; if he wins the vole, he marks only one; if he wins the point when his adversary has played without proposing or has refused the first proposal, he marks only one. But if the adversary himself holds the King, there is no penalty.

23. If a player proposes he cannot retract.

24. The dealer, having accepted or refused, cannot retract. The dealer, if required, must inform his adversary how many cards he has taken.

25. Each player, before taking cards, must put his discard face down on the table, apart from the stock and from his adversary's discard. Cards once discarded must not be looked at.

26. If the nondealer takes more cards than he has discarded, and mixes any of them with his hand, the dealer may claim a fresh deal. If the dealer elects to play the hand, he draws the superfluous cards from the nondealer's hand. Should the nondealer have taken up any of the cards given him, the dealer is entitled to look at the cards he draws.

27. If the dealer gives himself more cards than he has discarded, and mixes any of them with his hand, the nondealer may claim a fresh deal. If the nondealer elects to play the hand, he draws the superfluous cards from the dealer's hand. Should the dealer have taken up any of the cards he has given himself, the nondealer is entitled to look at the cards he draws.

28. If the nondealer asks for less cards than he has discarded, the dealer counts as tricks all cards that cannot be played to.

29. If the dealer gives himself less cards than he has discarded, he may, before playing, complete his hand from the stock. If the dealer plays with less than five cards, the nondealer counts as tricks all cards that cannot be played to.

30. If the dealer give his adversary more cards than he has asked for, the nondealer may claim a fresh deal. If the nondealer elects to play the hand, he discards the superfluous cards, and the dealer is not entitled to see them.

31. If the dealer give his adversary less cards than he has asked for, the nondealer may claim a fresh deal. If the nondealer elects to play the hand, he completes it from the stock.

32. If a faced card is found in the stock after discarding, both players have a right to see it. The faced card must be thrown aside, and the next card given instead.

33. If, in giving cards, the dealer exposes any of the nondealer's cards, the nondealer has the option of taking them. Should he refuse them, they must be thrown aside,

The Rules of the Game

and the next cards given instead. If the dealer expose any of his own cards, he must take them.

34. If, after giving cards, the dealer turns up a card in error, as though it were the trump card, he cannot refuse another discard. If another is demanded, the non-dealer has the option of taking the exposed card.

35. If the dealer accepts when there are not sufficient cards left in the stock to enable the players to exchange as many cards as they wish, the nondealer is entitled to exchange as many as there are left, and the dealer must play his hand. The dealer is at liberty to accept on the condition that there enough cards in the stock.

36. A card led in turn cannot be taken up again. A card played to a lead may be taken up again to save a revoke or to correct the error of not winning a trick when able, and then only prior to another card being led.

37. If a card is led out of turn, it may be taken up again, prior to its being played to. After it has been played to, the error cannot be rectified.

38. If the leader names one suit and plays another, the adversary may play to the card led, or may require the leader to play the suit named. If the leader has none of the suit named, the card led cannot be withdrawn.

39. If a player abandons his hand when he has not made a trick, his adversary is entitled to mark the vole. If a player abandons his hand after he has made one or two tricks, his adversary is entitled to mark the point. But, if a player throws down his cards, claiming to score, the hand is not abandoned, and there is no penalty.

40. If a player renounces when he holds a card of the suit led, or if a player fails to win the trick when able, his adversary has the option of requiring the hand to be played again, notwithstanding that he may have abandoned his hand. If the offender wins the point he marks nothing; if he wins the vole he marks only one; if he wins the point when his adversary has played without proposing or has refused the first proposal, he marks only one.

41. A player may call for new cards, at his own expense, at any time before the pack is cut for the next deal.

42. If a pack is discovered to be incorrect, redundant, or imperfect, the deal in which the discovery is made is void. All preceding deals stand good.

43. A player winning the point is entitled to mark one; a player winning the vole is entitled to mark two.

44. If a player plays without proposing and fails to win a point, his adversary is entitled to mark two.
    These scores apply only to the first proposal or refusal in a hand, and only to the point, the score for the vole being unaffected.

45. If a player omits to mark his score, he may rectify the omission at any time before the trump card of the next deal is turned up.

46. An admitted overscore can be taken down at any time during the game.

The Secrets of the Game

1. The pack should be thoroughly shuffled after every deal. Otherwise, the cards will get packed in suits in the course of play.

2. The dealer should not look at his hand until after his adversary has decided whether to propose or not.

3. A player holding the King should not announce it until he is in the act of playing his first card.

4. It is important to propose quickly, as hesitation exposes the nature of the hand. In order to be quick in proposing, the Jeux de Règle should be known by heart.

5. Never discard less than three cards, unless you hold the King of trumps. With this card in hand you may discard freely until you get cards that you are happy with. For example, two small trumps and a guarded Queen is a hand that should be played without proposing. But if one of the trumps is the King, cards should be asked for, unless the second card in the Queen suit is at least as high as the Ten. Hands that contain two trumps with weak cards in plain suits should be proposed on, whether one of the trumps is the King or not.

6. When discarding, throw out all cards except trumps and Kings. Consequently, hands from which only two cards can be discarded, without throwing a trump or a King, should be played without proposing. Most likely your adversary, if he accepts, will exchange more than two cards, and he may exchange four or five; therefore, he has a better chance than the proposer of strengthening his hand, and of taking the King.

7. All hands should be played without proposing when (the King of trumps not being in hand) the odds are two to one in favor of winning the point with the hand dealt. Some hands should be played with which the odds are rather less than two to one in favor of winning the point. The reason for playing these is that, if you exchange, the chance of scoring will be more against you than it was before, even allowing for the penalty, if you fail to win the point.

All the hands that should be played without proposing, called Jeux de Règle, have been calculated and are found on pages 90–92.

Hands stronger than those given should be played without proposing, with the following exceptions:

A. If you hold the King of trumps and cards that ensure the point you should propose, even for one card, unless you hold all court cards and trumps. For, by proposing, you have the chance of a refusal, which gives you two points on winning three tricks; and, if the proposal is accepted and you take in one good card, it may give you the vole.

B. If you hold the King of trumps and can only throw two cards without discarding a card at least as high as a Ten from your guarded suit. While the odds are more than two to one in favor of your winning the point, your chance of scoring is increased by exchanging, taking into account the absence of penalty if you fail to win the point. There is

also the chance of a refusal.

C. If you have proposed once and, after discarding, you hold the King of trumps and have the point certain, but have one or two weak unguarded cards, it is advisable to ask for cards a second time, for the chance of the vole.

8. The general rule is for the dealer to accept, unless he is guarded in three suits, or is guarded in two suits and has a trump, or is guarded in one suit and has two trumps. He may play such hands with rather weaker cards than the nondealer.

9. The general system of play is to lead from two or more of a suit, and to lead the highest. The lead from a strong suit is the one most likely to force the adversary; if the trumps are equal, the first force will probably win the point.

10. When playing a weak hand after a refusal, with no hope of the point and fear of the vole, you should lead the strongest single card, so that the guarded suit may be led up to. The rule does not apply to a King, which in such case should be played out at once. Having only one Queen guarded, or one Jack guarded, it is never right to lead the guarded card.

11. If the strong suit led is not trumped, it should continue, as a rule. But if the leader has the King of trumps or Queen (King not having been announced in the other hand), or Jack and Ace, it is advisable to take out a trump before going on with the suit.

12. Another exception to continuing with

the suit is when playing for the vole with a weak trump and high cards in the other suits. In this case you should change the suit each time. If three tricks are made in this way, then the single trump should be played.

13. When playing with two trumps and an unguarded King, it is usually recommended to begin with a low card rather than with the King. If the low cards are of the same suit, it is better to begin the game with them; but if of different suits, the King is the best card to play.

14. If cards are refused, it is better to lead from two small consecutive cards than with a high combination.

15. If you have won two tricks, your opponent one, and you hold a trump and a plain card, lead the plain card; but if your adversary has won two tricks and you win the third, lead your trump, though only the Seven.

16. Having made two tricks, and finding the adversary has no trump, it is better to lead a King than a trump. Then lead the trump. Your adversary, if he has another card of your King suit, will be in doubt whether to keep that suit or not; if the trump was first, he would have kept the suit in which he was guarded.

17. When the dealer is at four and the King is not in your hand nor turned up, you should play any cards without proposing that give an even chance of three tricks. If the point is lost, the adversary wins the game, and by not changing cards all chances of his taking the King are

avoided. When the nondealer is at four, the dealer should also refuse on a light hand, but he ought to have some protection in three suits, as, for instance, three Jacks, or a Jack and two guarded Tens.

18. If the dealer has four points, and you don't have the King in your hand nor turned up, you should play any hand that contains one trump, unless the cards out of trumps are of different suits and very small. Similarly, the dealer should refuse cards, if he holds a trump when his adversary is at four. With one trump and four small cards of a suit, the nondealer should play at this point of the game, but the dealer should not.

19. If the dealer has four points, the rule to ask for cards with three certain tricks in hand is invalid, unless the player proposing has the King of trumps, or the King is turned up.

20. If either player plays without proposing when he is at four to the opponent's three, the player, if he holds the King, ought not to mark it; if he wins the point he scores two and the game; and marking the King would unnecessarily expose his hand.

21. At four, a forward game should not be played in trumps, as there is no advantage in winning the vole. Thus, with Jeu de Règle No. 6, if the trump is the Queen, the leader at this score should continue the suit, and not play the trump after passing the King of his suit. By playing in this way it is possible to make three tricks, even against two trumps in the other hand. For, if the adversary holds Jack and another trump, and trumps the second card of the strong suit, he will probably lead his Jack to pass his other cards. If he does so he loses the point.

Jeux de Règle: Hands to be Played Without Proposing

Spades are trumps throughout. It is also assumed that neither player has scored any points.

No. 1. Any hand with three or more trumps: Lead the highest trump.

No. 2. Two trumps, and three cards of a suit: Lead the highest card of the suit not trumps, and continue until trumped. If one of the trumps is the King, ask for cards, as then there is no risk of the opponent's taking the King.

No. 3. Two trumps, Queen and another of a suit, and a small card of a third suit: This is a Jeu de Règle, but some players are afraid to risk it without another card as high as a Ten, instead of one of the small cards. If the trumps are high, the guarded Queen should be led.

Jeux de Règle: Hands to be Played Without Proposing (cont.)

If the trumps are low, commence with the single card, in hopes of forcing the adversary, and of being led to in the guarded suit. This is an exception to the rule of beginning the game with the guarded suit.

If one of the trumps is the King, ask for cards. But with King and another trump, Queen and another of the second suit, and an honor in the third, the hand should be played.

With Queen in each of the three suits, begin with the Queen of trump; if the King is encountered, the other suits are led up to. If the guarded plain card is a King, lead the King.

No. 4. Two trumps, Eight, Seven of a suit, and King of a third suit: Commence with the guarded Eight, and if it wins continue the suit. If one of the trumps is the King, ask for cards.

With similar but rather stronger hands—as, for example, King and another trump, Queen, Jack of the second suit, and a Jack—commence with the guarded Queen, and then, if it wins, play the King of trumps. To start with the King of trumps for the vole is too risky.

Hands of intermediate strength between No. 3 and No. 4 should be played. The guarded card should always be led.

No. 5. Two trumps, a King, a Jack, and an Eight or Seven of different suits: Lead the single King. Similarly, hands containing King, Ace, Nine of different suits; or King and two Tens of suits different from the King, should be played. Also hands containing two Queens; Queen, Jack, Ace of different suits; or three court cards should be played. In all these hands the highest single card should be led.

No. 6. One trump, a tierce major, and a small card of a third suit: Lead one of the tierce, and continue the suit. If trumped, the lead is regained with the trump. If not trumped, play the tierce major and then the trump. If the trump is the King, commence with the trump. If the trump is the Queen, and the King is not declared after the first lead, the Queen should be led, except at the point of four.

With King, Queen, and a small card of the strong suit, the hand should not be played unless the other card out of trump is an honor, or the cards held are King, Queen, Ace, and Eight or Nine of the third suit; or King, Queen, Ten, and another Ten.

No. 7. One trump and King, with three small cards of the same suit as the King: Lead the King, and continue the suit. If the trump is the King, ask for cards. If the trump is the Queen and the King is not declared after the first lead, the Queen should be led, except at the point of four.

No. 8. One trump, a Queen single, and a Queen with two small cards: Start with the guarded Queen, and continue the suit. If the suit is trumped, play it again on obtaining the lead. If the trump is the King, ask for cards, unless the guard to the Queen is at least as high as the Ten. If each Queen is singly guarded, ask for cards, unless one of the guards is at least as high as the Ten.

No. 9. Four court cards, except the four Jacks: Play four Jacks if the Jack of trumps is guarded (see Jeu de Règle No. 5). As a general rule, these hands should be played by commencing with the guarded card of the strongest suit out of trumps.

No. 10. Hands from which only two cards can be discarded without throwing a King or a trump; also hands guarded by a Queen in three suits, i.e., with three Queens: Begin with a guarded Queen.

No one can play Écarté without knowing the Jeux de Règle and being able to recognize them at a glance. It will be observed that (except when the King is taken into consideration), the value of the trumps does not influence any of the hands that should be played without proposing. The reason is that it is scarcely ever the game to lead trumps originally with two trumps, neither being the King. The general scheme of the game is to get the first force on the dealer, and to use the trumps for trumping his winning cards. For this purpose high trumps are no better than low ones.

The classification of the Jeux de Règle is therefore based on the *number* of trumps held and not on their *value*. The nondealer should be guided in deciding whether to propose by the number of trumps he holds, and by the value of the plain cards, and by whether they belong to one or more suits.

Euchre

Euchre is played with a pack of thirty-two cards—the sixes, fives, fours, threes, and twos are removed from a complete pack. Two, three, or four persons may play, but the four-handed game is the most popular. The object is to win a minimum of three tricks.

Dealing

The players having cut for the deal, the pack is shuffled, and the player to the right of the dealer cuts. The dealer gives five cards to each player, two cards at a time to each in rotation, beginning with the player to his left, then three cards at a time. After each player has received five cards, the dealer turns up the next card for trump, and places it face up on top of the stock.

Rank of the Cards

The cards in suits, not trumps, rank as in Whist, the Ace being the highest and the Seven being the lowest. In trumps, the cards rank differently. The Jack of the suit turned up is called the *right Bower*, and is the highest trump. The other Jack of the same color (black or red, as the case may be) is called the *left Bower,* and is the next highest trump.

Ordering Up, Assisting, Passing, and Taking Up

When the trump is turned, the eldest hand (the player to the left of the dealer) examines his hand to see what he will do. He may either order up the trump or pass. If he thinks his cards are strong enough to win three tricks, he says, "I order it up." The dealer then discards one card from the player's hand and puts it under the stock, face down, and takes the trump card, instead of the card the player discarded. But if the player is not satisfied with his cards, he says, "I pass."

If the eldest hand passes, the partner of the dealer then has the option of saying what he will do, and he may either assist his partner or pass. If his hand is strong enough to win three tricks with the help of the trump his partner has turned, he says, "I assist," and his partner discards as before, and the trump card belongs to him. If the partner of the dealer has a weak hand, he says, "I pass," and the third player has the option of saying what he will do. The third player proceeds exactly as the eldest hand, and, if he passes, the dealer has the next say.

If all the other players pass, the dealer may either take up the trump or pass. If his hand is strong enough to take three tricks, he says, "I take it up." The dealer then discards the weakest card from his hand, and takes the trump card. If the dealer has a weak hand, he says, "I turn it down," and, at the same time, places the trump card face up under the stock.

If the dealer turns down the trump, the eldest hand has the option of naming any suit (except the one turned down) for trumps, or of passing again. If he passes, he says, "I pass the making." If the eldest hand passes the making, the partner of the dealer then has the option of making the trump, and so on in rotation up to and including the dealer. If all the players, including the dealer, decline to make the trump, a fresh deal ensues, and the eldest hand deals.

If either side adopts (plays with the suit turned up for trump) or makes the trump, the play of the hand begins. When the trump is made of the same color as the turnup (that is, black if the turnup is black, or red if it is red), it is called *making it next in suit.* If the trump is made of a different color from the turnup, it is called *crossing the suit.*

Playing Alone

If a player holds a hand so strong that he has a reasonable hope of taking all five tricks without the assistance of his partner, he may play alone. If he plays without his partner, he says, "I play alone." His partner then places his cards face down on the table, and remains silent during the play of the five tricks.

If the eldest hand orders up or makes the trump, either he or his partner may play alone. If the dealer's partner assists or makes the trump, either he or the dealer may play alone. If the player to the right of the dealer orders up or makes the trump, he may play alone (but his partner cannot). If the dealer takes up or makes a trump, he may play alone (but his partner cannot).

A player cannot play alone after having passed a trump or passed the making of a trump. A player cannot play alone when the opposing side adopts or makes the trump; nor can he play alone unless he announces his intentions to do so before he, or the opposing side, makes a lead.

Playing

The eldest hand leads a card and each player in rotation plays a card to the lead. The four cards thus played constitute a trick. A player must follow suit if he can, but if not able to follow suit, he may play any card he chooses. The highest card of the suit led wins the trick; trumps win all other suits. The winner of the trick leads to the next, and so on until the five tricks are played.

Scoring

The game is five points. If the side that adopts, or makes a trump wins all five tricks, they make a *march* and score two. If they win three tricks, they make the *point* and score one. Four tricks count no more than three tricks. If they fail to take three tricks they are *euchred,* and the opposing side scores two points. When a player plays alone and takes all five tricks he scores four points. If he takes three tricks he scores one point. If he fails to take three tricks he is euchred, and the opposing side scores two points. The Three and Four are used in marking game. The face of the Three being up, and the face of the Four down on it, counts one, whether one, two, or three pips are exposed; the face of the Four being up, and the Three over it, face down, counts two, whether one, two, three, or four of the pips are shown; the face of the Three uppermost counts three; and the face of the Four uppermost counts four.

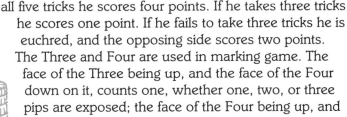

The Rules of the Game

1. At the outset of the game each player cuts for the deal, and the lowest cut deals. If there is a tie, the parties tied cut again. The players cutting the two highest cards play against those cutting the two lowest.
2. In cutting, the Ace is lowest, and the other cards rank as in Whist.
3. Should a player expose more than one card, he must cut again.
4. The cards may be shuffled by any player who demands that privilege, but the dealer always has the right to shuffle last.
5. The cards must be cut by the right-hand opponent before they are dealt. A cut must not be less than four cards removed from the top.
6. After the first deal, the right of dealing goes to the left.
7. A misdeal forfeits the deal, and the following are misdeals: (A) Too many or too few cards given to either player; (B) Dealing the cards when the pack has not been properly cut. The claim for a misdeal must be made prior to the trump card being turned, and before the adversaries look at their cards.
8. Whenever a misdeal is attributable to any interruption by the adversaries, the deal will not be forfeited. If an adversary touches his cards during the deal, and the dealer's partner has not done so, no misdeal can be claimed.
9. If a card is exposed by the dealer or partner, should neither of the adversaries have touched their cards, a new deal may be claimed, but the right to deal is not lost.
10. If, during the deal, the dealer's partner touches any of his cards, the adversaries may do the same without losing their privilege of claiming a new deal.
11. If an opponent displays a card dealt, the dealer may make a new deal, unless he or his partner have examined their own cards.
12. If a deal is made out of turn, and it is not discovered before the dealer has discarded and the eldest hand has led, it is good.
13. If a card is faced in dealing, unless it be the trump card, a new deal may be demanded, but the right to deal is not lost.
14. If the pack is discovered to be defective, by reason of having more or less than thirty-two cards, the deal is void; but all the points made before are good.
15. The dealer, unless he turns down the trump, must discard one card from his hand and take up the trump card.
16. The discard is not complete until the dealer has placed the card under the pack; if the eldest hand makes a lead before the discard is complete, he cannot take back the card thus led, but must let it remain. The dealer, however, may change the card he intended to discard and substitute another, or he may play alone, when a card has been prematurely led.
17. After the discard has been made, the dealer may let the trump card remain upon the stock until it is necessary to play it on a trick. After the trump card has been taken in hand, no player has a right to demand its denomination, but he may ask for the trump suit and the dealer must inform him.
18. Should a player play with more than five cards, or if the dealer forgets to discard

or omits to declare the fact before three tricks have been turned, the deal is lost. However, should the adverse side win, they may score all the points they make.

19. All exposed cards may be called, and the offending party compelled to lead or play the exposed card or cards when he can legally do so, but in no case can a card be called if a revoke is thereby caused. The following are exposed cards: (A) Two or more cards played at once; (B) any card that a player indicates he holds in his hand; (C) any card dropped with its face upward; (D) all cards exposed, whether by accident or otherwise, so that an opponent can distinguish and name them.

20. If any player leads out of turn, his adversaries may demand of him to withdraw his card, and the lead may be compelled from the right player; the card improperly led may be treated as an exposed card and called at any time during that deal, provided it causes no revoke.

21. If any player leads out of turn and the mislead is followed by the other players, the trick is completed and stands good; but if only the second, or the second and third, have played to the false lead, their cards, on discovery of the mistake, are taken back, and there is no penalty against anyone except the original offender, whose card may be called.

22. If any player trumps a card in error, and thereby induces an opponent to play otherwise than he would have done, the latter may take up his card without penalty, and may call upon the offender to play the trump at any period of the hand.

23. If two cards are played or if a player plays twice to the same trick, his opponent can elect which of the two shall remain and belong to the trick, provided, however, that no revoke be caused.

24. If a player, thinking that he can take every trick, or for any other reason, throws down his cards upon the table with their faces exposed, the adverse side may call each and all of the cards so exposed, and the delinquent party must play the exposed cards accordingly. This cannot be done, however, in the case of a lone hand.

25. When a revoke occurs, the adverse parties are entitled to add two points to their scores.

26. If a suit is led and any one of the players, having a card of the same suit, shall play another suit to it, a revoke is committed. But if the error is discovered before the trick is quitted or before the party having so played a wrong suit (or his partner) shall play again, the penalty amounts to only the cards being treated as exposed, and being liable to be called.

27. When the player who has made a revoke corrects his error, his partner, if he has played, cannot change his card played; but the adversary may withdraw his card and play another.

28. When a revoke is claimed against adversaries, if they mix their cards, or throw

The Rules of the Game

them up, the revoke is taken for granted, and they lose the two points.

29. No party can claim a revoke after cutting for a new deal.
30. A revoke on both sides forfeits to neither; but requires a new deal.
31. If a player makes a revoke, his side cannot count any points made in that hand.
32. A party refusing to play an exposed card on call forfeits two cards to his opponents, as in a revoke.
33. Any player making a trump cannot change the suit after having once named it; if he should by error name the suit previously turned down, he forfeits his right to make the trump, and such privilege must pass to the next player.
34. A player may only play alone when he orders up, takes up, or makes a trump, or when his partner assists, orders up, or makes a trump. He cannot play alone with a trump he has passed, or with a trump the making of which he has passed; nor can he play alone after a lead has been made.
35. A player cannot play alone when he or his partner is ordered up by an opponent, or when the opposite side adopts or makes the trump.
36. When a player elects to play alone, his partner cannot supersede him and play alone instead.
37. When a player announces that he will play alone, his partner must place his cards upon the table face down. Should he accidentally expose the face of any of his cards, his opponents may compel him to play or not to play with his partner, at their option.
38. A player who goes alone must clearly announce his intention. If he is not clearly understood by his adversaries and he or they make a lead, he forfeits his privilege and must play with his partner.
39. If a partner indicates his hand by words or gestures to his partner, including telling him to follow the rules of the game, the adversary scores one point.
40. No player has a right to see any trick but the last one turned.

The Secrets of the Game

1. Don't order up unless your hand is strong enough to win the trick.

2. If the eldest hand holds the right Bower, Ace, or King, another small trump, and a card of the same color as the trump suit, pass; for if his adversaries adopt the trump, he will, in all probability, euchre them; and if they reject it, he can make the trump next in suit, and the chances of scoring a point are in his favor.

3. When you have four points and hold commanding trumps sufficient to make a sure point, order up, particularly if you are the eldest hand, for then you will take your opponent's deal.

4. The eldest hand should not order up the trump unless he has good commanding cards, which would include: right Bower, King, and Ten of trumps, with an Ace of a different suit, or left Bower, King, and two small trumps. The player at the right of the dealer should hold a very strong hand to order up the trump, because his partner has shown weakness by passing, and if the opposing side turns down the trump, his partner has the advantage of having the first say to make a new trump.

5. Two picture cards usually form a good assisting hand, but when the game is very close, it is advisable to assist, even on a lighter hand.

6. When assisted by your partner, and you hold a card next in denomination to the card turned up (whether higher or lower), play it. If, for instance, you turn up the Ace, and hold either the left Bower or King, play the Bower or King when a chance occurs, and thus inform your partner that you have the Ace remaining. The same policy should be adopted when your partner assists and you have a sequence of three trumps, the trump card being the smallest of the three; in such a situation invariably play the highest card of the sequence, which will inform your partner that you hold the balance of the sequence, and with this knowledge he can shape his play.

7. Always assist when you can win two tricks.

8. In case the dealer turns the trump down, the eldest hand has the privilege of choosing a new one. The best choice would be to make it next in suit, or the same color as the trump turned. If Diamonds should be the trump turned and the dealer refuses to take it up, you can assume that neither of the Bowers were in the hands of your opponents; if the dealer's partner had held one of them he would in all probability have assisted. Then in the absence of either Bower an otherwise weak hand could make the point in the same color. For reverse reasons, the partner of the dealer would cross the suit and make it Clubs or Spades; his partner having evidenced weakness in the red suits, by turning a red card down, it would be but fair to presume that his strength was in the black suits.

9. Be careful how you make the trump when your adversaries have scored

three points, and do not make or order up a trump unless you are the eldest hand, or the dealer's partner.

10. If one side has scored four, and the other side only one, such position is called a *bridge*.

11. The eldest hand is the only one who should order up at the bridge. If he passes, his partner should realize that he holds commanding cards sufficient to prevent the adversaries making a lone hand. If the eldest hand passes and his partner is strong in trumps, the latter may then order up the trump to make a point and go out; because, by the eldest hand passing, his partner is informed that he holds one or more commanding trumps, and may therefore safely play for the point and game.

12. The eldest hand should always order up at the bridge when not sure of a trick: the weaker his hand, the greater the necessity for doing so.

13. In playing alone, it is to your advantage to have the lead. The next advantage is to have the last play on the first trick, therefore the eldest hand and the dealer may assume the responsibility of playing alone on a hand weaker than that of either of the other players.

14. When your opponent is playing alone and trumps a suit you or your partner leads, be sure and throw away all cards of that suit upon his subsequent leads, provided you do not have to follow suit.

15. When opposing a lone hand, and your partner throws away high cards of any particular suit, you may be

sure that he holds good cards in some other suit; you should hold onto the highest card of the suit he throws away (if you have one) in preference to any other card, unless it be an Ace of some suit for the last trick.

16. Where the dealer takes up the trump voluntarily, the eldest hand is then on the defensive, and to lead trump under such circumstances would be a mistake.

17. Should your partner have the right Bower turned, lead a small trump as soon as you can; by so doing, you will weaken your adversary's hand.

18. When your partner makes the trump or orders it up, lead him the best trump you hold.

19. When you hold the commanding cards, they should be led, to make the *march*; but if you are only strong enough to secure your point, cards of other suits should be used.

20. When opposed to a lone hand, always lead the best card you have of another suit, so that the possibility of your partner's retaining a card of the same suit as yourself may be averted. It would be even better to lead with a card of an opposite color from the trump.

21. The exception to the above rule is when you hold two or three cards of a suit, including Ace and King, and two small cards in other suits; in this case your best play would be to lead one of the latter and save your strong suit, because your partner may hold commanding cards in your weak suits, and you can give him a

chance to make a trick with them. If this does not occur, you have your own strong suit as a reserve, and may secure a trick with it.

22. When playing alone, always lead your commanding trump cards first, reserving your small trumps and other suit for the closing leads. When you have exhausted your commanding trumps, having secured two tricks, and retain in your hand a small trump and two cards of another suit, lead the highest of the lay suit to make the third trick, then your trump.

23. When you hold three small trumps and good lay cards and want to euchre your opponents, lead a trump, because when all the trumps are exhausted you may possibly make your commanding lay cards win.

24. When you make the trump next in suit, always lead a trump, unless you hold the tenace of right Bower and Ace, and even then it would be good policy to lead the Bower, if you hold strong lay cards.

25. When you hold two trumps, two lay cards of the same suit, and a single lay card, lead one of the two lay cards, for you may win a trick by trumping the suit of which you hold none, and then, by leading your second lay card, you may force your opponents to trump, and thus weaken them. With such a hand it would not be good play to lead the single lay card, for you might have to throw it away on your partner's trick.

26. When your partner has made or adopted the trump, it is bad play to win the lead, unless you possess a hand strong enough to play for a march.

27. If your partner assists you and has played a trump, and you have won a trick and the lead, do not lead him a trump unless you hold commanding cards and are pretty certain of making the odd trick or a march, for your partner may have assisted on two trumps only, in which case such a lead would draw his remaining trump and ruin his own strategy.

28. When you have lost the first two tricks, and secured the third, if you hold a trump and a lay card, play the former, as it is your only chance to make or save a euchre. There are only two exceptions to this rule: (A) when you have assisted your partner, and (B) when he has adopted the trump and still retains the trump card in his hand. In both cases you should lead the lay card.

29. Never lose sight of the state of the game. When both teams have four points, adopt or make the trump upon a weak hand. A euchre will put your adversaries out.

30. When you are alone and your opponents have scored four, you can try and make it upon a weaker hand than if the score were more favorable to you.

31. When you are the eldest hand and the score stands four for you and one for your opponents, do not fail to order up the trump to prevent them from going alone, unless you hold the right Bower, or the left Bower, guarded.

The Secrets of the Game

32. Never trump your partner's winning cards, but throw out your losing or single cards.

33. If your partner adopts or makes the trump and you hold the right or left Bower alone, ruff with it as soon as you get the opportunity.

34. When playing second, be careful how you ruff a card of a small denomination the first time around, for it is an even chance that your partner will take the trick if you let it pass. Throw away any single card lower than an Ace, so that you may ruff the suit you throw away when it is led.

35. When your partner assists and you hold the next highest card to the turned-up card, ruff with it when an opportunity occurs, thereby giving valuable information to your partner.

36. When you are in the position of third player, ruff with high or medium trumps. This line of play forces the high trumps of the dealer and thereby weakens your adversaries.

37. When your partner leads a lay Ace, and you have none of that suit, do not trump it; if you have a single card, throw it out.

38. If you are the second hand on your team, and are compelled to follow suit, head the trick if possible; this greatly strengthens your partner's game.

39. When you cannot follow suit or trump, throw out your weakest card.

40. When opposed to a lone player, be careful how you separate two cards of the same suit. Throw away a single King rather than separate a Seven and Queen. Be cautious how you separate your trumps when you hold the left Bower guarded.

Lap

The *Lap* game may be played by two, three, or four persons. A lap is simply counting in the score of the ensuing game all the points made over and above the five of which the game consists. For example, if one party, having made four points, should euchre his opponents or make a march, either of which entitles him to score two points, he not only wins the game then being played, but counts one point on the next game; or, if a player in a four-handed game, having four points, plays a lone hand and makes his five tricks, he wins the game and scores three points on the next game. When the Lap game is played, it is usual to count four points when a lone hand is euchred.

Slam

To make a *slam* is to win a game before the opposing side has scored a point. When the slam is played, it counts as two games. For instance, if a player has four points, and his adversaries nothing, plays a lone hand and makes his five tricks, he not only wins that game, which is to be counted as two games, but counts the extra three points on the score of the third game, by means of the lap.

Jambone

A *jambone* is to play a lone hand with the cards exposed on the table, and to give to that adversary who is entitled to the lead, the privilege of calling one of the exposed cards to the first trick played. If the jambone player has the lead, he may lead with any one of the exposed cards. Under these conditions, if the jambone player wins all five tricks, he is entitled to score eight points.

A jambone hand may be played by either party, subject to the same rules that govern playing alone in the regular game. The right to the call is forfeited when the partner of the player having the lead gives an intimation that enables the two to win the first trick.

When the adverse party orders up or makes the trump, a jambone hand cannot be played, and the holder must limit his strategy to euchring his opponent.

The jambone player being entitled to lead, his left-hand opponent only has the right to say which of the exposed cards shall be led.

No call can be made after the first trick has been played, after which the jambone player may exercise his own judgment and lead whichever card he pleases.

When the dealer plays jambone, and the eldest hand leads a card not a trump, but which the dealer will trump, he should call for the lowest exposed card, so that his partner may have a chance to play a higher trump than the one called, and thus win the trick. If the dealer holding a jambone hand finds that by discarding and taking up the trump, he weakens his hand, he is not obliged to discard, so that the turnup card merely indicates the trump suit.

The player calling the card for the first trick must call it the moment he leads, or he forfeits his right to the call.

If the lead belongs to the jambone player, his opponent entitled to the call must call before a card is played, otherwise the jambone player may play any card he chooses, the right to the call being forfeited.

If the jambone player wins less than five tricks, he can only score one point; and should he fail to win three tricks, his adversaries are entitled to score eight points.

Jamboree

Jamboree signifies the combination of the five highest cards, as, for example, the two Bowers, Ace, King, and Queen of trumps in one hand, which entitles the holder to count sixteen points. The holder of such a hand simply announces the fact, as no play is necessary.

When the parties are playing laps and slams, and one of the players has four points to his opponent's nothing and announces a jamboree, the sixteen points thus won, added to his four, making twenty points, equal to four games, each of them a slam, which entitles him to count eight games in all.

Jamboree, like Jambone, cannot be played if the adverse party orders up the trump or makes it, in which case the hand can only make two points, as in ordinary Euchre.

Two-Handed Euchre

In Two-Handed Euchre the cards are dealt alternately to each player, beginning with the nondealer. The nondealer then examines his hand, and decides whether he will play or not. If his hand is strong, he will order up the trump; if weak, he will pass. If the nondealer orders up the trump, the dealer discards and takes up the trump card; if he passes, the dealer has the option of taking up or turning down the trump. If the dealer adopts the trump, he discards, and the play of the hand begins; but if he turns it down, then the nondealer has the option of naming a suit for trump, or of passing. If the nondealer passes the making, then the dealer has the privilege of making a suit trump; but if the nondealer makes a trump, then the play of the hand commences.

If neither player adopts or makes a trump, the deal passes to the opposing player.

As soon as a trump has been adopted or made, the nondealer leads a card, the dealer plays to it, and the two cards thus played constitute a trick. The winner of the trick leads to the next.

Two-Handed Euchre is governed by the same laws given for the four-handed game. Each player may adopt or even order up the trump with weaker cards than when playing three- or four-handed.

In the two-handed game, it is best to lead your strongest trumps first, until you have won two tricks, and then, having a trump left, lead the strongest card of another suit; if your adversary takes it, you may have a chance to trump the card he leads, and thus make your point. Having won two tricks, and your adversary being without a trump, play for a march by leading trumps or your highest cards.

The deal is considered equal to a point, therefore never pass the deal unless to save a euchre.

Three-Handed Euchre

After the cards have been dealt, the option of passing or playing goes to each player in rotation, commencing with the player to the dealer's left. The eldest hand leads, and each of the other two players plays in his turn a card to the lead. These three cards constitute a trick, and the winner of the trick leads to the next. After the hand is played, the eldest hand has the next deal. The player who adopts, orders up, or makes the trump has to play against the other two.

Railroad Euchre

Railroad Euchre is played with a pack of thirty-three cards, consisting of a regular euchre pack and a Joker. The Joker is always a trump, no matter what suit is turned up or made trump, and will beat the right Bower. Railroad Euchre is more rapid than the regular four-handed game, and differs in the following particulars:

A) The game is five points, but may be ten, if agreed upon.
B) If a player elects to go alone, he may call for his partner's best card, and discard any one from his own hand; in this case either player of the opposing side may also call for the best card held by his partner, and if the latter succeeds in gaining a euchre, his side is entitled to a score of four points.
C) If the Joker is turned up for trump, the dealer must turn up the next card to determine the suit of trump, but this does not hold him from discarding and taking the Joker in hand, provided his side adopts the suit turned up, or the opposing side orders it up.

The addition of the Joker to the pack, as well as the privilege of calling for a partner's best card, create a game in which it is often best to play a lone hand.

Set-Back Euchre

This game may be played by two or more people. It is governed by the same rules as the ordinary three-handed game of Euchre, except in scoring.

Suppose four people sit down to play for four chips. Each player contributes a chip to the pool. The chips may represent any amount the players agree upon. At the beginning of the game each player has five points marked to his score. The player who is the first to reduce his score to nothing wins the game and the pool.

Each player plays for himself; therefore, the player who orders up, takes up, or makes the trump, has to play single-handed against all the other players combined.

If any player fails to take a single trick, he is set back one point, which is added to his score.

If a player adopts or order ups the trump, and takes three tricks, he wipes one point from his score. If he makes a march, he wipes two points from his score. If a player is euchred, he is *set back* two points, which are *added* to his score, and he must deposit another chip into the pool.

The player who thinks he cannot take a trick has the right to throw up his hand, and thus save himself from being set back.

Napoleon

This is a French modification of Euchre, in which each of the participants plays alone. The number of players should not be over six.

The dealer gives five cards to each player, two and three at a time, as in Euchre, beginning with the eldest hand. The eldest hand has the first say. He bids to make as many tricks as he thinks his hand will warrant, or he may pass. Each player, in turn, has the right to bid more, or pass. The player who bids to make the most tricks plays against the others, who combine to defeat him.

The successful bidder names the trump and always leads. If he names no trump, the first card he leads is trump.

If a player bids to make all five tricks, this bid is called *Napoleon,* and its payment is ten chips. When the bid is for less than five tricks, the payment is one chip for each trick bid. If a successful bidder makes the number of tricks he announced, he receives from each of his opponents one chip for each trick bid; if he fails, he pays each of them the same.

If a player has made an accepted bid of three, as soon as he has made three tricks, he throws down his remaining cards (if any), as his object has been attained. If he bids to make three and, having made the first three tricks, he continues to play by leading his fourth card, he is then compelled to play for all five tricks, and he loses the game if he fails. If he makes all five, he is paid by each player for five; if he fails, he must pay each for five tricks.

Some other differences in the game are as follows:

A) Suit must be followed. If this is not possible, a trump must be played.
B) A bidder must play his bid, unless outbid.

C) A trick, once turned, cannot be examined until the end of the game.
D) A revoke forfeits the game.
E) When six play, sometimes the Seven cards of the two red suits may be rejected, so that all the cards are dealt out.
F) In cases where four or less are playing, the Seven and Eight cards of each suit are eliminated, reducing the pack to twenty-four cards.
G) If seven are playing, you can add the four Six cards.

Six-Handed Euchre

This is a variety of Napoleon, played by six people, forming two partnerships of three, seated alternately. Two of the Sevens are discarded from the pack, so that all the cards are dealt. The winning side can only claim exactly the amount of the bid, even if more tricks are taken. If the side having the successful bid fails to make the number of tricks bid, the other side adds the same number of tricks to their score.

The game is usually twenty-five points, which are scored as in Napoleon. When a bid is made, the suit on which the bid is based must be declared; but it is not obligatory to lead the suit declared. In other respects Six-Handed Euchre is identical to French Euchre.

French Euchre

This variety is played with a pack of twenty-four cards, with all cards below the Nines being discarded. The game is played by four people, playing as partners, who sit opposite each other.

Five cards are dealt, to each player as in the ordinary game, but no trump is turned.

After the deal the players bid for the privilege of making the trump, beginning with the eldest hand, and going in rotation to the dealer, who, unless some other player anticipates him by bidding five tricks, has the last say.

When a player proposes to take a certain number of tricks in any named suit, and the opposing side declines to outbid him, the suit named becomes trump. The eldest hand then leads, and the play proceeds as in the regular four-handed game.

The player who makes the highest bid must accomplish all he proposes, and if, with the assistance of his partner, he fails to take the required number of tricks, he is euchred, and the adverse side scores all he would have counted had he been successful. Should either side take more tricks than they bid, they can only score the number proposed, and not the actual number taken. In all other particulars French Euchre is governed by the laws of the ordinary game.

Go Fish

Go Fish is played with two or more players, with a pack of fifty-two cards.

Dealing

The dealer deals one card to each player in rotation, until the entire deck is dealt. While doing this, the dealer also creates an additional pile that is called the *fish pile,* placed face down in the center of the table. Any cards left from the deal go to the fish pile. The object of the game is to collect all four suits of every card denomination, called *books.* Before the play begins, each player removes from his hand all existing books, and puts them face down in front on him.

Playing

The first player asks any one opponent for a card he needs. For example, if the first player is holding two Fours, one Six, one Jack, one Seven, and two Eights, he may say to one opponent, "Do you have any Sixes?"

If that person has the card requested, he must give it to the player, and if he has more than one he must hand over all of them. The player then continues in this fashion, by asking the same opponent, or any other opponent, for another card. This continues until a request made is denied. If the opponent does not have the card requested, he says, "Go fish," and the player takes one card from the fish pile. If, by chance, he picked the card he asked for, the player gets to continue his turn. Otherwise the turn is over.

The next player to take a turn is the one who rejected the first player, and the game continues in much the same fashion. Each time a book is made, the cards are withdrawn from the hand and placed with the other books face down in front of the player. The game continues until one player has played through his hand. All of the players then count up the number of books they have created. The player who has the most books at the end of the game wins.

Grabouche

Grabouche may be played by two, four, six, or eight people. Three complete decks of fifty-two cards each are required if two, four, or six people play; when eight play, four decks are necessary. The cards rank as in Whist.

When four people play, they divide into two teams, each player sitting opposite his partner. When six people play, they form two teams of three, and the players composing the two sets sit in alternate order. When eight people play, two teams of four each are formed, and the players are similarly seated alternately. The partnerships are determined by cutting.

Dealing

The player who cuts the lowest card deals. Ties are cut over. The dealer counts out twenty cards for each team face down. The top card of each pile is turned up. When six or eight people play, the number of cards in the two piles are sometimes increased.

A second set of cards is dealt: five to each person, beginning with the player to the left of the dealer. The remaining cards are made up into groups of five, to be given to each player when his hand is played out.

Playing

The player on the left of the dealer opens the play and may begin by placing an Ace (if he has one) face up in the center of the table. A player is entitled to use cards from his hand, the top cards of his own or his partners' table piles, or the top card of his twenty pile. He may build upon the Ace in sequence with all the suitable cards contained in his hand. For example, he may then put out the Two, the Three, etc., in their regular upward sequence. He may do this not only to get rid of his hand and take a fresh one, but, if possible, to reach the denomination of the card turned up on his pile of twenty, so that he or his partner may play it off.

The Aces must always be placed in the center, and cards built upon the Aces are known as the *center piles*. When a player plays his last card in the center, he may take a fresh hand and continue playing. When the player has finished playing in the center, he lays one card, face up, in front of him, and this is known as a table card. No more than four piles of table cards are permitted in front of each player; it is therefore best to arrange them in sequence, placing the lower cards on the higher; or, when possible, making one pile all of the same denomination.

It is not obligatory to play the Ace at once, and it is advisable not to be too hasty in playing it when the exposed card on the adversaries' pile is a low one, and you have no cards to build up the Ace to the denomination of their card, or beyond it. If you hold no cards in sequence with the Ace, it is better to first play your other cards upon the table, retaining your Ace to the last. This is particularly beneficial when your last two cards are both Aces, as it affords you an opportunity of getting a fresh hand that may contain cards that will continue your play advantageously.

After the first player has completed his play, the next player similarly plays, and so on all around. When a player cannot or does not choose to play upon the center piles, he deposits a table card in front of him.

A player is not obliged to build upon the center piles unless he chooses to do so; and when it comes his turn, he may play a card on either of his table piles as often as he likes; whether such card is in sequence with the cards in the center piles or not.

The object of the game is to play off the cards from the twenty pile; therefore, if by playing on the center piles you lead up to the denomination of the card on your own pile, do so; but you should refrain from playing on the center when it will help your opponents to accomplish the same object. Instead, play upon the table piles, because your adversaries cannot use the cards on your table and the cards thus exposed may be advantageously employed by your partners to prevent the opponents from playing off their pile. This is called *blocking*.

It is occasionally advisable to play up to the adversaries' card when by doing so you can get rid of all your cards and take a fresh hand.

The Aces are built upon without any regard to suit. When the King is finally put on, the pile is removed from the center, shuffled, and made up into books of five each ready for use when needed.

When the top card of a twenty pile is played off, the next card is immediately turned up, and this operation is continued until the last card of the pile is played. The side who first plays off all the cards in their twenty pile wins the game.

The Secrets of the Game

1. Be careful, in playing to your own pile, not to give your opponents a chance to play off theirs. Block their game all you can.
2. Keep a strict account of the cards in your own and your partners' table piles.
3. When your hand is out, call for a fresh one before you play from your own or your partners' table. As soon as you play a card from your twenty pile, turn up the next one at once, and use it if possible.
4. Get rid of your hand as quickly as possible, and always play from your hand, in preference to playing the same card from the table, unless, of course, the corresponding card is the top one on your pile of twenty; always give that the preference.
5. An exception to the Rule #4 is when you desire to release a card on a table pile that is covered by one of a higher denomination.
6. No remarks of any kind are allowed between partners regarding a play. Should a player, by word or gesture, express disapproval or approval of a partner's play, the opposing players may each place a card from their hand in the center of the pile of the offending side. If a player holds no card, he may employ a card for the above purpose from his fresh hand, as soon as he receives it.

Hearts

Hearts is played by four players (each playing independently), with a full pack of fifty-two cards. The cards rank in play in the following order: Ace (highest), King, Queen, Jack, Ten, Nine, Eight, Seven, Six, Five, Four, Three, and Two (lowest). The object of the game is to avoid taking any trick that contains a Heart.

Dealing

The deal is determined by giving a card to each player, and the one with the lowest card deals. After the cards have been shuffled and cut, the dealer delivers to each player in rotation, beginning with the player to his left, one card at a time until the whole pack is dealt out; thus giving to each player thirteen cards.

Playing

When the deal has been completed, the eldest hand (the player to the left of the dealer) leads any card he pleases. Each player plays a card to the lead, and the highest card of the suit led wins the trick.

Each player must follow suit if he can, but if not able to follow suit, he may play any card he chooses. The winner of the trick leads to the next, until the thirteen tricks are played.

The Rules of the Game

1. There is no trump suit.
2. Tricks do not count, but each trick must be kept intact until the close of the game, to verify a possible revoke.
3. At the close of the game each player reports how many (if any) Hearts he has taken.
4. Any player who has taken tricks containing Hearts must deposit in the pool one chip for each and every Heart captured. If one player takes the whole thirteen Hearts, he must pay thirteen chips into the pool, which is then divided: the other three players receive four chips each, and the odd chip goes to the winning player who sits nearest the left of the dealer.

   If only one player does not have any Hearts, he takes all the chips in the pool. If two or more players have not captured Hearts, the pool is divided among them as equally as possible, any odd chips remaining after the division going to the winning player nearest to the left of the dealer.

   When all four players capture Hearts, the player who takes the least number of Hearts is paid by the other three.

   When all four players capture Hearts, the player who takes the least number of Hearts is paid by the other three.
5. If a card is exposed during the deal, the dealer must deal over again, unless the exposed card belongs to the dealer.
6. If a misdeal occurs, the dealer must deal over again.
7. A card exposed in the course of play cannot be called.
8. In case of a revoke, the delinquent must pay into the pool as many chips as the pool then contains (if any), plus thirteen additional chips .
9. A revoking player cannot win anything in the round in which the revoke occurred; after the penalty has been paid, the entire pool is divided among the other players.
10. Any player has the right to look at the last trick turned.
11. Every trick must be gathered and turned before a card can be led for the next trick.

1. It is desirable to dispose of the highest cards in each suit. For example: Suppose a player holds Ace, King, Queen, and Two of Spades; Ace, Queen, Jack, and Four of Diamonds; Three and Six of Clubs; and Three, Four, and Eight of Hearts. Having the lead, his best play would be to lead a Club, because as soon as this suit is exhausted he can discard some of the commanding cards in Spades and Diamonds when the short suit is subsequently led.

2. Always get rid of the commanding Hearts, except in cases as in the above example, where Hearts were all low in denomination. It would then be better to discard the high cards in the other suits.

3. As a general rule, it is better to avoid taking a trick in a suit that has been led the second time. There is no harm in the last player in a trick to capture it, provided it contains no Heart, particularly if he takes the trick with a commanding card of the suit, and has a good card for the next lead.

4. When a player plays a low card of a suit led in the first round, provided he is second or third player, it may indicate that he is short of the suit. It may also be, however, that it is his long suit, and he declines playing a high card, fearing that some of the other players may be short of it and discard a Heart.

5. If the fourth player plays a very low card of a suit led the first time, and no Heart has been discarded to the trick, the inference is that he is short of the suit.

6. Remember all the cards that have been played, and particularly the denomination of the cards in the Heart suit that remain unplayed.

7. Lead from a single card of any suit except Hearts; from the highest card of a short suit; from a low card of a long suit, or when you have three or more low cards of that suit. Lead a low Heart whenever the opportunity presents itself—the object being to eliminate this dangerous suit before some other player develops a short suit. Do not lead the highest card of a suit that has already been led more than once, and do not lead a thirteenth card. When a suit has been led three times, and one or two cards of other suits have been played to the leads, do not lead the suit again unless you are sure that you are leading the lowest card of the suit.

VaRiATiONS

Five- or Six-Handed Hearts

The game of Hearts may be played by five or six players by removing a sufficient number of small cards of any suit except Hearts from the pack, in order to insure the same number of cards being dealt to each player.

Heart Jackpot

This is an interesting modification of Hearts. To open the jackpot, which is kept entirely separate from the ordinary pool, each player deposits a chip in a small dish provided for that purpose.

If, in the ensuing game, only one player takes no Hearts, each of the other players pay him a chip for each of the Hearts they may have captured, as in the regular game, but the four chips must remain in the pot.

If two or more players take no Hearts, twelve chips are equally divided among them, but the odd (thirteenth) chip must be put into the jackpot, thus increasing its value.

If all the players capture Hearts, the thirteen chips do not go into the jackpot, but form a double pool, and the whole is divided equally among the players who do not capture any Hearts in the next deal.

If three players take no Hearts, then the odd chip remaining after the division has been made goes into the jackpot.

For every new deal, each player deposits one chip in the jackpot; this continues until some fortunate player takes *no trick at all,* and thus captures the jackpot, together with all the chips he may be entitled to in the regular pool.

If it should happen that two players take no trick, then the Jackpot is divided, and any odd chip that may remain after the division has been made is left as a nest egg for the new jackpot.

I Doubt It

This game can be played with two or more people, with a regular deck of fifty-two cards. The object of the game is to dispose of the player's entire hand.

Dealing

The dealer deals one card to each player in rotation, until the entire deck is dealt.

Playing

As soon as the players have examined their hands, the eldest hand (the player on the left of the dealer) plays the lowest card or cards he has, beginning with an Ace. He must place the card or cards face down on the table, at the same time calling out what it is. The next player must put down the next highest card or cards, face down, and so on. For instance, if the first player puts down a card and says, "One Ace," the second player says, "Two Two's," and so on.

It is not necessary for the player to be honest about their turn. The fun of the game is to put down the wrong card without anyone suspecting you. Naturally, it is not often that the cards run straight on, as no one may play out of turn.

If any other player thinks someone has put down the wrong card, he calls the bluff by saying, "I doubt it." The player must then show his card, and if it is not the one he said, he must take all the cards laid down and add them to his pack. If the card(s) happens to be the right one, then the accuser must take the pile of cards. The player who first succeeds in getting rid of his cards wins the game.

Old Maid

Old Maid is played with two or more players, using a full deck of fifty-two cards. The object of the game is not to be stuck holding the Queen of Diamonds, called, the *Old Maid.*

Dealing

The Queen of Hearts is taken out of the deck, and all the cards are dealt among the players. Each player takes out all the pairs of cards he has in his hand and places them face down in a pile in front of him. A player with three cards of the same value can only put down two, but if he has four of the same value he can put all four down as *two pairs.*

Playing

In a clockwise fashion, the players take turns picking from each other's hands to try to create a match with their own cards. If a player creates a pair, he removes it from his hand and places it in his pile and his turn continues. Otherwise the new card becomes part of that player's hand and the next player takes a turn. The game continues in this manner until all the cards are played out and only the Queen of Diamonds is left. The player with that card is the Old Maid.

Pinochle

Pinochle is played with two packs of cards, retaining only the Ace, Ten, King, Queen, Jack, and Nine of each pack, or with a special pinochle deck. The game may be played by two, three, or four people. The object of the game is to make points, 1,000 points being game.

Two-Handed Pinochle

Dealing

In cutting, the highest card wins the deal, Ace being highest, the Ten next, followed by the King, Queen, Jack, and Nine. After the cards have been shuffled by the dealer and cut by the player on his right, the dealer deals the cards four at a time to each player, until each has twelve cards; the next card is turned up for trump, and is placed face up by the side of the stock.

Playing

The first player leads any card he pleases; his opponent lays a card on top of it, constituting a trick. In playing to a card led, the second player need not follow suit, nor play a card to win the trick, unless he chooses. Trumping is optional.

The player who takes the trick leads for the next; but before he leads, he can then (and then only), announce or meld any one combination that he may be holding in his hand. After the *meld* (if any) has been made, and before he leads, he must draw the top card from the stock, and his opponent draws the next; thus again filling both their hands with twelve cards.

After each trick is taken, the same routine is followed until the stock has been exhausted, the trump card being the last to be drawn.

Each player takes up into his hand all the cards exposed; suit must be followed, if possible, otherwise a trump must be played; if neither is possible, any card may be played. The second player to a trick must take the trick, if he can; failure to do so constitutes a revoke, and the player loses all the points he has made in that hand.

The points depend upon the face value of the cards contained in tricks won, and the value of melds declared in course of play. The last trick counts 10 points for the player who takes it. The total points, therefore, of the cards and last trick combined, amount to 250. The score is kept by one of the players, or a third person, and the points are scored to each player as they accrue.

Rank and Value of the Cards
Ace highest, counts for 11 points
Ten counts for 10 points
King counts for 4 points
Queen counts for 3 points
Jack counts for 2 points
Nine counts for 0 points

Value of Announcements or Melds
Eight Aces count for 1,000
Eight Kings count for 800
Eight Queens count for 400
Eight Jacks count for 400
Two Queens of Spades, Double-Pinochle, count for 400
Two Jacks of Diamonds count for 400
Ace, Ten, King, Queen and Jack of trumps count for 150
Four Aces of different suits count for 100
Four Kings count for 80
Four Queens count for 60
Four Jacks count for 40
Queen of Spades, Pinochle, counts for 40
Jack of Diamonds counts for 40
King and Queen of trumps, Royal Marriage, count for 40
King and Queen of a suit not trumps, Marriage, count for 20

When the dealer turns up a Nine for trump, he scores 10 points for the Nine, or *Dix* (pronounced *deece),* at once. When a Nine is not turned up for trumps, the player who holds the Nine can exchange it for the trump card and meld 10 points at any time when he has obtained the privilege of melding, that is, after he has taken a trick; he cannot meld anything else he may have in his hand.

When a player melds any combination, he must lay down the cards of which his meld consists, face up on the table beside him; he can make use of any of these exposed cards to play to a trick.

Cards that have been melded cannot be used to make any new combinations of the same nature. For example, if four Kings have been melded, none of those four can be combined with other Kings for a new meld. Or, if the Queen of Spades and Jack of Diamonds have been melded for Pinochle, that Queen cannot be used to combine with another Jack of Diamonds for a new Pinochle.

Melded cards can be used to form different combinations, however. For example, if King and Queen of Spades have been melded, the Queen of Spades may be combined with a Jack of Diamonds to meld Pinochle. It must be noted, however, that a Royal Marriage must have been melded first.

It requires two Queens of Spades and two Jacks of Diamonds to form a double Pinochle. The cards composing a single Pinochle, already melded, cannot be employed to form a double Pinochle.

Points are awarded only to those players who hold better hands than the dealer.

Pinochle Without a Trump

This is a variety of the game of Pinochle, which applies only to the two-handed game.

The dealer does not turn up the twenty-fifth card for trump, as in the regular game, but the trump suit is determined by the first marriage (King and Queen of a suit) melded. There is, therefore, no trump suit until the first marriage has been melded.

With this single exception, the game proceeds in exactly the same manner as the regular two-handed game.

Three-Handed Pinochle

Three-Handed Pinochle differs from the two-handed game in the following particulars:

A) The dealer deals out the cards, four at a time, to the players until all the cards have been dealt.

B) He turns up the last card for trump.

C) If any other card is turned up, either of the other players who holds a Nine of trumps may exchange it for the trump card, and claim 10 points for Dix; the eldest hand having the preference.

D) Each player, beginning with eldest hand, melds whatever he has in his hand, and the value of his melds are noted; but no melded points (Dix included) can be added to a player's score until he has taken a trick. The cards being all dealt, there is no stock; therefore, suit must be followed, and the cards played exactly in the same manner as in the two-handed game after the stock is exhausted.

E) When a player has scored 1,000 points, he wins the game; but he must play the hand out, and then retire, leaving the two remaining players to continue the two-handed game to decide the victor.

F) The delinquent player cannot claim any points after he has wrongly called game.

Four-Handed Pinochle

This game is sometimes played in the same manner as Three-Handed Pinochle, each player for himself. It is usually played two against two as partners sitting opposite each other.

The cards are all dealt out, twelve to each, and the method of playing is similar to the three-handed game, except that partners score together.

As it would be evident that the premature declaration of melds might give the eldest hand (the player to the left of the dealer) information that would influence his first lead, no melds are permitted until he has led a card for the first trick; he then announces his melds. Each of the other players in turn must play his card to the first trick and then declare his melds.

Each can meld only what is in his own hand.

A player cannot score any points he has melded, and which are standing to his credit, until he has taken a trick.

The four-handed game is played with partners for a given number of points. The score is tallied the same as the two-handed game, the partners in the game combining their points.

If a player makes a build, the fact that he holds the necessary card to redeem it is sufficient authority for his partner to make a similar build, or to call a card upon the build, without having a card of the same denomination in his hand.

Poker

NOW WHAT'S IT CALLED AGAIN WHEN THEY'RE ALL THOSE LITTLE CLOVER LEAFS?

There are many varieties of Poker played, and we've chosen the most popular ones to list here. All are played with a regular pack of fifty-two cards, and by any number of persons from two to six. Many of the games can be easily modified to include more players. The object of the game is for a player to have the best hand at the table.

Draw Poker

Dealing

Before the dealer begins to deal the cards, the eldest hand (the player to the left of the dealer), must deposit in the pool an *ante* not exceeding one-half the limit previously agreed upon; this is called a *blind.*

The dealer then gives five cards to each player, one at a time, beginning with the eldest hand.

Going in on the Original Hand

After the cards have been dealt the players look at their hands, and each player, in rotation, beginning with the player to the left of the eldest hand, determines whether he will *go in* (to play for the pool) or not. Any player who decides to go in must put into the pool double the amount of the ante, except the eldest hand, who contributes the same amount as his original ante.

Those who pass throw their cards face down on the table in front of the dealer.

Any player, when it is his turn and after contributing his ante, may increase the ante (called a *raise)* any amount within the limit of the game; the next player, after making good the ante and raise, may then also raise it any amount within the limit; and so on.

Each player who raises the ante, must do so in rotation, going around to the left, and any player who remains in to play must put in the pool as much as will make his stake equal to such increase, or abandon all he has already contributed to the pool.

Straddling

Another feature that may be introduced when betting on the original hand is the *straddle.* The straddle is nothing more than a double blind. For example:

A, B, C, D, and E play. A deals. B, the eldest hand, antes one chip. C can straddle B's ante by putting in the pool two chips, provided he does so before the cards are cut for the deal. D may double the straddle by putting in four chips, and so on up to the eldest hand, provided the bets do not exceed the limit.

The straddle gives a player the first opportunity to be the last in before the draw. After the draw, the player to the left of the eldest hand must make the first bet, provided he remains in. A good player very rarely straddles.

Filling the Hands

After the bidding, each player has the right to draw any number of cards he chooses, from one to five, or he can retain his cards as originally dealt to him. If a player draws cards, he must discard a like number from his original hand, and the rejected cards must be placed face down on the table near the next dealer.

The dealer asks each player in rotation, beginning with the eldest hand, how many cards he wants, and when the player has discarded, he gives the number requested from the top of the pack. When the other hands have been helped, the dealer, if he has gone in and wants cards, then helps himself last.

Betting, Raising, and Calling

When all the hands are filled, the player to the left of the eldest hand has the first say, and he must either bet, or retire from the game, forfeiting what he has already staked. The other players must do the same in rotation, up to the eldest hand.

When a player makes a bet, the next player must either *see him,* by putting in the pool an equal amount of chips, or better by raising the bet any amount not exceeding the limit; or he must pass out. This continues either until one player drives all the others out of the game, and takes the pool without showing his hand, or until all the other players who remain in see the last raise (no one going better) and *call* the player who made the last raise. When a call is made, the players remaining in all show their hands, and the strongest hand takes the pool.

Rank of the Hands

The rank of the hands is as follows, beginning with the lowest:
1. *One Pair* (accompanied by three cards of different denominations). If two players each hold a pair, the highest pair wins; if the two are similar, the highest additional card wins.
2. *Two Pair* (accompanied by a card of another denomination).
3. *Triples.* The highest three of a kind win. Triples beat two pairs.
4. *A Straight.* A sequence of five cards not all of the same suit. An Ace may either begin or end a straight. For example: Ace, King, Queen, Jack, Ten is the highest straight. Five, Four, Three, Two, Ace, is the lowest straight. If more than one player holds a straight, the straight headed by the highest card wins. A straight will beat three of a kind.

     Straights are not always played; it should therefore be determined whether they are to be admitted at the beginning of the game. If straights are counted in the game, a straight flush outranks four cards of the same denomination.
5. *A Flush.* Five cards of the same suit, not in sequence. If more than one player holds a flush, the flush holding the highest card wins; if the highest cards tie, the next highest cards in those two hands wins. A flush will beat a straight, and three of a kind.
6. *A Full House.* Three cards of the same denominations and a pair. If more than one player holds a full house, the highest three of a kind wins. A full house will beat a flush.
7. *Four of a Kind.* Four cards of the same denomination, accompanied

by any other card. If more than one player holds fours, the highest fours wins. When straights are not played, fours beat a straight flush.

8. *A Straight Flush.* A sequence of five cards, all of the same suit. If more than one player holds a straight flush, the hand headed by the highest card wins. When straights are not played, the straight flush does not rank higher than a common flush, but when straights are played, it is the highest hand that can be held, and beats four of a kind.

When none of the foregoing hands are shown, the highest card wins; if these tie, the next highest in those two hands, and so on.

If two or more players hold hands identical in value, and those hands are the best out, the players divide the pool equally.

The Rules of the Game

1. The deal is determined by giving one card to each player, and the player who gets the lowest card deals.
2. In determining the deal, the Ace is lowest and the King highest. Ties are determined by cutting.
3. The cards must be shuffled above the table; each player has a right to shuffle the cards, but the dealer shuffles last.
4. The player to the right of the dealer must cut the cards.
5. The dealer must give each player one card at a time, in rotation, beginning to his left, and in this order he must deliver five cards to each player.
6. If the dealer deals without having the pack properly cut, or if a card is faced in the pack, there must be a fresh deal. The cards are reshuffled and recut, and the dealer deals again.
7. If a card is exposed during dealing, the player to whom such card is dealt must accept it as though it had not been exposed.
8. If the dealer delivers more or less than five cards, and a player discovers and announces the fact before he raises his hand, it is a misdeal. The cards are reshuffled and recut, and the dealer deals again.
9. If the dealer delivers more or less than five cards, and a player does not realize this before reviewing his hand, no misdeal occurs, and the player must sit out that game.
10. After the first hand the deal proceeds in rotation, beginning with the player to the left of the dealer.
11. After the deal has been completed, each player who remains in the game may discard from his hand as many cards as he chooses, or his whole hand, and the dealer gives him an equal number from the top of the remaining pack. The eldest hand must discard first, and so in regular rotation around to the dealer, who discards last.

The Rules of the Game

12. Any player, after having asked for fresh cards, must take the exact number called for; and after cards have once been discarded, they must not again be taken in hand.

13. Should the dealer give any player more cards than the player has demanded, and the player discover and announce the fact before raising his cards, the dealer must withdraw the superfluous cards and restore them to the pack. But if the player looks at the cards before informing the dealer of the mistake, he must retire from the hand. The same rule holds true if the dealer gives fewer cards.

14. If the dealer exposes one or more cards when refreshing any player's hand, the dealer must place the exposed cards on the bottom of the pack and give to the player a corresponding number from the top of the pack, before serving the next player.

15. In opening the pool before the cards are dealt, the eldest hand makes the first ante, which must not exceed one-half the limit. After the cards are dealt, every player in his proper turn, beginning with the player to the left of the eldest hand, must make this ante good by depositing double the amount in the pool, or retire from that hand.

16. After the hands are filled, any player who remains in the game may, in his proper turn, beginning with the player to the left of the eldest hand, bet or raise the pool any amount not exceeding the limit of the game.

17. After the draw has been made, the eldest hand has the privilege of deferring his say until after all the other players have made their bets or passed. The eldest hand is the last player to declare whether he will play or pass. If, however, the eldest hand passes out of the game before the draw, then the next player to his left in play must make the first bet or, failing to bet, must pass out.

18. If a player, in his regular turn, bets or raises a bet any amount not exceeding the limit of the game, his adversaries must either call him, go better, or retire from the game for that hand. When a player makes a bet, he must deposit the amount in the pool.

19. If a player makes good (or sees) a bet and calls for a show of hands, each player must show his entire hand, and the best poker hand wins the pool.

20. If a player bets or raises a bet and no other player goes better or calls him, he wins the pool and is not compelled to show his hand.

21. Upon a show of hands, if a player miscalls his hand, he does not lose the pool for that reason, for every hand shows for itself.

22. Any player betting with more or less than five cards in his hand loses the pool, unless his opponents all throw up their hands before discovering the foul hand. If only one player is betting against the foul hand, that player is entitled to the ante and all the money bet; but if there are more than one betting against him, then the best hand among his opponents is entitled to the pool.

23. If a player makes a bet, and an adversary raises him, and the player who made the previous bet does not have enough chips to see the raise, he can put up all the chips he may have and call for a show of cards. If the player calling for a

The Rules of the Game

show has the best hand, he wins the ante, and an amount from each player who bets over him, equal to the sum that he himself has bet.

24. None but the eldest hand has the privilege of going a blind. The party to the left of the eldest hand may double the blind, and the next player straddle it, the next double the straddle, and so on, but the amount of the straddle, when made good, must not exceed the limit of the game.

25. If the player to the left of the eldest hand declines to straddle a blind, he prevents any other player from doing so.

Jackpot

The Jackpot is a modification of Draw Poker, and is played as follows:

When all the players pass up to the blind hand, the latter allows his blind to remain in the pot, and each of the other players deposits a similar amount. The blind now deals, and any player in his regular turn may open or break the pot, provided he holds a pair of Jacks or better.

Each player in turn, beginning with the eldest hand, declares whether he can and will open the pot; if he declines to open he says, "I pass." If he elects to open, he says, "I open."

If no player opens the pot, then each player deposits in the pool the same amount that was previously contributed, and the deal passes to the next player. This continues until some player holds the necessary cards, and is willing to break the pot.

A player may break the pot for any amount within the limits of the game, and each player in turn must make the bet good, raise it, or pass out.

After all the players who determine to go in have made good the bet of the player who opened the Jackpot, and the hands have been filled, then the opener of the pot makes the first bet.

If all pass up to the player who broke the pot, the latter takes the pool and can only be compelled to show the Jacks, or better, necessary to break the pot.

A player who breaks the pot on a pair may split the pair in order to draw to a four flush or straight. When a player breaks the pot without holding the requisite cards to do so, he must deposit in the pool, as penalty, twice the amount of his original bet.

Progressive Jackpot is played as follows:

When, after a deal, no one opens the game, the players each place another chip in the pot, new hands are dealt, and no player can, under the second deal, open with less than Queens or better. If a third deal becomes necessary, it requires Kings or better to break the pot; and should it come to a fourth deal, it takes Aces or better, and so remains for any subsequent deals, until some player can break the pot.

Straight Poker

Straight Poker, or Bluff, as it is sometimes called, is played with a pack of fifty-two cards. The game is governed by the same rules as Draw Poker, except for the following variations:
1. The winner of the pool has the next deal.
2. Each player antes before the cards are dealt.
3. Any player may pass from the game, but only before the cards are dealt.
4. No player is permitted to draw or discard any cards from his original hand.

Whiskey Poker

Each player contributes one chip to the pool, and the same rules govern as in Draw Poker, except that the strongest hand is always a straight flush.

Five cards are dealt to each player, one at a time, and an extra hand is dealt on the table, which is called the *widow*. The eldest hand then examines his cards, and either passes or takes the widow. If he passes, the next player then has the privilege of the widow, and so on. Whoever takes the widow lays his discarded hand face up in the center of the table, and the player to his left selects from it the one card that might help his hand, and so on, each player discarding one card and picking up another, until someone is satisfied, which he signifies by knocking upon the table.

When a player knocks, the other players have the privilege of one more draw, after which the hands are shown, and the strongest wins. If a player knocks before the widow is taken, the widow is then turned face up, and the remaining players have one draw.

If no one takes the widow, the dealer turns the widow, and the game proceeds as in Draw Poker.

Stud Poker

Five cards are dealt, one at a time; the first is dealt face down, all others face up. The best hand wins, as in Draw Poker. For example, if the dealer's four exposed cards are a King, Four, Seven, and Five; and his opponent's a Queen, Ten, Six, and Nine; the dealer's hand in sight is the better hand, but the call being made and the unknown cards turned over, the nondealer shows an Ace, and his opponent an Eight, and the dealer loses.

Mistigris

This variety is also called Fifty-Three Deck Poker. Mistigris is a name given to the Joker; the player holding it can call it any card not already in his hand. For example, a pair with Mistigris becomes a three of a kind; two pairs and Mistigris make a full house; three of a kind with Mistigris are the same as four of a kind; four of a kind filled with Mistigris constitute a flush, and when straights are played, a sequence of four cards with Mistigris count as a straight. In all other respects, this game is played in the same manner as Draw Poker.

Rounce

Rounce may be played by any number of persons not exceeding nine, but five or seven make a good game. The game is played with a pack of fifty-two cards, which rank as in Whist.

Dealing

The dealer gives five cards to each player in rotation, beginning with the player to his left, by alternate rounds of two and three at a time. He also deals an extra hand of six cards in the center of the table, called a dummy.

The dummy must be dealt before the dealer deals to himself, and should be filled immediately preceding his own hand. The dealer then turns up the top card on the pack, which is the trump. After the first hand, the deal passes to the left.

Declaring to Play

After the deal has been completed, each player in rotation, beginning with the eldest hand, looks at his cards and declares whether he will play his hand, take the dummy, or resign. If he is satisfied with his cards, he says, "I play"; if he resigns, he says, "I pass," and throws down his cards. If a player resigns, his interest in the pool ceases, unless he elects to exchange his hand for the dummy.

The eldest hand has the first privilege of taking the dummy, and if he wants it, he places his original hand in the center of the table, face down, and discards one card from his new hand. If he declines to take the dummy, the option passes to the next player to his left. Whoever takes the dummy must play it.

When all refuse to play, then the player to the right of the dealer must play his hand, take the dummy, or, in default of doing either, give the dealer five points. The dealer, when he elects to play, may discard any card in his hand, and substitute for it the card turned up for trump.

Playing the Hand

After all have declared, the first player leads a card, and each person in rotation (to the left) plays a card to the lead; the cards played constituting a trick. The trick is won by the highest card of the suit led, or, if trumped, by the highest trump played. Suit must be followed; but if this is not possible, a player may trump or not, at his option. The winner of a trick must lead a trump; however, if he holds no trump, he may lead any card he chooses.

Scoring

Each player begins the game with fifteen points. The player who is the first to reduce his score to nothing wins the game. Each trick taken counts as one point taken off a player's score, and if a player fails to take a trick after entering to play his hand, he is *rounced,* and five points are added to his score at once.

The Rules of the Game

1. One of the players shuffles the pack, and, after having it cut by the player to his right, deals a card face up to each player in rotation, beginning to his left. The player who receives the lowest card deals. If two or more players receive the same low card, they must cut the pack, and again the lowest deals. Ace is low.
2. Each player has a right to shuffle the deck. The dealer has the right of shuffling last.
3. The player to the dealer's right cuts the cards, and if there is a card exposed in cutting, the pack must be reshuffled, and cut again.
4. The dealer must deliver the cards face down, two at a time, and then three at a time to each player in rotation, beginning with the player to his left; and before giving any cards to himself he must deal six cards to the dummy. After he deals to himself, the dealer turns up for trump the card remaining on top of the pack.
5. If, before the deal is completed, it is discovered that a card is faced in the pack, there must be a fresh deal.
6. If the dealer deals without having the pack cut; or shuffles the pack after it has been cut with his consent; or deals out of order, for instance, misses a hand or deals too many or too few cards to any player (even though the hand has been partly played out when the error is discovered); or exposes a card in dealing, he is rounced. The cards are reshuffled and recut, and the deal passes.
7. The player to the left of the dealer has the next deal.
8. If a player deals out of turn, and is not stopped before the trump card is turned, the deal stands good, and the player to the left of the player who dealt out of turn has the next deal.
9. Players must declare in rotation, beginning to the dealer's left.
10. If a player exposes a card before declaring to play, or declares to play before his turn, he is rounced.
11. The eldest hand has the first privilege of taking the dummy. If he declines to take the dummy, the next player to his left has the option, and so on up to the dealer. Whoever takes the dummy must play it, and whoever takes it must similarly place his rejected hand face down in the center of the table, and discard one card from his new hand.
12. Any player who thinks he cannot take a trick may decline to play his hand.
13. If all the players up to the right of the dealer decline to play, then he must play his hand or take the dummy, or, in default of doing either, must allow the dealer to score five points.
14. If the dealer elects to play, he may discard any card in his hand and substitute for it the card turned up for trump. (If the dealer plays the dummy, he cannot take the turned-up trump.)
15. If a player, having declared to play, exposes a card before it is his turn to play; or plays a card out of turn or before all have declared; or exposes a card while playing so as to be named by any other declared player, he is rounced.
16. If a player, having declared to play, fails to win a trick, he is rounced.

The Rules of the Game

17. If a player fails to follow suit when he has a card of the suit led; or if he fails to lead a trump after taking a trick, when it is possible for him to do so, he is rounced.

18. When a revoke or any error of play occurs, the cards must be taken up and the hand replayed, if so desired by any player except the offender.

19. If a pack is discovered to be imperfect, the deal in which the discovery is made is void. All preceding deals stand good.

Rummy

There are several versions of this very popular game. The difference is usually the number of cards originally dealt. The object of the game is to create sets of three or more cards to gain points, eventually adding up to 500. Two versions of the game given here are Rummy 500 and Gin Rummy.

Rummy 500

This game is can be played with two or more people, using a standard deck of fifty-two cards.

Dealing

The dealer deals each player seven cards, one at a time. The remainder of the deck, or the stock, is placed face down on the table, and the top card is flipped over to create a discard pile.

The players look over their hands and, if possible, group the cards in sets of threes. The cards can be grouped as a *run* or a *lay*. A run consists of three or more cards of the same suit in consecutive order; a lay consists of three or more cards of the same rank (for example, three Kings). If a player begins the game with either a run or a lay, he removes them from his hand and places them on the table face up.

The eldest hand (the player to the left of the dealer) goes first, and picks a card from either the stock or the discard pile. If he can use the card he picks up to form either a run or a lay, he keeps it, puts the run or lay face up ont the table, and discards another from his hand face up into the discard pile. If a player can use a card that is in the discard pile, he may pick it up instead, but he must take *all* the cards in the pile, and he must use the top card immediately to form a lay or a run. As soon as a player discards, his turn is finished, and the next player goes.

The game ends when the first player has created sets with all of his cards. Any player who still has cards in his hand after the first person goes out must subtract the total number of points he is holding from his score. If he does not have enough points laid down in front of him to cover what is in his hand, he must subtract this score from a previous hand. There are no additional points given for going out first.

Scoring

The cards are worth the following number of points:

Ace	= 15 points
Picture cards	= 10 points
All other cards	= 5 points

The Secrets of the Game

1. As soon as you can group cards together, take them out of your hand and lay them on the table in front of you. If you hold them in your hand and another player goes out, you won't be able to add those points to your score; instead you will have to subtract the cards in your hand from your points on the table.

2. If a player can make a rummy, that is, if he has a card that can be added to one of your sets, he places his card or cards with your set and add the addi-tional points to his score.

3. If a rummy is discarded without the player realizing it the player who first notices can pull that card or cards from the discard pile, and add the points to his score. For example, if a player puts down three Fours, and there is a Four on top of the discard pile, the next player to pick up from the discard pile may use it. However, the player pulling the card from the discard pile will have to take up the entire pile into his hand.

Gin Rummy

This game is played by two or more people. If you are playing with two people, use one standard deck of fifty-two cards. If playing with more than four people, you might want to use two complete decks to make the game more interesting. The object of the game is to form matched sets of runs and lays consisting of three or four cards each.

Dealing

The dealer deals ten cards to each player, and to himself. The top card from the stock is turned over to create a discard pile.

Playing

The eldest hand plays first, and must pick a card from either the stock or the discard pile. If he chooses to take a card from the discard pile, he only has to take the top card. He then tries to use the new card in either a run or a lay, and discards one card from his hand that he will not need. Once the first player has discarded, his turn is over and the player to the left of him continues the game.

In this version of rummy, the player holds onto his sets in his hand instead of laying them on the table. Whoever can use all of his cards except for one in matched sets wins. The single card left is thrown onto the discard pile, face down, and the player announces, "Gin," to signify that the game is over.

Each hand that wins is worth 25 points. Complete games are usually played to reach 100 points.

Sixty-Six

Sixty-Six is played with two players, using twenty-four cards: the Ace, Ten, King, Queen, Jack, and Nine of each suit. The cards rank in value in the order named above; trumps are the superior suit.

Dealing

The player who cuts the highest card deals. The dealer gives each player six cards, three at a time, turning up the last card for trump, which is laid on the table. The remainder of the pack (called the *stock*) is placed face down apart from the trump card.

The nondealer leads and may play any card in his hand. The dealer may play to it any card he pleases, without restriction as to suit or value, and the two cards played constitute a trick. The highest card of the suit led wins the trick, but trumps beat all inferior suits.

The player who wins the trick places it, face down, in front of himself, and then draws the top card from the stock; his adversary draws the next card; this restores the cards in hand to six, as before the lead.

When all the cards are played out, the player who wins the last trick receives ten extra points toward sixty-six.

In the course of play, if either player reaches sixty-six points or more, he declares it at once.

If the hand is played to its conclusion, and both players count only sixty-five, neither can score, but the winner of the next hand scores one point extra.

No more cards are played after sixty-six has been declared; the unplayed cards in hand are void and have no value.

When a player announces sixty-six, his adversary may examine the tricks to ascertain whether the announcement is correct.

Closing

If, at any time before the stock is exhausted, a player thinks he can make sixty-six without further drawing, he may, when it is his turn to lead, turn down the turned-up trump. This is called *closing*.

A player may close before a card is led, and consequently before a trick has been taken.

The leader has the option of closing either before or after drawing from the stock, but his adversary has no choice about the matter, and must play either with or without drawing, as the leader elects.

All drawing is discontinued as soon as the leader closes, and the last cards are played subject to the same rules and conditions as those in operation when playing the last six tricks after the stock is exhausted, with the exception that the winner of the last trick does not count ten points.

If the player who closes fails to count sixty-six, his adversary scores two points.

If a player closes before his adversary has won a trick, and fails to count sixty-six, his adversary scores three points.

The Rules of the Game

1. A cut must consist of at least two cards. When cutting for deal, the player cutting first must leave sufficient cards for the player cutting last to make a legal deal. The player who cuts last must not leave less than two cards in the remainder of the lower packet.

2. When cutting, if more than one card is exposed, the player must cut again.

3. Each player has the right to shuffle, and it is the dealer's right to shuffle last, but if the dealer shuffles after the pack is cut, there must be a fresh cut.

4. The players deal alternately throughout the game.

5. The dealer must deal six cards to each player, three at a time, and turn up the next or thirteenth card for trump.

6. If the dealer fails to give the proper number of cards and the error is discovered before the trump card is turned, there must be a fresh deal.

7. If there is a faced card in the pack, or, if the cards have been dealt without having the pack cut, there must be a fresh deal.

8. If a player deals out of turn, his adversary may stop him at any time before the trump card is turned; but if the trump card is turned, the deal stands good.

9. If a player draws out of turn, and his adversary does not discover the error previous to drawing himself, there is no penalty. If the adversary discovers the error before drawing, he may draw and proceed with the game; or he may end the hand and score one point.

10. If a player forgets to draw, and plays a card before discovering the error, his adversary may allow the offending player to draw, and proceed with the game, or he may end the hand and score one point.

11. If a player draws when he has six cards in his hand, his adversary may require the delinquent player to play next time without drawing, or he may end the hand and score one point.

12. If a player lifts two cards in drawing, his adversary may have them both turned face up, and then choose which the player may take.

13. If a player leads out of turn, or, leads a wrong card, there is no penalty. If the adversary plays to the card led, the error cannot be rectified.

14. If, after the stock is exhausted or there is a close, a player does not follow suit or win the trick when able, he can score no point that hand, and his adversary scores two points, or three if the offender has no points toward sixty-six.

15. If a player announces sixty-six, and on examination it appears that he has fewer points, his adversary scores two points, and the hand is ended.

16. The turned and quitted tricks must not be searched during the play of the hand.

Skat

This game is played with a Euchre pack of thirty-two cards, (Sixes, Fives, Fours, Threes, and Twos removed from a regular pack) and is played by three players for each deal. Four or five people may alternate in the game, but must play in rotation. The game is played by two players against one. If there are remaining or silent players, they share the fortunes of the two opponents of the lone player. The object of the game is to make at least sixty-one points, which depend on the value of the cards contained in the tricks taken.

Dealing

The dealer deals ten cards to each player, one at a time, in rotation, starting with the player to his left, and two cards are laid aside, face down.

Playing

The eldest hand (the player to the left of the dealer) goes first, and if his cards are favorable, says, "I ask"; the player next on his left then makes a bid into the pool as his cards may warrant; if the eldest hand thinks he can do as well or better, he replies, "Yes"; the asker must then bid higher or pass; if he bids higher, the eldest hand must answer, "Yes," or pass. The players are then asked again by the third player (the dealer), who must overbid or pass.

In case none of the players are able to make or accept a bid, and all three pass, the game is void, and the deal passes.

The successful bidder then names the trump suit and plays against the other two. The eldest hand leads first, any card he chooses. Each player plays to the trick in turn, and the highest card of the suit led wins the trick, unless trumped.

Each player must follow suit if he can; if not able, he may play any card he chooses, trumping being optional. The winner of a trick leads for the next trick.

If the lone player makes 61 points, he wins the game; if he makes 91 points, he makes his opponents *Schneider;* or if he makes 120 or all the points, he makes his opponents *Schwartz,* and his winnings are increased accordingly. He then receives from each of his opponents (and the silent players, if any) the value of his game.

If, however, he fails to make 61 points, he loses the game; if his opponents make 91 points he is Schneider; or if he makes no points at all, he is Schwartz and he pays each of his opponents (silent players included, if any) the value of his game, increased, as the case may be, by the additional payment for Schneider or Schwartz.

The lone player may bid or announce to win 91 points (Schneider) or 120 points (Schwartz); but loses unless he makes the points announced.

If he announces to win a Schneider or a Schwartz, and is himself made Schneider or Schwartz as the case may be, his losses are proportionally increased. The announcement or bid to win a Schneider or a Schwartz is only permitted in a *solo-bid*.

If the lone player, after the first trick has been played and before another lead is made, sees that his case is hopeless, he can throw down his cards, and pay the value of the game as announced, thus securing himself against further possible loss.

Rank of the Suits

The value of a bid is regulated by the suit. The suits rank in the following order: First, Clubs; second, Spades; third, Hearts; and fourth and lowest, Diamonds.

Rank and Value of the Cards

The cards in each suit rank in the order here given, and count their respective points toward game:

Ace counts for 11 points

Ten counts for 10 points

King counts for 4 points

Queen counts for 3 points

Nine, Eight, and Seven rank in the order of their spots, but have no counting value.

Jack does not rank in the suits, but counts 2 points toward the game. This does not apply to *Null*, in which the cards have no counting value, and their rank is changed.

The Matadores

The four Jacks are called *Matadores,* and are the four highest trumps. Each trump suit, therefore, contains eleven trumps.

The Matadores rank in the following order:
First, Jack of Clubs; second, Jack of Spades; third, Jack of Hearts; and fourth and lowest, Jack of Diamonds.

All trump cards, in unbroken sequence, beginning with the highest Matadore down, are reckoned as Matadores in bidding and payments. The possession of Matadores is of great importance in adding to the value and payment of a bid.

The failure to possess them also counts in exactly the same manner. Thus, a lone player who does not have the highest Matadore can bid *without one;* if he does not have the highest and second Matadore, he can bid *without two,* making the value of his game the same as if he had bid *with one, two.*

The Skat

The two cards that are dealt face down on the table constitute the *Skat* or discard pile. The Skat is the property of the lone player in all cases, except in Null.

Description of the Bids

The bids are divided into three classes:
First—Simple bids ranking in the order of the suits.
Second—The bid to play in Tournée. These two bids are played with the assistance of Skat cards.
Third—Bids in Solo, in the order of the suits. These are played without the Skat cards although they belong to the successful bidder; at the close of the game, he adds to his score all the points they may contain.

The Simple Game

This bid includes the Skat cards, and the privilege of naming the trump suit. If any suit is bid, the successful bidder must adopt the suit bid as trump, or he may name a higher suit, if he prefers it; but he cannot adopt a lower suit. The *Simple* is not much used, the biding generally beginning with *Tournée.*

Tournée

This is a bid to play alone, and decide the trump suit by turning up either one of the Skat cards. If this bid be accepted, the player takes up both the Skat cards and discards two from his hand, as in the Simple. He may discard one or both of the original Skat cards.

If the turnup card should be a Matadore, before he has seen the other Skat card, he may either adopt the suit of the turned-up Jack as trump, or he may declare to play Grand. If the turn-up card is a Seven, the player may announce to play Null.

Solo

A bid for Solo must be based on the cards in hand, without the help of the Skat cards, and requires a strong assurance of the ability to make at least 61 points. The lone player makes the trump. He must make it the suit he has bid, or a higher suit, but not a lower one. The skat cards remain untouched until the close of the game; any counting cards or Matadores they may contain are then added to the player's count.

Grand

In *Grand,* all the suits are of the same value, and the four Matadores are the only trump cards; the highest bid, therefore, is *with* or *without* four Matadores. *Grand Solo,* played without the Skat cards, outbids any other Solo of equal value.

Grand Ouverte

This bid is similar to Grand, with the exception that, after the first trick has been taken, the three players complete the game with their cards exposed upon the table before them, thus affording them the better opportunity of defeating the lone player.

Grand Ouverte with or *without* four Matadores is the highest bid in Skat, taking precedence over all other bids.

Grand Tournée

When in Tournée, the Skat card turned up for trump is a Matadore, the player has the privilege of declaring Grand, but he must declare it before he looks at the remaining Skat card.

Null

The object of *Null* is to avoid taking any trick at all. If the lone player takes any (even only one) trick, he loses the game. A *Null Solo* ranks below any Solo Game of the same or greater value, but takes precedence over any simple game of the same or less value.

Null Ouverte

This is played on the same principles as Null, except that, after the first trick, the player must expose his cards on the table before him, and thus finish the game while his opponents play against him, each with his cards visible to himself only.

Grand Null Ouverte

This is also called *Revolution.* The cards of all the three players are exposed face up on the table before the first card is led. Before the play begins the opponents are permitted to exchange as many cards as they want, so as to make each of their hands as effective as possible; also, throughout the game they may consult with each other as to the play of their cards.

Null Tournée

When, in Tournée, the Skat card turned for trump is a Seven, the lone player is permitted to play Null, but this must be announced before he looks at the remaining Skat card. When he has announced a Null, after taking up the other Skat card, he is allowed to declare Null Ouverte.

The Value of Bids

The following table exhibits the fundamental units of value for the various bids:

	Diamonds	Hearts	Spades	Clubs
Simple	1	2	3	4
Tournée	5	6	7	8
Solo	9	10	11	12

In addition to these are bids that are irrespective of suit:

Tournée	12	Tournée	16
Grand Solo	16	Solo	24
Ouverte	24	Null Tournée Ouverte	32
		Solo Ouverte	48
		Revolution	72

The foregoing units of value are increased by two conditions. First, the amount of points reached in the play of the hands, either Schneider and Schwartz. Second, the number of Matadores held in hand, including those (if any) contained in the Skat cards. The first and second added together form a multiplier of the unit-values, and are reckoned as follows:

A) Schneider and Schwartz. There is a difference between a Schneider and a Schwartz, not announced but reached in play, and if bid or declared beforehand.

Schneider made, not bid	1	Schwartz made, not bid	3
Schneider bid and won	2	Schwartz bid and won	4

B) The number of Matadores. Each Matadore counts for one unit-value of the game bid or declared.

With (or without) one Matadore   1
With (or without) two Matadores   2
With (or without) three Matadores 3
With (or without) four Matadores   4

Bids and Payments

Figure 15 exhibits the value and payments of each bid. This table includes up to six Matadores; for every additional Matadore (if any), add one more unit-value of the bid to the amount given for six Matadores.

Bidding

The main object of a bid is the expectation to make at least 61 points. Success in this depends first on the value of such cards in hand as are sure to win a trick, second on those counting cards that may be captured. The relative position of a bidder is of great importance; it makes a wide difference if the bidder has the first lead.

Figure 15

	Unit value	With or without one Matadore.					With or without two Matadores.					With or without three Matadores.				
		Game.	Schneider.	Schneider announced.	Schwarz.	Schwarz announced.	Game.	Schneider.	schneider announced.	Schwarz.	Schwarz announced.	Game.	Schneider.	Schneider announced.	Schwarz.	Schwarz announced.
Simple. Diamonds.	1	2	3	4	5	6	3	4	5	6	7	4	5	6	7	8
Hearts.	2	4	6	8	10	12	6	8	10	12	14	8	10	12	14	16
Spades.	3	6	9	12	15	18	9	12	15	18	21	12	15	18	21	24
Clubs.	4	8	12	16	20	24	12	16	20	24	28	16	20	24	28	32
Tourné. Diamonds.	5	10	15	20	25	30	15	20	25	30	35	20	25	30	35	40
Hearts.	6	12	18	24	30	36	18	24	30	36	42	24	30	36	42	48
Spades.	7	14	21	28	35	42	21	28	35	42	49	28	35	42	49	56
Clubs.	8	16	24	32	40	48	24	32	40	48	56	32	40	48	56	64
Grand.	12	24	36	48	60	72	36	48	60	72	84	48	60	72	84	96
Null.	16	..	..	..	..	..	..	..	..	..	..	..	..	..	..	..
" Ouvert.	32	..	..	..	..	..	..	..	..	..	..	..	..	..	..	..
Solo. Diamonds.	9	18	27	36	45	54	27	36	45	54	63	36	45	54	63	72
Hearts.	10	20	30	40	50	60	30	40	50	60	70	40	50	60	70	80
Spades.	11	22	33	44	55	66	33	44	55	66	77	44	55	66	77	88
Clubs.	12	24	36	48	60	72	36	48	60	72	84	48	60	72	84	96
Grand.	16	32	48	64	80	90	48	64	80	96	112	64	80	96	112	128
" Ouvert	24	..	..	..	..	144	..	..	..	..	168	..	..	..	..	192
Null.	24	..	..	..	..	..	..	..	..	..	..	..	..	..	..	..
" Ouvert	48	..	..	..	..	..	..	..	..	..	..	..	..	..	..	..
Revolution.	72	..	..	..	..	..	..	..	..	..	..	..	..	..	..	..

	Unit value	With or without four Matadores.					With or without five Matadores.					With or without six Matadores.				
		Game.	Schneider.	Schneider announced.	Scwarz.	Schwarz announced.	Game.	Schneider.	Schneider announced.	Schwarz.	Schwarz announced.	Game.	Schneider.	Schneider announced.	Schwarz.	Schwarz announced.
Simple. Diamonds.	1	5	6	7	8	9	6	7	8	9	10	7	8	9	10	11
Hearts.	2	10	12	14	16	18	12	14	16	18	20	14	16	18	20	22
Spades.	3	15	18	21	24	27	18	21	24	27	30	21	24	27	30	33
Clubs.	4	20	24	28	32	36	24	28	32	36	40	28	32	36	40	44
Tourné. Diamonds.	5	25	30	35	40	45	30	35	40	45	50	35	40	45	50	55
Hearts.	6	30	36	42	48	54	36	42	48	54	60	42	48	54	60	66
Spades.	7	35	42	49	56	63	42	49	56	63	70	49	56	63	70	77
Clubs.	8	40	48	56	64	72	48	56	64	72	80	56	64	72	80	88
Grand.	12	60	72	84	96	108	..	..	..	..	..	..	..	..	..	..
Solo. Diamonds.	9	45	54	63	72	81	54	63	72	81	90	63	72	81	90	99
Hearts.	10	50	60	70	80	90	60	70	80	90	100	70	80	90	100	110
Spades.	11	55	66	77	88	99	66	77	88	99	110	77	88	99	110	121
Clubs.	12	60	72	84	96	108	72	84	96	108	120	84	96	108	120	132
Grand.	16	80	96	112	128	144	..	..	..	..	..	..	..	..	..	..
Grand Ouvert	24	120	144	168	192	216	..	..	..	..	..	..	..	..	..	..

The Rules of the Game

1. To determine the order of play, each player draws a card from a pack spread out face down on the table. The player drawing the lowest card is the dealer. The drawer of the next higher card takes his seat to the left of the dealer; the drawer of the next higher card sits next, to the left of the second player already seated, and so on, until all are seated. Ties are drawn over again.
2. The cards are shuffled by the dealer, and cut by the player on his right.
3. When only three are playing, the dealer deals five cards to each in rotation, beginning with the eldest hand; he then lays the next two cards face down on the center of the table, which constitute the Skat; finally he deals five cards more to each.
4. If the dealer exposes a card while dealing, the player to whom the card belongs can either accept it or order the dealer to deal again.
5. After the first deal, the deal passes in rotation to the left.
6. If the dealer gives to any player too few or too many cards, and it is detected *before* a card has been led, there must be a fresh deal, and the dealer must pay a penalty of five points to each of the other players. If the deck is imperfect, or one or more cards are faced in the pack, or either of the players touch their cards or in any way interfere with the dealer, the dealer deals again without penalty.
7. If it is found, after play has commenced, that the lone player does not have the correct number of cards, he loses the game. If, after play has commenced, it is discovered that either of the opposing players has an incorrect number of cards, his side loses the game.
8. If a misdeal is not discovered until after the lone player has won a Schneider, the Schneider holds good. If, however, the opponents have won a Scheider, and the lone player has correct cards, they can only win a plain game of 61 points.
9. If the lone player and one or both of his opponents have incorrect cards, the game is void, and the deal passes.
10. Any player dealing out of turn may be stopped before the deal is completed. If the deal has been completed and play commenced, the deal stands good; and the next deal passes to the player on his left in regular routine.
11. The eldest hand retains the right to play alone, until overbid by one of the other players. The rank of a bid is decided by its value, and in cases of bids of equal value, the elder hand takes the preference.
12. A successful bidder must play his bid, or a higher one.
13. If a player leads out of his turn and it is discovered before the trick has been turned, each player must withdraw his card.
14. If an incorrect lead is not discovered until *after* the trick has been turned, the lead and play must stand good.
15. If any card is exposed by either of the opponents, the offender must pay to the lone player a penalty of five points, not only for himself, but also for each of his

The Rules of the Game

partners; the game may be played to its conclusion, or a new deal be demanded by the lone player, at his option.

16. When a player, holding one or more cards of the suit led, plays a card of a different suit, he makes a revoke.

17. If a revoke is discovered before the trick has been turned, the error can be rectified; otherwise, the revoke is established.

18. If the lone player makes a revoke, he loses the game and must pay the price of the game to each of his opponents, including silent partners (if any). This holds true as well for the opposing players.

19. Any player has the right to inspect only the trick last turned.

20. If any player, who is not entitled to them, takes up one or both of the Skat cards, he (or his side) loses the game. This applies also to silent players (if any).

21. If either or both of the Skat cards are improperly lifted before the play begins, the offender pays ten points to the lone player, who can continue the play or order a new deal at his option.

22. When the lone player, after the first trick has been turned and before another lead has been made, sees that his game is hopeless and may possibly result in a Schneider or Schwartz, he can throw down his cards and pay for the game.

23. Either side, having passed 61, can insist on the hands being played out, so as to secure the opportunity of winning a Schneider or Schwartz. The same principle holds good in case of 91 points (a Schneider announced) having been made.

24. During the play, no remarks are permissible, either by active or silent players, or the offender pays ten points to the lone player. The only exception is when Grand Null Ouvert is played, in which consultation between partners is a feature of the game.

The Secrets of the Game

For the Lone Player

1. The lone player has one great advantage in his favor: the cards in his own hand tell him exactly what his opponents have in their combined hands.

2. His first care should be to work out his opponent's trumps as soon as possible, especially if he has a long suit to bring in. This is particularly the case in playing Grand, in order to prevent any commanding cards from being trumped. When a trick is against him, he should not play any counting card to it, or as low a card as possible, because every point tells against him.

3. If the Skat cards are taken in hand, it requires some judgment to determine what cards to discard in their place. It is advisable to discard any suit of which only two cards are in hand. This leaves the suit free for trumping. It is also important to discard cards that will add to the final count: Tens, for instance, especially when unguarded; or even Ace and Ten of a suit unguarded. This is especially the case in Ace and Ten of trumps, unguarded, with other suits evenly represented. These two trumps are likely to fall to the Matadores; but they should be retained in case the hand is bare of one or more suits, in order to trumps such suit or suits when led.

4. If he has two or three highest Matadores, he may lead the lowest of them first; it may induce his first opponent to fatten the trick in the supposition that his partner will take the trick.

5. If he is weak in trumps, he should stop leading them if he finds the remainder of the trumps are all held by one of his opponents.

6. It is advisable to retain the lead if possible, until sufficient points have been gathered in to make the game fairly secure.

7. In Grand, with first and third (or fourth) Matadore, and a long suit, the lone player should lead highest Matadore, then the suit.

For the Opponents

1. The first consideration for the two opponents is to assist each other to defeat the lone player: by baffling him in play, by contributing as few points as possible to his tricks, and by fattening a partner's trick with available counting cards.

2. They should try to make the lone player second or middle man in the play. This gives the leader's partner the advantage of being third in play, and affords him an opportunity of fattening their own trick with an Ace or Ten, or of playing a low card to the trick if it is against them.

3. If it is found that the lone player is weak in trumps, the opponents should lead them.

4. If the lone player is bare of any suit, the opponents should lead it, so as to draw his trumps, and retain their own.

5. It is usual to answer a partner's lead and, when the partner is third hand, to lead a suit in which he renounces.

6. If each of the partners has a strong suit in which the other renounces,

The Secrets of the Game

and either of them has the lead, they can lead into each other's hands, fattening their tricks, while the lone player is sandwiched in between them, and loses every trick in which he can follow suit.

7. Early in the game, an opponent should lead from a short suit, there being less chance of it being trumped by the lone player.

8. In playing Grand, if the lone player leads a Matadore and one of the opponents has the first and either the third or fourth Matadore, the opponent, if he has a strong suit, should not play his highest Matadore, but reserve it to regain the lead, and bring in his own long suit, defeating the lone player.

9. When the Ace and Ten of a suit are out, an opponent should not lead in it again unless his partner renounces.

10. When one of the opponents holds the majority of trumps, he should not lead trumps, but reserve them.

11. If the lone player at the start does not lead trumps, or leads them and fails to follow up his trump lead, the opponent in second hand should trump if he can.

12. When the lone player has failed to lead out the trumps, and an opponent, on his first lead, also refrains from doing so, his partner should follow his example when he gets the lead and avoid leading trumps, unless very strong in them.

13. When an opponent's first lead is an Ace and his partner cannot follow suit, the partner should fatten from his shortest suit, rather than weaken a commanding one.

14. If an opponent leads an Ace and his partner has the Ten and King, he should fatten with the Ten.

Slapjack

This game is played by two people, with a standard deck of fifty-two cards. The object of the game is to end up with all fifty-two cards.

Playing

The entire deck is dealt between the two players, face down. Neither player is allowed to look at his cards.

The first player puts down a card, face up, onto the table. The second player does the same, on top of the first card, and so on, until a player puts down a Jack. When a Jack is faced on the table, each player tries to slap their hand over it. The first person to slap it gets all the cards underneath, including the Jack. This process continues until one player holds all the cards, and is declared the winner of the game.

Slobberhannes

This is a game for four players, each playing for his own hand. A Euchre pack is used, the cards ranking in value from Ace (highest) to Seven (lowest).

Playing

The players cut, not for the deal, but for the lead, the highest having the preference, and the player on his right dealing. After the first hand has been played, the deal passes in rotation to the left. The deal is no advantage, and a misdeal, therefore, involves no penalty. The dealer gives out cards to the other players, rotating to the left, two cards at a time. There is no trump, all suits being alike in value.

Each player is bound to follow suit if he can. The highest card wins the trick, and the winner leads to the next. The object is to *avoid* making tricks, for the players who first makes ten points loses the game, and has to pay an agreed stake to each of the other players.

Scoring

Points are scored as follows:

1. For the first trick, one point.
2. For the last trick, one point.
3. For the trick containing the Queen of Clubs, one point.
4. If, in the same hand, any one player wins all three tricks above mentioned, he is said to make Slobberhannes, and scores an extra point.
5. The penalty of a revoke is also one point added to the score of the offender.

The Secrets of the Game

1. The lead is a great advantage, for the player is pretty sure to hold one safe losing card, which he will lead accordingly.
2. The general policy of the other three players will be to follow suit with the lowest card possible, unless the player sees that he is bound to win the trick, he should in such case do so with his *highest* card, to avoid the possibility of being compelled to win a damaging trick at a later stage.
3. The main interest of the game lies in the general struggle not to be saddled with the Queen of Clubs, which the holder will try to play to a Club trick, or discard to some other lead when he happens to be short.
4. The Ace and King of Clubs are very dangerous cards to hold.
5. The eighth card of a suit, or the best card of any suit of which there are only two or three remaining, is a very bad lead, as, being a certain winner, it gives the adversaries a safe opportunity to discard several of the above-mentioned cards of higher value.

Solo

Unlike its name suggests, Solo is played by three or four (usually four) players, with a Euchre pack of thirty-two cards. Five players may play, but then you'll need to increase the number of the cards to forty, by adding the Fives and Sixes of each suit. The game, as described here, is for four players.

Dealing

The dealer shuffles the cards, and after the player to his right has cut, he deals to each player eight cards, by three and two and three at a time. The deal, after the first round, passes to the left in rotation.

The Pool

Before the cards are dealt, the dealer puts a stake into the pool. The amount of the stake is agreed upon before the game, and is usually two or four chips. The pool is increased by the forfeits (or *Béte)* that occur in the game.

A béte can never exceed sixteen chips, and when the pool contains sixteen, it is called a *Stamm.*

Rank of the Cards

The Queen of Clubs is called *Spadilla,* and is always the best trump. The Seven of the trump suit (whatever it may be) is called *Manilla,* and ranks second, or below Spadilla. The Queen of Spades is called *Basta,* and is always the third trump. These three cards are natural *Matadores.* When Clubs or Spades are trumps, they are termed *short suits,* as they contain nine trumps; when Hearts or Diamonds are trumps, they are *long suits,* because they contain ten trumps.

Rank of Bids

One of the suits is selected, which is termed *couleur,* and bids in that suit are worth twice as much as in either of the other three suits. Couleur is generally Clubs or, after the first game, that suit in which the first game was won. The rank and value of the bids follows:

Simple game, in Suit	2 chips
Simple game, in Couleur	4 chips
Forcée Partout, in Suit	4 chips
Forcée Partout, in Couleur	8 chips
Solo, in Suit	4 chips

Solo, in Couleur	8 chips
Tout, in Suit	16 chips
Tout, in Couleur	32 chips

Forcée Partout outranks a *Simple; Solo* outbids *Forcée Partout,* and *Tout* supersedes any *Solo.*

Forcée Simple. When all have passed, the holder of Spadilla is forced to call for an Ace, and play with his friend against the other two players. The holder of the called Ace then names the trump, but not the suit of the called Ace. *Forcée Simple* is not a bid; but, in the absence of any bid, a compulsory play of at least a *simple* game, with corresponding payments.

Matadores or Honors

Higher Matadores. Spadilla, Manilla, and Basta are called *higher Matadores.* When all three are in a player's hand (or in his and his friend's hands), they count as one chip for the three in the payment of the game.

Lower Matadores. When all three of the higher Matadores are held by either side, all trump cards that are also held in uninterrupted succession from Ace downward, are also counted as Matadores. Each lower Matadore counts as one chip.

Reservation or reneging is allowed when a trump or lower Matadore is led; in that case a higher Matadore unguarded may be *reserved* without penalty for a revoke. No Matadore need be played to a lead of trumps, even if a higher Matadore has been played, unless the higher Matadore has been led. A higher Matadore, when led, forces a lower Matadore unguarded; a lower Matadore or any trump card led does not force a higher Matadore. Sometimes Solo is played without the element of reservation being introduced.

Object of the Game

The object of the game is for a player to get the privilege of naming the trump, and playing either alone against the other three, or with the assistance of a friend against the remaining two players. This privilege is accorded to the bidder or announcer of the highest play. A successful bidder must take five tricks in order to win from the opponents the value of his bid; if he fails to take five tricks, he must pay the same price to each of the opponents.

Bids and Payment

Simple Game. This is when the player is unwilling to play a solo; he names the trump suit, and calls for an Ace; the holder of the called Ace then acts as his partner or friend. Until the called Ace falls in play, it is not necessarily known who the friend really is; but, acting on his own knowledge, he is bound to assist the player to the best of his ability.

The payment for a simple game in suit is two chips; or, if in couleur, four chips. If the player and friend win five tricks, each receives the value of the game (including the price of the Matadores, if any), from his left-hand neighbor. Or, if they lose, each pays the same to,

If the player holds all four Aces and is not willing to play a solo, he can call for a King instead of an Ace.

Forcée Partout. The holder of Spadilla and Basta must always announce it, unless a higher bid has already been made by himself or a previous bidder. It may be played as a solo or with a called Ace. The holder of the called Ace then names the trump, but not in the suit of the called Ace.

Solo. A solo is when the player attempts to take five tricks unaided. He names the trump, and plays alone against the other three. The payment of a solo in suit is four chips; in couleur, eight chips. The player alone receives payment for the game (and Matadores, if any) from the other three. If he loses, he pays each of them the same amount.

If the solo is in couleur, and he wins it, he also draws a stamm from the pool. If he lose the game, he puts a béte into the pool, in addition to the regular payments.

A *tout* is when the bidder proposes to take all the tricks, either playing solo, or with a called Ace. The payment for a tout is sixteen chips if in suit, or thirty-two chips if in couleur.

In some places, the winner of a Solo-Tout in couleur draws a stamm from the pool; or, if he loses, he pays a béte into the pool.

If in the course of playing a solo or a simple, the player having succeeded in taking the first five tricks, and believing it possible to make all the eight, should lead his sixth card. This act signifies that he proposes incidentally to play for tout. By doing this, he forfeits his right to any payment to which the winning of the five tricks would have entitled him. If he succeeds, he wins double the value of the game if in suit, or four times the value if in couleur, from each of the others, and also the price of any Matadores. If he fails to take all the tricks, he must pay in the same proportion.

If no bid is made, the holder of Spadilla is obliged to assume the play.

Bidding

After the hands are dealt, the eldest hand has the first say. If his hand is not good, he can pass, and the next player can do the same, and so on. If the eldest hand considers his cards good enough (with the assistance of an Ace) to make five tricks, he says, "I ask." The next player can outbid him, or pass, the other two players having the opportunity in turn to bid higher or pass. The highest bidder then plays alone against the other three, or, with the assistance of a friend, against the other two; in either case, the bidder names the trump. If the called Ace is in the caller's own hand, the game then ranks in value as a Solo. If the caller holds all four Aces, and will not play Solo, he can call for a King in the same manner as for an Ace.

If all pass, then the player who hold Spadilla is compelled to play a Forcée Simple; that is, to call for an Ace, the holder of which becomes his partner or friend.

The bidding is done in this manner: Suppose A has a hand good for playing a solo in Hearts. He says, "I ask." B says, "Is it in couleur?" A answers, "Yes." B says "Is it Solo?" A answers, "Yes." B again asks, "Is it solo in couleur?" A replies "No," and therefore passes. B then has the say, and unless either C or D can bid a tout, B must play solo in couleur. A player is compelled to play at least the game he bids.

Playing

After the bidding has been concluded, the eldest hand leads any card he chooses. The player to his left plays a card to it, and so on in rotation until each player has played a card to the lead. The four cards thus played constitute a trick. The highest card of the suit led wins the trick. Trumps win other suits. Suit must be followed, except with Matadores. If suit cannot be followed, trumping is optional. The winner of the trick leads to the next, and so on.

The Rules of the Game

1. The deal is determined by one of the players delivering a card face up to each player in rotation, beginning to his left; the player to whom the first Club falls is dealer.

2. After the dealer has shuffled the cards, and the pack has been cut by the player to his right, he delivers to each player in rotation, beginning with the player to his left, eight cards: three and two and three at a time. After the first hand has been played, the deal passes in rotation to the left.

3. If the dealer deals without having the pack properly cut; or if he exposes any of the cards of the other players, or if he gives any player too few or too many cards; or if a card is faced in the pack, there must be a fresh deal.

4. A player who has once passed cannot afterward bid to play that deal.

5. If a player asks, he must play, unless he is superseded by a higher bid.

6. If all the players pass, the holder of Spadilla is forced to call for an Ace, and play with his friend against the other two players.

7. If a player passes, having Spadilla and Basta in his hand, unless solo or a higher bid has already been made, he must pay a forfeit or béte, and a new deal ensues.

8. If a Solo player leads a card before naming the trump, it is assumed that he means to play in couleur, and he must so play.

9. If a player, having made the first five tricks, leads his sixth card, he is bound to play for Tout, or all the tricks, with all the payments that Tout involves. If he make all the tricks, he is paid for all. If he fails to make all the tricks, he loses all.

10. If, when a solo is played, either of the three opponents lead or play a card out of turn, or expose a card, they all equally lose the game. There is no penalty for the solo player if he commits any of these errors.

11. If the game is played with a called Ace, two against two, and any player commits either of the errors enumerated in Rule #10, he and his partner equally forfeit the game, the guilty player alone paying a béte into the pool.

12. If a player calls for the Ace of a suit of which he has none, he must announce that fact before he plays. If he fails to announce it, he loses the game at once.

13. If a player has announced that he has none of the suit of the called Ace, he is at liberty to trump or overtrump the trick to which the called Ace has been played.

14. The holder of a called Ace must play it at the first opportunity.

15. Each player must follow suit, if possible. If a suit is led, and any player having a card of that suit should play a card of another suit to it, and the trick has been turned and quitted, that constitutes a revoke. However, a player is entitled to renege or reserve a Matadore when a lower trump is led, and also to renege a higher Matadore when a lower one is led; but a higher Matadore when led always forces the lower one, when the latter is unguarded.

16. If a player revokes when not entitled, or reneges when not entitled, his side forfeits the game.

Solitaire

There are hundreds of variations of this game. However, what they all have in common is that they are created for one player. The object of all the games is to build sequences (called families) on different foundations, using either one or two standard decks of fifty-two cards. Some games are very quick to play; others require patience and quite a bit of skill. What follows is a sampling of some of the more interesting solitaire games.

Classic Solitaire

The object of this game is to build complete families upon the foundations, beginning with the King, in descending sequence, alternating colors. One deck of cards is used.

Playing

The cards are dealt, face down, into seven packets in a row, the first (or left-hand) packet contains seven cards; the next packet to the right, six cards; and each succeeding packet to the right, one card less than the preceding packet, so that the seventh packet will consist of one card. These cards are referred to as the *auxiliary piles*. The top card from each auxiliary pile is then turned over, exposing the face of the card.

If any Kings appear, remove them from their pile and place them in a separate row above the *auxiliary piles*. These Kings will form the foundations on which you will build the families. The rest of the face up cards are then matched up in descending order, alternating in color (this is called a *marriage*) if possible. If any piles are left unexposed, you may turn up the next available card in that pile and see if you can use it.

Once all the preliminary marriages are complete, flip over one card from the stock, and see if it can be used. If it is King, place it in the separate row above the piles. A Queen of an alternating color can be placed atop the King, and so on, until you reach an Ace. Cards from the stock can also be used to create marriages within the auxiliary piles.

The deal is repeated over and over again until you have exhausted the auxiliary piles. If no play has been possible during a deal, the game is blocked and ended. A winning game will consist of the four families, all ending with an Ace.

Anno Domini

Figure 16

The object of this game is to build complete families upon the foundations in suit and in ascending sequence. The game board is formed with four foundation cards, one of each suit, each card selected so that if the families are successfully completed, the result will show the date of the year.

To produce this result, each of the foundation cards must be one card higher in denomination than the digits that form the date. One deck of cards is used.

Playing

The game board given here is for 1997: The foundation cards are therefore the Deuce of Spades, Ten of Hearts, Ten of Diamonds, and Eight of Clubs. In case a zero (0) should occur in the date—2000 for instance—zero is represented by the Ten-spot, and the foundation card to correspond would be a Jack. (See Figure 16.)

One redeal is permitted. If no play has been possible during a deal, the game is blocked and ended.

Fascination

Figure 17

The object of this game is to build complete families upon the foundations in suit and ascending sequence. Marriages are made in descending sequence and alternate colors between the auxiliary cards or packets, and upon them from the pack and from the reserve. One deck of cards is used for this game.

Playing

Count off thirteen cards face down from the pack, which will be used for the reserve packet, which is then turned face up. Deal one card from the pack, and place it below the reserve packet; this is the first of the foundations; the other three cards of the same denomination are placed in a row to the right of the first, as they appear in play. Deal four more cards in a row below the foundation row. These are the auxiliary cards. (See Figure 17.)

Vacancies in the auxiliaries are filled from the reserve only until the reserve is exhausted, and then by the next undealt card of the pack.

Next, the cards are lifted from the pack, face down, in bunches of three at a time; each bunch as dealt is turned face up; the exposed or released card of each successive bunch is then available for play.

Marriages between auxiliary cards are not confined merely to exposed cards; any number of cards in a packet may be lifted and transferred, provided that the bottom card of those lifted fits exactly in color and sequence upon the top card of another packet.

The deal is repeated over and over again as long as a suitable card has appeared in the previous deal. If no play has been possible during a deal, the game is blocked and ended.

Double or Quits

Figure 18

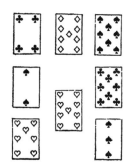

All the cards count for their face value from Ace (one) up to Ten; the Jack counts for eleven; the Queen, twelve; and the King, thirteen. Each succeeding card placed on the foundation must be double the value of the card preceding it. The exposed card of the stock and the auxiliary cards are available for play. One deck of cards is used for this game.

Playing

Six cards are placed in two columns of three each, and a seventh card between the top cards of the columns; these seven cards are auxiliaries, and vacancies as they occur are filled from the pack. (See Figure 18.)

An eighth card is laid between the four lower cards of the columns; this is the foundation on which building is made. In this game, cards go by value only, regardless of suit. Unsuitable cards form a stock.

If any one of the auxiliary cards first laid out should be a King, it is placed at the bottom of the pack, and another card is substituted. If, in the course of play, a King becomes an auxiliary card, it must remain so.

If the double of a card is over thirteen, the excess of the double over thirteen denotes the card required. For example, if the last card played on the foundation were a Nine, the double of nine is eighteen, which is five more than thirteen, and the next required card must be a Five; the next following, the double of five, etc.

Two redeals are allowed, if necessary. If no play has been possible after the second deal, the game is blocked and ended.

Marguerite

Figure 19

The object of the game is to build families upon the foundations in suit and descending sequence. The exposed card of the stock, and any card or cards in the A group, are available. One deck of cards is used for this game.

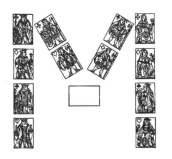
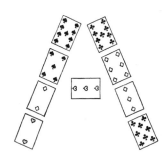

Playing

The game board is formed by the Kings, Queens, and Jacks of each suit, taken from the pack and arranged in the form of an M with a vacant space below the Jacks. (See Figure 19.) The foundations are completed by three cards on each in descending sequence, as follows:

On each King—the Ten, Nine, and Eight of the same suit;
On each Queen—the Seven, Six, and Five of the same suit;
On each Jack—the Four, Three, and Two of the same suit.

Deal from the pack nine cards, arranged in the form of letter A. As vacancies occur in the A group, they are filled from the pack; if no vacancies occur, the cards are dealt from the stock until suitable cards appear.

If two cards of the same suit should be dealt upon the stock in descending sequence—a Three on a Four, for instance—it is clear that the game is blocked. Aces, being of no use in the game, are placed, as they are dealt, upon the vacant spot below the Jacks.

There is no redeal allowed. If no play has been possible during a deal, the game is blocked and ended.

The Royal Widows

Figure 20

The object of this game is to form families upon the foundations in suit and ascending sequence from Ace to Queen. The Kings are defunct. The exposed card in each packet and all released cards are available. One deck of cards is used for this game.

Playing

The cards are divided, face up, into eight packets in a row, the first (or left-hand) packet contains ten cards; the next packet to the right, nine cards; and each succeeding packet to the right, one card less than the preceding packet, so that the eighth packet will consist of three cards. (See Figure 20.)

If the top card of any packet is an Ace, it is placed below the row for a foundation, on which an ascending sequence in suit is to be built. If a King appears on top of a packet, he is taken off and slipped under the bottom card of the same packet.

If the exposed card of a packet is of the same suit and next lower in rank to the exposed card of another packet, it can be transferred in descending sequence.

After all possible changes have been made, take the left-hand packet up, and, without disturbing their order, search for a card of the same suit and next in rank below the exposed card of any other packet. If such a card is found, the discovered card and all cards above it are transferred just as they are.

The same routine is followed with each successive packet to the right, over and over again in regular rotation, transferring where possible, and employing all suitable and released cards for forming the families, until all the packets are exhausted and the board is complete, or the game is blocked and ended.

Perseverance

Figure 21

The object of the game is to build families upon the foundations in suit and ascending sequence from Ace up to King. Marriages can be made between exposed cards of the auxiliary packets, in suit and descending sequence. Exposed cards of the auxiliary packets are available. One deck of cards is used for this game.

Playing

Take the four Aces from the pack and place them in a row. These are the foundations. Deal the remainder of the pack into twelve packets of four cards each. These are the auxiliary packets (See Figure 21.)

Play all suitable cards upon the foundations. Marry suitable exposed cards. When the game is blocked, gather the packets and deal them again into as many packets of four cards each as the cards allow. This may be repeated as often as necessary until two such deals in succession fail to produce any suitable card for the foundations. The game is then finally blocked and ended.

The Necklace

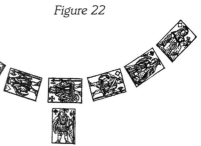

Figure 22

In this game families are built upon the foundation cards, following suit in descending sequence from the Ten down to the Ace. Cards as dealt, the three auxiliary cards, and the exposed card of the stock, are available. One deck of cards is used for this game.

Playing

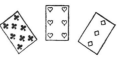

The game board is formed by degrees as the necessary cards are dealt; the four Tens, as they appear, are placed in the form of a cross, and are used as the foundation cards. (See Figure 22.)

In dealing, the first three cards are laid in fan-shape below the lower Ten, for auxiliary cards, and their places filled up from the stock as vacancies occur.

If a card dealt is of the same suit and next higher in rank of any one of the auxiliary cards, it may be placed upon such auxiliary card.

The court cards are merely ornamental, being placed, as they appear in dealing, in their respective positions in the game board; the four Kings in a packet in the space between the Tens, and the Queens and Jacks forming the necklace above the Tens.

If the game is successful, the cards will have all been used, and the packet of kings will be surrounded by the four Aces. One redeal is allowed. If no play has been possible during a deal, the game is blocked and ended.

Forwards and Backwards

Figure 23

In this game the King counts for thirteen; the Queen, for twelve; the Jack, for eleven; and the remainder of the cards for the pips on their face, the Ace being one. A card, as dealt, is suitable to use only when it can make fourteen points with the foundation card or packet upon which it is played. Two decks of cards are used for this game.

Playing

Deal twenty cards from the pack, arranging them in four rows of five cards each. These are the foundation cards to be played upon. In case a Seven should fail to appear in these twenty cards, any one card must be replaced in the pack, and the vacancy filled by a Seven selected from the pack. (See Figure 23.)

The cards are dealt, one by one. The first card dealt that is not suitable blocks the game.

The Privileged Four

Figure 24

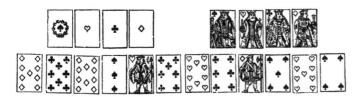

In this game families are built upon the foundations in suit; upon the Aces in ascending sequence; upon the Kings in descending sequence. The free cards are always available. During the deal, only such cards in the auxiliary rows are available as are in direct line below the Ace or King of the same suit. After all the cards have been dealt, the above restriction ceases, and the lowest card in any column, as well as released cards, is available. Two decks of cards are used in this game.

Playing

Select the four Aces and Kings of one pack, and place them in a row, leaving a space the width of two cards between the Ace and King groups. These Aces and Kings are the foundations.

Deal twelve auxiliary cards in an unbroken row from left to right, placing the second card exactly below the left-hand Ace; in this manner two cards in the middle, and one card at each end of the row. These four cards are the free cards.

After any suitable cards have been placed upon the foundations, vacancies are filled from the pack, and another row of twelve cards is dealt, partially covering but not concealing the cards in the row above.

Suitable cards are played upon the foundations, in the same manner as in the first row. Vacancies are filled as before, and new rows of twelve cards are laid in the same manner, until the pack is exhausted.

Only after the pack is exhausted can marriages be permitted between available cards in suit and in ascending or descending sequence. When further play is impossible, the remaining cards in each column are run together in packets from left to right and dealt again, and the entire routine of play repeated.

This repetition is allowed a second time if necessary, making three deals in all.

After the last deal and as a last resource, if a column has been formed, only one card can be transferred to reopen the column.

Odd and Even

Figure 25

In this game families are built in suit upon Ace foundations in ascending sequence of odd numbers, i.e., Three, Five, Seven, Nine, Jack, King; then in sequence of even numbers, i.e., Two, Four, Six, Eight, Ten, ending finally with Queen. The families are built in suit upon the Deuce foundations in ascending even numbers, i.e., Four, Six, Eight, Ten, Queen; then in odd numbers, i.e., Ace, Three, Five, etc., finally ending with King. Cards as dealt, the auxiliary cards, and the exposed card of the stock, are available. Two packs of cards are necessary for this game.

Playing

The first nine cards dealt are placed upon the table in rows of three each. These are the auxiliary cards. One Ace and Deuce of each suit are placed, as they appear in dealing, side by side in a row above the auxiliary cards, and are the foundations upon which the families are built.

In dealing, cards that are not suitable form a stock. Vacancies in the nine auxiliary cards are filled from the stock. One redeal is allowed. The game, if successful, will result in the Kings and Queens of the four suits.

The Solid Square

Figure 26

In this game families are formed upon the foundations in suit, first in ascending sequence from Ace to King, and then in descending sequence from King to Ace. The cards as dealt, the auxiliary cards, and the exposed card of the stock, are always available. Two packs of cards are necessary for this game.

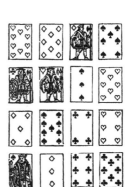

Playing

The first sixteen cards as they are dealt are arranged in a solid four square, and are the auxiliary cards. The four Aces of different suits are placed at the four corners of the square as they appear in the course of the deal, and are the foundations. Suitable auxiliary cards should be played upon the foundations without delay, and vacancies occurring at any stage of the game, filled up at once from the stock, or, if there is no stock, from the pack. Marriages in suit and in ascending or descending sequence may be made among the auxiliary cards. A card dealt, which is next in rank above or below any auxiliary card and of the same suit, may be similarly married. There is no redeal. If no play has been possible during a deal, the game is blocked and ended.

The Wedding

Figure 27

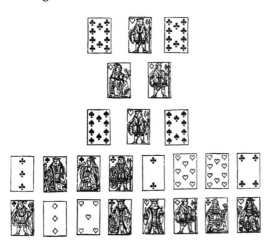

The game is played by building a single family upon the foundation of the Queen of Diamonds, in suit and ascending sequence, from Queen, King, Ace, Deuce, etc., ending with the Jack. Families upon each of the three Jacks are built in suit and in descending sequence from Jack down to Ace, then King and ending with Queen. The families upon each of the four Tens are built in suit and in similar manner, but from Ten, Nine, etc., down to Ace, then King, Queen, ending with Jack. Cards as dealt, and exposed auxiliary cards, are available. Two packs of cards are necessary for this game.

Playing

Select from the pack a Queen and Jack of Diamonds, and place them side by side, the Queen on the left of the Jack. Then deal two rows of eight cards each for auxiliary cards. As soon as they appear, the two Jacks of Hearts are placed one above and the other below the Queen and Jack of Diamonds.

Also, as they appear, the two Tens of Spades and of Clubs are placed, a Ten of Spades on each side of the lower Jack of Hearts, and a Ten of Clubs on each side of the upper Jack of Hearts. The Queen of Diamonds, the three Jacks, and the four Tens are the foundations for building. (See Figure 27.)

After the sixteen auxiliary cards have been dealt, and all suitable cards for the foundations and for play have been used, sixteen more cards are dealt from left to right upon the auxiliary cards and vacancies, if any, and suitable cards played.

This is repeated until all the pack has been dealt. The sixteenth auxiliary packet is dealt, first to fill the vacancy then from left to right, upon the remaining fifteen packets. After this, the fifteenth packet is in like manner dealt, first filling vacancies and so on; the first card of each new deal beginning next to the right of the last card previously dealt. If the foundation is finally blocked, the game is over.

If, however, it has succeeded, the wedded Jack and Queen of Diamonds will appear surrounded by a bridesmaid and two groomsmen.

The Fan

In this game families are built upon the foundations in sequence without following suit. Sequences may be ascending or descending at the option of the player, but the one selected at first must be adhered to in respect to all the foundations. The right-hand exposed or released card in the fan, the four auxiliary cards, the exposed card of the reserve packet, and the top undealt card of the pack, are always available. This game requires two complete decks of cards.

Figure 28

Playing

Turn the pack face up; lay out in the shape of a fan twelve cards, from left to right, each successive card partly covering, but not concealing, its left-hand neighbor. Next, place a reserve packet of twelve cards to the right of the fan; then deal four auxiliary cards in a row, a little distance below the fan, so as to leave space between for the foundations. Vacancies in the auxiliary cards are filled from the pack.

The next card dealt from the pack is laid below the left end of the fan. This card, together with the other seven cards of the same denomination, placed in a row to the right as they appear in dealing, are the eight foundations for families. Suitable cards are played upon the foundations as available. As it is important that the fan and reserve should be used up, suitable cards should be played from them in preference to playing from the pack, when such choice presents itself.

Two redeals are allowed, if necessary.

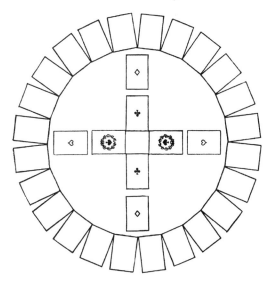

Figure 29

The Wheel

For this game, you will be selecting cards to form the packets; two cards of the same denomination are prohibited. During each dealing of the cards there must be no interruption; play is not allowed until a deal is completed. Exposed auxiliary cards are available. Two decks of cards are necessary for this game.

Playing

The eight Aces are taken from the pack and arranged in the form of a cross, the black Aces in the center, and the red Aces outside, suit opposite suit, as shown in Figure 29. These Aces are merely ornamental, and represent the spokes of the wheel. Deal from the pack twelve auxiliary card in two rows of six cards each. Select from them first a court card; then any three other cards whose combined pips count exactly 18. The court card does not enter in to the count. Gather the four cards into a packet, the court card at top, and place the packet in one of the spaces that represent the circumference of the wheel in the game board. Fill up vacancies as they occur from the pack. When all packets have been made, or no packet is possible, deal twelve more cards upon the rows. Continue the same routine until all the pack has been dealt. If the game is successful, the wheel will contain twenty-four packets. There is no redeal.

Figure 30

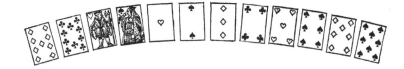

The Sickle

Twelve foundation cards are laid out in sequence from left to right; they do not follow suit, but must be of alternate colors. Cards that match or pair with the original twelve cards must be played upon them in alternate colors. The exposed card of the stock is always available. This game requires two decks of cards.

Playing

The top card of the pack is turned up and placed at the left hand of the game board. The pack is then turned face up and dealt onto a stock until a card of the next higher denomination, but of different color, appears; this is then placed to the right of the first card already laid in the game board. The same process is continued until the entire sequence of twelve cards up to the Queen, then Ace, etc., has been laid from left to right. At all times during the dealing, cards that match or pair with the original twelve cards must be played on them in alternate colors. (See Figure 30.)

The Kings take no part in the game but are put aside as they appear, and are only used to make an ornamental handle for the sickle if the game is successful, in which case there will be eight cards of the same denomination, in alternate colors, upon each of the twelve original cards.

Until all of the original twelve cards have been laid out, care must be taken not to entirely conceal the color of each by the matched cards played upon them.

Two redeals are permitted.

Speculation

This game is played with a deck of fifty-two cards. Any number of people may play.

Dealing

The deal is determined by giving a card to each person and the player to whom the first Jack falls has the deal. Before the cards are dealt, the players each stake a sum agreed on to form a pool; the dealer stakes double.

Playing

The dealer gives three cards, face down, to each player in rotation, beginning with the eldest hand (the player to his left), and turns up the top card of the stock for trumps.

The eldest hand then turns up one of his cards. If it is not a trump, or a smaller trump than the turnup, it is of no value, and the next player to his left turns up a card, and so on, until a higher trump than the turn up appears. The cards rank Ace (highest), King, Queen, Jack, Ten, etc., down to the Two (lowest).

The player who shows a better trump than the turnup may sell it, if a price is offered that he approves. If more than one player desires to buy, the card is sold to the highest bidder. If the price offered is not approved, or there are no bidders, the player keeps the card. The others then proceed to turn up their cards; but the holder of the highest trump shown (whether by purchase, or by not being able to sell) does not turn up again until his card is beaten by a higher trump. This higher trump may be kept or sold, and the holder of it is similarly exempt from turning up. The dealer does not turn up any of his cards until the trump card is beaten. The player who turns up or purchases the highest trump takes the pool.

No one looking at his card out of turn or when not entitled, can take the pool.

Speculation is not confined to the cards shown. The trump card may be bought or kept either before or after it is turned up. If sold, the dealer turns up, and the purchaser is exempt until the card is beaten. Unseen cards or hands may be speculated upon. This is frequently done toward the end of a hand, either when no high trump has been turned, or by the possessor of a high trump, to prevent its being beaten.

Sometimes, when a player turns up a Jack or a Five, he is required to pay a chip to the pool. If this rule is adopted, and the card has been purchased unseen, the buyer has to pay instead of the holder.

When the Ace of trumps is turned, the hand is ended, and the holder or purchaser (if it was an unseen card) takes the pool. When no trump is turned from any of the hands, the dealer or purchaser of the turnup card takes the pool.

Sometimes an extra hand is dealt, which is turned up when all the other hands have been shown. If the extra hand contains the best trump, the pool remains for the next deal, and the players contribute again, so that the pool is doubled.

Spoil Five

This game is played with a complete pack of fifty-two cards. Any number may play, from three to ten, but five make the best game. The object of the game is for a player to win a minimum of three tricks, or to block other players from doing so.

Dealing

The dealer gives five cards to each player in regular rotation, beginning with the eldest hand (the player to the left of the dealer). The cards must be distributed two at a time, and then three at a time.

After the dealer has served five cards to each player, one card from the top of the pack is turned face up and placed on top of the stock. This card determines the trump, and is called the *trump card.* After the first hand has been played, each player takes the deal in succession, beginning with the eldest hand.

Robbing

If the turnup card is an Ace the dealer has the privilege of *robbing,* i.e., he discards from his hand any card he pleases (placing it face down on the table or under the pack), and substitutes for it the Ace turned up. The suit to which the Ace belongs still remains the trump suit. The dealer must discard before the eldest hand plays; but the rob should not be completed until it is the dealer's turn to play to the first trick.

If an Ace is not turned up, and any player holds the Ace of the trump suit in his hand he must rob, i.e., he must reject a card from his hand, and take in the turnup. A player is not bound to declare that he is about to rob until it is his turn to play; but he must declare the rob before he plays his first card. The usual way of making the declaration is to place the rejected card face down on the table. If the player neglects to do this before he plays, the power of robbing becomes void, and he is liable to a penalty. No one is allowed to inspect the card put out in robbing.

After robbing, the dealer may employ the turn-up card to trump the first trick, or he may use it to follow suit to a trump that has been led by the eldest hand, but no other player has this privilege.

Each player plays one card at a time in rotation, beginning with the eldest hand. The player of the highest Spoil Five card wins the trick. Trumps win other suits. The winner of the trick leads to the next, and so on until the hand is played out, or until three tricks are won by one player. A player who wins three tricks in one hand wins the game. If no one wins three tricks, the game is said to be *spoiled.*

The Pool

Before play begins, each player pays to the pool a certain sum or number of chips agreed on. Should the game be won in that deal, the winner takes the pool; but if a spoil occurs, the pool remains, and each player puts an additional sum (generally a half or a third of the original stake) into the pool. This is repeated after every spoil until a game is won.

Rank of the Cards

The rank of the cards differs in the red and black suits, and again in the trump suit. In *suits that are not trumps,* the order of the cards is as follows, beginning with the highest:

Red Suits When Not Trumps: King, Queen, Jack, Ten, Nine, Eight, Seven, Six, Five, Four, Three, Two, Ace. The Ace of Hearts always ranks as a trump. Therefore, in the above-mentioned order for red suits when not trumps, the Ace of Hearts must be omitted from the Heart suit.

Black Suits When Not Trumps: King, Queen, Jack, Ace, Two, Three, Four, Five, Six, Seven, Eight, Nine, Ten. The order of the cards below the Jack is thus commonly expressed, "The highest in Red and the lowest in Black."

In the trump suit, which includes the Ace of Hearts, the rank of the cards is as follows, beginning with the highest:

Red Suits When Trumps: Five, Jack, Ace of Hearts, Ace of trumps, King, Queen, Ten, Nine, Eight, Seven, Six, Four, Three, Two.

Black Suits When Trumps: Five, Jack, Ace of Hearts, Ace of trumps, King, Queen, Two, Three, Four, Six, Seven, Eight, Nine, Ten.

The order of the cards in trumps below the Jack adheres to the rule, "The highest in Red, and lowest in Black." Of course when Hearts are trumps there is only one Ace in the trump suit. It is as though the Ace of

Hearts were thrust into all other trump suits, between the Jack and the Ace of that suit.

Reneging

The Five of trumps, Jack of trumps, and Ace of Hearts, may *renege,* i.e., they are exempt from following suit when an inferior trump is led.

The Five of trumps may renege to any trump led. No trump can renege when the Five is led.

The Jack of trumps can renege to any trump led except to the one superior to it, the Five. If the Five is played (not led) the Jack can renege. If the Jack is led, no trump can renege except the Five.

Similarly, the Ace of Hearts can renege to any trump led, except to the trumps superior to it, including the Five and the Jack. If the Ace of Hearts is led when Hearts are trumps, the Five and Jack are entitled to renege. If the Ace of Hearts is led when hearts are not trumps, a player holding no trump need not play a Heart.

Jinking

Sometimes by mutual agreement *jinking* is allowed. A jink is when a player plays for and wins all five tricks, the winner being paid in addition to the pool the amount originally staked by each player.

When jinking is allowed, and a player, having won three tricks, continues to play for a jink but fails to win every trick, he scores nothing that hand, and cannot, therefore, win the game that deal. It is optional on the player's part whether he will run the risk of scoring nothing for the chance of obtaining a jink.

VaRiATiONS

Forty-Five

This game is nearly identical to Spoil Five, omitting the spoil. The cards rank the same as in Spoil Five.

Playing

The hand is played the same as Spoil Five. The eldest hand leads, and each trick won counts five. Sometimes, by previous agreement, the trick won by the best trump out counts ten instead of five. If tricks are won sufficient to make game before the holder of the best trump out plays it, the tricks win the game. When this variation is adopted, a player can rob with the Ace only.

The game consists of forty-five points, and the player (or players, if partners) first scoring that number wins the game. The King or Ace, when turned up by the dealer, counts five.

Any player holding the King of trumps must, when it comes to his turn to play, lay out a card for it, face down, and if the Ace should not be in play, the trump turned up is his. Should the Ace, however, be out, the turned-up trump belongs to the holder of the Ace, who lays out any card he chooses and takes in hand the turned-up card, and the player who holds the King takes up the card he previously laid out.

Reneging the superior to the inferior trump led is the same as in Spoil Five.

The Rules of the Game

1. The deal is determined by cutting; the player cutting the lowest card has the deal. When cutting for the deal the cards rank as in Whist, but Ace is low.
2. The dealer gives five cards to each player, two at a time, and then three at a time.
3. If a card is faced in the pack (not by the dealer), there must be a fresh deal by the same dealer, except if the faced card happens to be the trump.
4. If there is a misdeal the deal passes to the next dealer. It is a misdeal if the dealer deals without having the pack cut; if the dealer shuffles the pack after it is cut with his consent; or if the dealer deals out of order, including giving too many or too few cards to a player.
5. If the dealer gives too many or too few cards to any player, and the error is not discovered until the hand is partly or wholly played out, it is still a misdeal.
6. Each player is entitled to a deal. The game must not be abandoned except at the conclusion of a round, unless there is a spoiling in the last deal of a round, when the deal continues in order until a game is won.
7. If a player deals out of turn he may be stopped at any time before the trump card is turned. If not stopped, the deal stands good, and the rotation of dealing proceeds to the dealer's left as though he had dealt in turn.
8. If a player neglects to declare his power of robbing before he plays to the first trick, he loses the right of robbing and forfeits the hand. He cannot win the game with that hand, but he may play his cards and try to spoil it.
9. If a player robs without the Ace, or leads or plays out of turn, or leads without waiting for the completion of the trick, or exposes a card, or omits to play to a trick, or revokes when not entitled, or reneges when not entitled, or plays to the first trick with too many or too few cards in his hand, he forfeits the pool. He cannot win the game that hand, and he cannot play again for that pool.
10. If a pack is discovered to be incorrect, redundant, or imperfect, the deal in which the discovery is made is void. All preceding deals stand good.

Twenty-One

Twenty-One may be played by any number of players. A pack of fifty-two cards is required. The Tens and court cards are each worth ten points, and the other cards according to their pips. The Ace in each suit may be valued as one or eleven, at the option of the holder, according to the requirement of his hand.

Dealing and Betting

After the deal is determined and the cards shuffled and cut, the players make their stakes into the pool. It is sometimes agreed that the players may all look at the first card dealt to them before making their bets. The dealer also has the privilege of seeing his first card, and may insist on all the players doubling their bets.

The dealer, holding the pack face down, takes the top card and places it upon the bottom of the pack. This is called the *burnt card,* or *brulet.* The dealer then delivers one card, face down, to each player in rotation, beginning to his left; he then repeats this operation, giving each player a total of two cards.

Playing

The players all examine their hands, and the dealer asks each in rotation, the eldest hand (the player to the left of the dealer) first, whether he will take any cards. If the player is satisfied with his hand, he says, "Stay," and places his hand upon the table, face down. If the player is not content he calls for a card, saying, "Hit me." The dealer then deals him a card face up on the table, and again asks, "Are you content?" This operation is continued until the player is satisfied, and so on until each player is served.

If the count of the pips in the entire hand of a player is more than twenty-one, he throws his hand face down, and is out of the hand. When a player overdraws, he *busts.*

After all the players have stood or drawn, or quit, the dealer exposes his hand, and either stands or draws. If he overdraws he pays, according to the sums staked, to each player who has not overdrawn. If he stands, or draws so that his hand does not exceed twenty-one, he receives from or pays to each player in rotation, the one winning whose cards amount most nearly to twenty-one. Players who have to pay the dealer throw their cards in the middle of the table without showing them. Players who claim anything from the dealer show their cards. Ties stand off.

If a player has an Ace and a court card dealt him, which totals twenty-one (called a *natural twenty-one),* he turns his hand face up on the table and receives double his stake from the dealer. The dealer, however, need not pay until he has looked at his own cards, to see if he also has a natural. When the dealer has a natural, he similarly receives payment (except from the player who also has a natural). In this instance, no one draws, as there is no chance of beating the dealer's hand.

If a player or the dealer has a pair dealt him originally, he may stake and draw on each card separately or not, as he pleases. If he goes on each, he separates the cards and puts a stake on each, and when it comes his turn to draw he says, "I go on each." In this case each party pays and receives on both hands. But if a natural occurs in a double hand, the holder receives only a single stake on each, because to obtain a natural the first two cards only may be counted.

Variations

Quinze

Quinze is played by two players, with a pack of fifty-two cards. The players cut for deal, and the lowest card deals. Ace is low. The game is similar to Twenty-One, except that the aim is to make fifteen points instead of twenty-one. In play, Ace counts as one, and court cards as tens that, other cards according to the number of their pips.

Playing

The stake having been agreed upon, the dealer deals one card to his adversary and one to himself. The nondealer has the option either to stand on the one card he has received, or to draw one or more additional cards in the hope of making fifteen or near that number. The dealer then examines his card, and either stands or draws in like manner.

The cards are then exposed, and the player who has made fifteen (or the nearest smaller number) wins.

The Rules of the Game

1. When the players have taken their seats, one player shuffles the pack, and (after having it cut by the player to his right) deals a card face up to each player in rotation, beginning to his left. The player to receive the first Ace becomes the dealer.

2. Only the dealer has a right to shuffle. The cards remaining undealt may not be reshuffled.

3. In cutting, at least four cards must be separated.

4. If a card is exposed in cutting or in reuniting the cut packets, or if there is any confusion of the cards, the pack must be reshuffled and cut again.

5. If two cards are dealt together to one player, the mistake may be rectified before a third card is dealt. But if a third card is dealt before the error is discovered, the player who has the surplus card, having looked at his hand, must reject one card and give it, face down, back to the dealer.

6. If a card is exposed in dealing, the player may keep it or reject it; if he rejects it, the rejected card is given to the dealer. If the dealer exposes one of his own cards, he must keep it.

7. Drawn cards must be dealt one at a time, face up on the table. Each player in rotation must be content before the next can draw a card. In drawing separately on split cards, the player must be content on one card before drawing on another.

8. If two drawn cards are dealt together, the player may keep either or both. If he keeps only one, he cannot draw another card.

9. If the dealer in drawing gives himself two cards together, he must keep them both.

10. If a player is missed in dealing or drawing, he may have his hand completed from the pack, or may throw it up.

11. If the dealer in dealing misses himself and a player draws cards before the error is discovered, the dealer must pay to each player the amount of his stake, and double to the natural. If the error is discovered before any cards are drawn, the dealer may complete his hand from the top of the pack, and there is no penalty.

12. The burnt card must not be dealt or drawn.

13. If a player (not the dealer) holds a natural twenty-one, it puts the dealer out. The holder of a natural has the next deal, except if it is the first hand of the deal, or the dealer also has a natural.

14. Each player is bound to place his stake in front of him, before a card is dealt. When content with his hand, he puts it face down on the table, and places his stake on top of it. No stake can be withdrawn, added to, or lessened after it has been made, but must be allowed to remain until the dealer declares his stand.

15. A player or dealer having a pair dealt may draw and stake on each separately. Cards worth ten points can only pair with cards of the same denomination, that is, Kings with Kings.

16. When the dealer and a player tie, the two cancel or stand off, and neither

The Rules of the Game

receives from or pays to the other.

17. When all the players have stood or drawn, the dealer exposes his hand on the table.

18. A natural twenty-one must consist of an Ace and a card worth ten points dealt in the first two rounds. The dealer pays to and receives from a player for a natural, unless a tie should occur. In case of a double hand, an Ace and a tenth card form *acquired* and not natural twenty-ones, and receive and pay only single stakes

War

This game is played with two players, using a pack of fifty-two cards.

Playing

The deck is evenly divided between the two players. Once stock is handed to each player, face down, and the player is not allowed to look at the cards. At the same time, the players each expose the top card from their stock. The player who shows the highest card takes both of the cards into his deck, a King being the highest card.

If both players show the same card, each player puts out three cards face down, and one card face up. The person with the highest card as their face up card wins all of the cards.

The game is won when one person holds the entire deck.

Whist

Whist is played by four people, with a pack of fifty-two cards, which rank as follows: Ace (highest), King, Queen, Jack, Ten, Nine, Eight, Seven, Six, Five, Four, Three, and Two (the lowest.) The four players divide themselves into two teams, each player sitting opposite his partner. The teams are determined by cutting; the two highest and the two lowest become partners.

Dealing

The dealer delivers to each player in rotation, beginning with the player to his left, one card at a time until the whole pack is dealt out (each player will be holding thirteen cards, and the dealer will have twelve). The last card, the trump card, is turned face up on the table, where it remains until the dealer plays the first trick; the dealer should then, before playing, take the trump card into his hand.

Playing

When the deal has been completed, and the players have arranged their cards, the eldest hand (the player to the left of the dealer) leads any cards he pleases; each player plays a card to the lead, and the highest card of the suit led wins the trick. Trumps win all other suits. Each player must follow suit if he can, but if unable to follow suit, he may play any card he chooses. The winner of the trick leads to the next, and so on, until the thirteen tricks are played. A second deal then occurs, the eldest hand having the deal, and so the game proceeds.

Solo Whist

Solo Whist is played by four people, with a pack of fifty-two cards, which rank as in Whist. The object is to make eight tricks out of the thirteen in conjunction with a partner; to make five or nine tricks out of your own hand against the other three players in combination; or to play your own hand against your three adversaries so as to avoid taking a trick.

Dealing

The deal is determined by cutting, and the player who cuts the lowest card deals.

After the cards have been properly shuffled and cut, the dealer distributes the whole pack, beginning with the player at his left, giving each of the four players three cards at a time, until there are only four remaining. Then these are dealt singly, the last card being turned up as the trump and becoming the property of the dealer.

Calling

After the deal has been completed, the eldest hand has the first call. He can pass or propose, i.e., ask for a partner with the object of making with that partner eight of the thirteen tricks; he can call a Solo, which is a declaration to make five of the thirteen tricks without having a partner; he can declare *Misère*, i.e., to lose all the thirteen tricks (in this phase of the game all the four suits are equal, the trump suit being annulled); or he can call *Abondance*, when, making whatever suit he likes trumps, and declaring the suit before the first card is led, he endeavors to make nine tricks out of the thirteen. The call of Abondance is, however, superseded by another player declaring to make Abondance in trumps, i.e., with the trump suit as it stands.

Further, he may call an *Open Misère*, or *Misère Ouverte*, thereby undertaking not only to lose all the thirteen tricks, but to expose his own cards on the table as soon as the first trick is played to and turned. Or he may announce his intention of taking the whole thirteen tricks by saying, "Abondance Declarée." In this case, as in the simple Abondance, he names his own trump suit, and in the case of this declaration, and this only, he leads, wherever he may chance to sit, the original lead to the first trick; in all other cases the lead comes from the eldest hand.

There are thus seven things the eldest hand may do after he has examined his cards.

The Rules of the Game

1. The *rubber* is the best of three games. If the first two games are won by the same players, the third game is not played.
2. A game consists of seven points. Each trick above eight counts for one point.
3. Honors, i.e., Ace, King, Queen, and Jack of trumps, are counted as follows:
    If a player and his partner, either separately or conjointly, hold the four honors, they score four points; any three honors, they score two points; only two honors, they do not score.
4. Players who, at the beginning of a deal, have six points, cannot score honors.
5. The penalty for a revoke takes precedence of all other scores. Tricks score next. Honors last.
6. Honors, unless claimed before the trump card of the following deal is turned up, cannot be scored.
7. Honors must be called at the end of the hand; if so called, they may be scored at any time during the game.
8. The winners gain three points, when their adversaries have not scored; two points, when their adversaries have scored less than three; or one point, when their adversaries have scored three or four.
9. The winners of the rubber gain two points (commonly called the *rubber points*), in addition to the value of their games.

The Rules of the Game

10. Should the rubber have consisted of three games, the value of the losers' game is deducted from the gross number of points gained by their opponents.

11. If there are more than four candidates, the players are selected by cutting: those first in the room having the preference. The four who cut the lowest cards play first, and again cut to decide on partners; the two lowest play against the two highest: the lowest is the dealer, who has choice of cards and seats, and, having once made his selection, must abide by it.

12. When there are more than six candidates, those who cut the two next lowest cards belong to the table, which is complete with six players; on the retirement of one of those six players, the candidate who cuts the next lowest card has a prior right to any latecomer to enter the table.

13. At the end of a rubber, should admission be claimed by any one or by two candidates, he who has (or they who have) played a greater number of consecutive rubbers than the others is (or are) out; but when all have played the same number, they must cut to decide who will go out; the highest are out.

14. Any one quitting a table prior to the conclusion of a rubber may, with consent of the other three players, appoint a substitute in his absence during that rubber.

15. The pack must be shuffled neither below the table nor so that the face of any card be seen.

16. The pack must not be shuffled during the play of the hand.

17. Each player after shuffling must place the cards, properly collected and face down, to the left of the player about to deal.

18. The dealer has always the right to shuffle last; but should a card or cards be seen during his shuffling or while giving the pack to be cut, he may be compelled to reshuffle.

19. The player on the dealer's right cuts the pack, and in dividing it must not leave fewer than four cards in either packet; if in cutting, or in replacing one of the two packets on the other, a card be exposed, or if there is any confusion of the cards, or a doubt as to the exact place in which the pack was divided, there must be a fresh cut.

20. If, while dealing, a card is exposed by the dealer or his partner, should neither of the adversaries have touched the cards, the latter can claim a new deal; a card exposed by either adversary gives that claim to the dealer, provided that his partner has not touched a card; if a new deal does not take place, the exposed card cannot be called.

21. If, during dealing, a player touches any of his cards, the adversaries may do the same, without losing their privilege of claiming a new deal, should chance give them such option.

22. If a player, while dealing, looks at the trump card, his adversaries have a right to see it, and may exact a new deal.

23. A misdeal loses the deal. It is a misdeal unless the cards are dealt into four packets, one at a time in regular rotation, beginning with the player to the dealer's left; should the dealer place the trump card, face down, on his own or any other

The Rules of the Game

pack; should the trump card not come in its regular order to the dealer; but he does not lose his deal if the pack be proved imperfect; should a player have fourteen cards, and either of the other three less than thirteen; should the dealer, under an impression that he has made a mistake, either count the cards on the table or the remainder of the pack; should the dealer deal two cards at once, or two cards to the same hand, and then deal a third; or, should the dealer omit to have the pack cut to him, and the adversaries discover the error, prior to the trump card being turned up, and before looking at their cards, but not after having done so.

24. A misdeal does not lose the deal if, during the dealing, either of the adversaries touches the cards prior to the dealer's partner having done so; but should the latter have first interfered with the cards, notwithstanding either or both of the adversaries have subsequently done the same, the deal is lost.

25. Should three players have their right number of cards but the fourth have less than thirteen, and not discover such deficiency until he has played any of his cards, the deal stands good; should he have played, he is answerable for any revoke he may have made as if the missing card, or cards, had been in his hand; he may search the other pack for it, or them.

26. If a pack, during or after a rubber, be proved incorrect or imperfect, that hand in which the imperfection was detected is void. All other hands stand good.

27. The dealer, when it is his turn to play to the first trick, should take the trump card into his hand; if left on the table after the first trick be turned, it is liable to be called; his partner may at any time remind him of the liability.

28. After the dealer has taken the trump card into his hand, it cannot be asked for; a player naming it at any time during the play of that hand is liable to have his highest or lowest trump called. However, any one may inquire what the trump suit is, at any time.

29. If the dealer takes the trump card into his hand before it is his turn to play, he may be desired to lay it on the table; should he show a wrong card, this card may be called, as also a second, a third, etc., until the trump card be produced.

30. If the dealer declares himself unable to recollect the trump card, his highest or lowest trump may be called at any time during that hand, and unless it causes him to revoke, must be played; the call may be repeated, but not changed, i.e., from highest to lowest, or vice versa, until such card is played.

31. All exposed cards are liable to be called, and must be left on the table; but a card is not an exposed card when dropped on the floor, or elsewhere below the table. The following are exposed cards: two or more cards played at once; any card dropped face up, or in any way exposed on or above the table, even if it is snatched up so quickly that no one can name it.

32. If anyone plays to an imperfect trick the best card on the table, or leads one that is a winning card as against his adversaries, and then leads again, or play several such winning cards, one after the other, without waiting for his partner to play,

The Rules of the Game

the latter may be called on to win, if he can, the first or any other of those tricks, and the other cards thus improperly played are exposed cards.

33. If a player, or players, under the impression that the game is lost or won, or for other reasons, throw his or their cards on the table and such cards are exposed, and liable to be called, each player's by the adversary; but should one player alone retain his hand, he cannot be forced to abandon it.

34. If all four players throw their cards on the table, the hands are abandoned; and no one can again take up his cards. Should this general exhibition show that the game might have been saved or won, neither claim can be entertained, unless a revoke is established. The revoking players are then liable to the following penalties: They cannot under any circumstances win the game by the result of that hand, and the adversaries may add three to their score, or deduct three from that of the revoking players.

35. A card detached from the rest of the hand so as to be named is liable to be called; but should the adversary name a wrong card, he is liable to have a suit called when he or his partner have the lead.

36. If a player who has rendered himself liable to have the highest or lowest of a suit called, fails to play as desired, or if when called on to lead one suit, lead another, having in his hand one or more cards of that suit demanded, he incurs the penalty of a revoke.

37. If any player leads out of turn, his adversaries may either call the card erroneously led, or may call a suit from the player or his partner when it is next the turn of either of them to lead.

38. If any player leads out of turn, and the other three have followed him, the trick is complete, and the error cannot be rectified; but if only the second, or the second and third have played to the false lead, their cards, on discovery of the mistake, are taken back. There is no penalty against anyone except the original offender, whose card may be called—or he, or his partner, when either of them next has the lead, may be compelled to play any suit demanded by the adversaries.

39. In no case can a player be compelled to play a card that would oblige him to revoke.

40. The call of a card may be repeated until such card has been played.

41. If a player called on to lead a suit has none of it, the penalty is paid.

42. If the third hand plays before the second, the fourth hand may play before his partner.

43. Should the third hand not have played, and the fourth play before his partner, the latter may be called on to win or not to win the trick.

44. If anyone omits playing to a former trick, and it is not discovered until he has played to the next, the adversaries may claim a new deal; should they decide that the deal stands good, the surplus card at the end of the hand is considered to have been played to the imperfect trick, but does not constitute a revoke.

45. If anyone plays two cards to the same trick, or mixes his trump or other card, with a trick to which it does not properly belong, and the mistake is not discovered

The Rules of the Game

until the hand is played out, he is answerable for all consequent revokes he may have made. If, during the play of the hand, the error is detected, the tricks may be counted face down, in order to ascertain whether there are too many cards; should this be the case, they may be searched, and the card restored; the player is liable for all revokes that he may have made.

46. The penalty for a revoke is at the option of the adversaries who, at the end of the hand, may either take three tricks from the revoking player, or deduct three points from his score, or add three to their own score. Penalty can be claimed for as many revokes as occur during the hand; is applicable only to the score of the game in which it occurs; cannot be divided, i.e., a player cannot add one or two to his own score and deduct one or two from the revoking player; or takes precedence of every other score.

47. At the end of the hand, the claimants of a revoke may search all the tricks.

48. If a player discovers his mistake in time to save a revoke, the adversaries, whenever they think fit, may call the card thus played in error, or may require him to play his highest or lowest card to that trick, in which he has renounced; any player or players who have played him may withdraw their cards and substitute others; the cards withdrawn are not liable to be called.

49. If a revoke is claimed, and the accused player or his partner mix the cards before they have been sufficiently examined by the adversaries, the revoke is established. The mixing of the cards only renders the proof of a revoke difficult; but does not prevent the claim, and possible establishment, of the penalty.

50. A revoke cannot be claimed after the cards have been cut for the following deal.

51. The revoking player and his partner may, under all circumstances, require the hand in which the revoke has been detected to be played out.

52. In whatever way the penalty is enforced, under no circumstances can a player win the game by the result of the hand during which he has revoked; and, he cannot score more than four points.

53. Anyone during the play of the trick, or after the four cards are played and before they are touched, may demand that the cards be placed before their respective players.

54. If any one, prior to his partner playing, should call attention to the trick—either by saying that it is his, or by naming his card, or, without being required to do so, by drawing it toward him—the adversaries may require that opponent's partner to play the highest or lowest of the suit then led, or to win or lose the trick.

55. In all cases where a penalty has been incurred, the offender is bound to give reasonable time for the decision of his adversaries.

56. Any player may demand to see the last trick turned, and no more. Under no circumstances can more than eight cards be seen during the play of the hand, including the four cards on the table that have not been turned and quitted, and the last trick turned.

The Secrets of the Game

1. When you open a suit with a low card, lead your fourth best card. Every suit, then, opened with a low card, whether of four or more cards, is treated as though the cards below the fourth were not in the leader's hand; and, whatever low card is led, the third player can always place, in the leader's hand, exactly three cards higher than the one first led. The fourth best card is sometimes called the *card of uniformity*.

2. No advantage is gained by showing your partner you hold six or seven cards of a suit. What you want to show is that you invariably hold exactly three cards, all higher than the one first selected.

3. To ascertain the number of cards, superior to the fourth best led, that are out against the leader, deduct the number of pips on the fourth best card from eleven, and the remainder will give the number of higher cards.

4. Play your lowest card.

5. It is an even chance that your partner has a higher card than the third player. You can therefore leave the trick to the third or fourth hand, without loss, and keep in your own hand any high cards you may hold over the original leader.

6. If you are the second hand and you hold certain combinations of high cards, it is in some cases advisable to play one of the high cards.

7. When a small card is led, and you are the second hand, hold Queen, Jack, and a small one, you should play the Jack.

8. If you are the second hand and hold King and one small card, the most approved practice is to follow the general rule, and to play the low card. An exception to playing the lowest, unsupported by another, is when you deem it advisable to grasp at an opportunity of obtaining the lead at once.

9. When a Ten or an honor is lead originally, and you, the second hand, hold a card or cards higher than the one led, you need to know, in nearly all cases, what combination of high cards the leader holds.

10. If an honor is led, and you, the second hand, hold a higher honor, not the Ace, play your lowest card.

11. The play of the second hand depends mainly on the fall of the cards in the first round.

12. When a medium or high card is led through you originally, you will generally know, on the second round, what other high cards the leader holds in the suit, and sometimes, whether those he does not hold are in the third hand or in the fourth hand. If you remain with a high card and a low card, you will generally be able to decide which of them to play by making use of this knowledge.

13. Failing indications to the contrary, play the winning card on the second round; do not play the second best card; and, not holding the winning card, play your lowest as a rule.

14. In trumps, with the winning trump on the second round, and good cards in plain suits, it is sometimes advisable to pass.

The Secrets of the Game

When a forced lead is made, the card led is generally the highest in the leader's hand. You can now do one of two things: (A) play your lowest, leaving the chance of the first trick to your partner; or (B) play the winning card, or the lowest of the two or more high sequence cards.

15. Late in a hand, you should bear in mind how many tricks are required to win or save the game or a point, and should play accordingly.

16. Your play, second hand, depends on your strength in trumps. If strong in trumps, you should pass a card of a suit of which your partner may hold the highest; if weak, the best use of your trumps is to make tricks by trumping, unless you are certain that your partner can win the trick.

Three-Handed Whist

In playing Three-Handed Whist, reject from the pack the Two, Three, and Four of each suit, and the Five of Spades. This gets rid of thirteen known cards, and the three players play each on his own account. Each player counts the honors contained in the tricks make a book, so that each player scores any trick he may make in excess of four, and ten is Game.

Part Three

Tile and Dice Games

Tile and Dice Games

Dice

MAKE SURE YOU DON'T GET LOADED

Dice games can usually be played by any number of players. In all dice games the six spot is always high; the one spot is always low. To constitute a fair throw all the dice must be thrown clean from the box and lie flat on the table. The dice, when thrown, must not be touched, until the result of the throw has been noted.

A throw is foul or unfair if one of the dice rolls off the table and falls on the floor; if any of the dice are touched while rolling; if a die is cocked, remaining tilted on edge against another die or other obstruction; or if one die rests flat on the top of another. Foul throws must be thrown over again.

Classic Dice

Each player throws the three dice, three times, and the sum of the spots are added together and act as the score of that player. Ties throw over again, if necessary.

For example: A is throwing dice; at the first throw he makes One, Four, Six, which added together count eleven. His second throw is Five, Two, and Three, together ten. His third throw is two Fives and a Four, making fourteen. The sum of eleven, ten, and fourteen, which is thirty-five, is his score. The one who scores the highest wins the game.

VaRiATiONS

Raffles

Three dice are used, which are thrown by each player until he succeeds in throwing two similar hands; the first throw containing a pair, adds its number of spots to the thrower's score. Triplets, or three alike, take precedence of pairs, so that three Ones (the lowest triplets) will beat two Sixes and a Five. This is sometimes played differently, triplets counting only as pairs. In this case three Fives would be counted as fifteen points and would be beaten by two Fives and a Six.

Draw Poker

Draw Poker is played with five Dice; each player has one throw, and may take a second throw if he wants. In the first throw all the five dice must be thrown. The player then decides if he wants to leave all of them on the table, or replace as many as he pleases and throws them again.

The throws rank in the same manner as in the card game, beginning with the lowest; one pair, two pairs, three of a kind, a Full House, four of a kind. The highest throw is five alike, ranking in the order of their denomination, from six down to one; so that five Sixes make an invincible hand.

Multiplication

This is played with three dice, and three throws, as follows: The first throw is with three dice; the highest one is left on the table and the other two taken up and thrown again; the higher one is left and the lower one taken up and thrown again. The spots on the two left on the table are added together and their sum multiplied by the spots on the third, or last die thrown, for the thrower's total score.

Going to Boston

This game is also played with three dice, which are thrown precisely as in multiplication. The difference is in the counting; the result of the last throw is added to, instead of multiplied by the sum of the two remaining on the table.

Centennial

This is played with three dice by two or more people, each scoring alone; or by partners, two or
three on each side. The object is to score the
numbers 1 up to 12, in exact numerical order.
When 12 is reached the numbers are then wiped
out in exact reverse order down again to 1. The spots
on any one of the dice, or on any of them combined, are
counted for the score.

Each player throws in turn, continuing to thrown until he
fails to score. The numbers are scored in line, as they are
made each player or party having his own line to score. The first
who succeeds in wiping out his entire line wins the game.

Ace in the Pot

Each player is supplied with two chips. In the center of the table a recepta-
cle is provided, which is called the Pot. One player begins by throwing two
dice. If he throws a One, he puts one of his chips in the Pot; and if he
throws a six he passes one chip to his next left-hand neighbor. All the other
spots are of no value.

Each player has one throw in regular rotation, provided he possess-
es a chip, and it goes around until all the chips but one have been
played into the Pot. The holder of the last chip has three throws; the Pot
is closed, and nothing but a Six will enable him to get rid of his chip by
passing it to his neighbor, who has also three throws. This continues
until the last chip holder fails in his three throws to throw a Six, and he
is then declared winner.

The Pot has always the preference during the open game, so that if
a player has only one chip, in a throw of Six, One, the chip must go in
the Pot, unless the Pot has been closed.

Twenty-One

This game is played with a single die, each player throwing it as many
times as is necessary to get the sum of the spots equal to or as near as
possible to, but not over twenty-one.

Throwing twenty-two or more *busts* the player, depriving him of further participation in the game for that round. The thrower who gets
twenty-one, or gets closest to twenty-one without going over, wins the
game.

Help Your Neighbor

This is game is also played with one die. Each player marks on a pad the numbers 1, 2, 3, 4, 5, 6.

One of the players then throws the die, and crosses off the number he throws; he continues throwing so long as he is able to cross out the number thrown; when he throws a number already thrown, his neighbor to the left crosses it out instead, and the latter takes the die and throws in the same manner.

The throwing goes round in regular rotation to the left. When a number is thrown that A and his next neighbor, B, have both already thrown, then the next player to the left, C, or if he has not got it, the next, D, etc., crosses the number out, but B then throws.

The player who first wipes out all his numbers wins the game.

Round the Spot

This is played with three dice, which are thrown three times, the sum of the spots being counted as such: those spots only count that lay around a central spot, including the Three and Five. The Three-spot counts for two points and the Five-spot counting for four points. Six, Four, Two, and One do not count at all; and therefore a player may throw three times and count nothing.

Dominoes

Dominoes were originally made from pieces of ivory or bone, with ebony backs. Today, you can find them made out of plastic, or wood, or other kinds of hard materials. On the face of each piece are two compartments, each of which is either blank or contains a number of black pits, from one to six. These are called, according to the numbers shown, Double Blank, Blank Ace, Blank Deuce, Blank Trey, Blank Four, Blank Five, Blank Six, Double Ace, Ace Deuce, Ace Trey, Ace Four, Ace Five, Ace Six; Double Deuce, Deuce Trey, Deuce Four, Deuce Five, Deuce Six; Double Trey, Trey Four, Trey Five, Trey Six; Double Four, Four Five, Four Six; Double Five, Five Six; and Double Six—twenty-eight pieces in all. They are shuffled on the table face down, and each player draws at random the number that the game requires. The pieces are played one at a time, and each piece to be played must match the end of a piece that does not join any other.

Most of the games can be played by any number of people. There are various games; but the most popular are Block, Draw, Muggins, and Bergen.

Block

Each player draws seven from the pool. The highest double leads in the first hand, and, after that, each player leads alternately until the end of the game. If a player cannot play, the next plays. If neither can play the set is blocked, and they count the number of spots on the pieces each still holds.

Whoever has the lowest number of spots adds to his count the number held by his opponents. If there are two with the same number of spots, and they are lower than their opponents, there is no count. If anyone is able to play his last piece while his opponents hold theirs, he cries, "Domino," and wins the hand, and adds to his count the number of spots the rest hold. The number required to win the game is 100, but it may be made less by agreement.

Draw

Each player draws seven as in Block, and the game is subject to the same rules as Block, except when a player cannot play he is obliged to draw from the pool until he can play, or has exhausted the stock of pieces.

The player may draw as many pieces as he needs to until he can match. After a lead has been made, there is no abridgment to his right. The object of drawing is to enable him to play. Once he has drawn the required piece, the rule to play remains as before.

Muggins

Each player draws five pieces. The highest double leads; after that the players lead alternately. The score is made by fives. If the one who leads can put down any domino containing spots that amount to five or ten, as the double five, six, four, five blank, trey deuce, etc., he counts that number to his score in the game. In matching, if a piece can be put down so as to make five, ten, fifteen, or twenty, by adding the spots contained on both ends of the row, it counts to the score of the one setting it.

For example, if a trey was at one end, and a five at the other, the next player could put down a deuce five, and would score five; or if double trey was at one end, and a player was successful in playing so as to get double deuce at the other end, it would score ten.

If a player cannot match he draws from the pool, the same as in Draw, until he gets the piece required to match either end, or exhausts the pool. As in Draw or Block, the one who plays his last piece first, adds to his count the spots his opponents have; and the same if he gains them when the game is blocked, by having the lowest count. But the sum added to the score is a multiple of five nearest the actual amount. So, if his opponents have twenty spots, and he has nineteen, he adds twenty to his score. The game is played until the first player reaches 200 points if two play, or 150 if there are three or more players.

Bergen

Each player draws six pieces from the pool. The lowest double leads at the beginning, and is called a double-header. After that the parties lead alternately. If no one has a double when his turn comes to lead, he plays the lowest piece he has. When a player sets down a piece that makes the extremities be a double, and the next player can lay a piece that will make the other extremity of the same value, or if a double can be added to one end of a double-header, it makes a triple-header. The two aces in the annexed engraving show the double-header, and the double ace added shows the triple-header.

If a player is not able to match from his hand, he draws one piece from the pool. If he is still not able to play, the next plays, or draws, and so on alternately. If domino is made, the one who makes it wins that hand. If it is blocked, players count their score, and the lowest wins; but if the lowest holds a double in his hand, and his opponent none, the opposite wins. If two players have doubles, and one has none, the last wins. If all the players hold one or more doubles, the lowest double wins.

The game is worth ten points when three or four play, and fifteen points for two players. A hand won by either domino or counting scores one. A double-header, either led or made, counts two. A triple-header counts three. But when either party is within two of being cut, a double-header or triple-header will count him but one, and if he is within three of being out a triple-header will count him but two.

Domino Poker

Domino Poker is governed by the same laws as the card game called Straight Poker, and is played in precisely the same manner. In this game only twenty pieces are employed, the Double Ace and all the Blanks being discarded. The hands rank in regular order, from one pair up to the Royal Hand, which is the highest hand that can be held, as follows:
One Pair—Any two Doubles; Double Six and Double Deuce will beat Double Five and Double Four.

Flush—Any five of a suit not in consecutive order: as Six Ace, Six Trey, Six Four, Six Five and Double Six.

Three of a Kind—Any three Doubles. The Double Ace and Double Blank being discarded, it follows that only one hand of Triplets can be out in the same deal.

Straight Four—A Sequence of Fours, as Four Six, Four Five, Double Four, Four Three and Four Deuce.

Full House—Three Doubles and two of any suit, as Double Six Double Three, and Double Deuce, together with Deuce Four, and Deuce Ace.

Straight Five—A Sequence of Fives.

Four of a Kind—Any four Doubles.

Straight Six—A Sequences of Sixes.

Royal Hand, or Invincible—Five Doubles.

When none of the above hands are out, the best is determined by the rank of the highest leading pieces. A hand led by Double Six is superior to a hand led by Double Five, but a hand headed by Double Deuce will beat Six Five, and Six Five will outrank Five Four.

Domino Euchre

Domino Euchre is like the card game of the same name, and the laws for the card game may be consulted to settle any dispute that may arise while playing with tiles. This game is usually played by four people. The pieces rank as follows: the Double of the trump suit is the Right Bower, and the next lower Double is the Left Bower. There is, however, an exception to this rule, for when Blank is the trump, it is impossible to have a lower Double than the Double-Blank, so the Double-Six is adopted instead, and becomes the Left Bower. In this instance the lowest Double is Right Bower, and the highest Double is Left Bower. After the Right and Left Bower the value of the dominoes is governed by the number of spots following the trump.

For instance, if Six is Trump, the Double Six is Right Bower, and the Double Five is Left Bower, followed by Six Five, Six Four, Six Trey, and so on, down to Six Blank. If Ace is the trump, the Double-Ace is Right Bower, and the Double Blank is Left Bower, the Ace Six is next in value, the Ace Five is next, and so on, down to the Ace Blank. But when Blank is trump, the Double Blank is Right Bower, and the Double Six becomes Left Bower, the next trump in importance being Blank Six, the next, Blank Five, and so on, down to Blank Ace, which is the lowest trump. When a suit is not trump, the value of the pieces take rank from the Double of the suit in regular order, downward.

At the beginning of the game the players usually draw to decide who shall turn up trump; whoever draws the lowest piece is entitled to the privilege, and is termed the dealer. When the dominoes have again been shuffled, each player draws five pieces, beginning with the eldest hand (the player to the dealer's left), and the dealer then turns up one of the remaining pieces for trump. That portion of the domino which has the highest number of spots upon it determines the suit of the trump. After the first hand, the privilege of turning trump passes to each player in succession.

The eldest hand does not have the lead unless he exercises the privilege of ordering up, or making the trump. Only the player who takes the responsibility of the trump—that is, the player who takes up, order up, assists, or makes the trump—has the right to lead. *(See Euchre, page 92.)*

Bingo

This game is played similarly to the card game of Sixty-Six. The rank of the pieces is the same as in other domino games, except that Blanks count for seven spots. The Double Blank, which is called *Bingo* and counts for fourteen spots, is the highest domino and will take the Double of trumps.

The game is played by two people, and begins as each draws for the lead; whoever draws the lowest piece has the lead. Each player then draws seven pieces, after which the next player turns up another piece, the highest spot on which is trumps. The second player then leads, and the play is conducted in the same manner as the card game of Sixty-Six. *(See Sixty-Six, page 130.)*

The game consists of seven points, which are made in the following manner: The player who counts seventy first scores one point toward game; if he makes seventy before his opponent has counted thirty, he scores two points; if before his adversary has won a trick, three points. If Bingo captures the Double of trumps, it adds at once one point to the winner of the trick.

The pieces count as follows to the winner of the trick containing them: The Double of trumps always twenty-eight; the other Doubles and all the other trumps according to their spots; the Six Four and Three Blank are always good for ten each, whether trumps or not; the other pieces have no value.

If a player has, at any time, two Doubles in his hand, he can, when it is his turn to lead, play one, show the other, and announce twenty points, which are added to his count as soon as he has won a trick. If he hold three Doubles, he counts forty; four Doubles, fifty; five Doubles, sixty; six Doubles, seventy points. If Bingo is among the Doubles held it adds ten more to the count.

In all other respects the game is conducted in the same manner as Sixty-Six, except that whenever sixty-six occurs, seventy must be substituted for it.

Matadore

In this game, instead of matching the pieces, each player must make up the complement of seven. For instance, a Five requires a Two to be played to it, because two added to five make *seven*. On a Six, an Ace must be played; on a Four, a Three spot.

However, there is no place capable of making a Seven of a Blank. To obviate this difficulty there are four *Matadores*: the Double Blank, and the three natural Seven spots, namely, Six Ace, Five Two, and Four Three. These four Matadores can be played anywhere, at any time, and are, of course, the only ones that can be played on a Blank.

Each player, at the beginning of the game, draws three pieces; the one who has the highest Double goes out first. If neither has a Double, then the holder of the highest piece plays first.

In this example, suppose Double, Four has been led. The next player must play a Three to it, or, failing to have a Three in hand, must draw until he gets one. If it is a Three Five, the end spots will be a Four and a Five; the next player must then either play a Three on the Four, or a Two on the Five, and so on.

This game may be played by two, three, or four persons. When two play, there must be three pieces left undrawn, to prevent each from knowing exactly his opponent's hand. When more than two engage in the game, all the pieces may be drawn. The player who makes domino first counts the spots on the other hand or hands, and scores them toward his game. The winner is the first to reach 100 points.

If Domino is not made before the drawing is ended, and a player cannot play in his turn, he must pass. He must play if he can; the failure to do so deprives him of any count he may make with that hand.

In playing, a Doublet counts only as a single piece. For instance, Double Six is a Six, and can only be played on an Ace spot, or on Double Ace; but, if left in hand after domino is called, it counts twelve points to the winner.

If the game is blocked, and neither player can make Domino, then the one whose hand contains the least number of spots wins; but only his own hand does not count to his score.

The Blanks are very valuable in this game—the Double Blank being the most valuable of all the Matadores. As it is impossible to make a Seven against a Blank, if you hold Blanks you may easily block the game.

The Secrets of the Game

1. When you have the worst of the game, guard against your adversary's Blanks, and prevent him from making them. You can do this by playing only those dominoes that fit with the Blanks already down.

2. Never play a Blank at the lead unless you have a Matadore or a corresponding Blank.

3. Keep back your Double Blank till your opponent makes it all Blanks; you can then force him to play a Matadore, or compel him to draw till he obtains one. It is better to have a mixed hand.

Domino Loo

This game is similar to the card game Division Loo on page 79. Domino Loo is often played by three or four players. When three play, there are two *misses* of six pieces each; when four play, there is only one *miss* of seven pieces (two being discarded). The deal goes to the players in succession to the left, and the players play to the trick in order to the left of the leader.

In this version, the hand consists of five pieces. The dealer (or adversary of the leader) turns up a piece for trump. Unless a Double is turned, the end having the greatest number of pits makes the trump suit.

The leader plays a piece from his hand and his adversary plays to it. The two dominoes played constitute a *trick*. The winner of the trick leads to the next. The highest piece of the suit led wins the trick. The pieces rank in order as follows: Trump suit (which wins other suits); Six suit; Five suit; etc.; down to Blank suit. The Double is the highest piece of each suit; the piece with the largest number of pips at its nonsuit end wins pieces of the same suit with a smaller number. The leader to each trick announces the suit when he leads. Thus, if he leads Six Five, and announces Six Five, Six is the suit led; if he announces Five Six, Five is the suit led. If a trump is led, the trump suit must be announced.

The rules of the game are as follows: Two trumps in hand lead one, otherwise any piece; lead a trump if able after winning a trick; follow suit to the piece led if able. A player is not obliged to win the trick if he holds a losing piece that he can legitimately play.

If a player is not satisfied with his hand, he may reject his pieces and take six others, and having looked at them may discard one, making his hand consist of five pieces. The dealer may exchange one of his

pieces for the turnup, or may take a miss, rejecting his hand and the turn up, but he cannot do both.

Each trick scores one. The game is fifteen up. A player who does not take any of the five tricks is *looed,* that is, he is set back five points; if he has no score, he owes five.

The score may be regulated as for two players; but a better plan is to form a pool. When played with a pool, each hand is a complete game in itself: each player contributes a stake divisible by five; the dealer puts in twice the amount contributed by any one of the others, and each trick entitles the winner to a fifth of the amount in the pool. If any player wins no trick, he is looed, and has to contribute to the next pool as much as there was in the previous pool. When there is a loo the other players do not stake, with the exception of the dealer, who only stakes a single. In order to prevent the accumulation of large amounts in the pool, no one can be looed more than twenty with three players, no more than twenty-five with four players.

When Domino Loo is played with a pool, each player has the option of *passing*, i.e., he may throw up his hand without taking a *miss,* when he only loses what he has contributed to the pool, and cannot be looed. Anyone taking a miss must play. If all pass but one, and the dealer wants to pass, he must play miss for the pool, or if no miss remains, he must play his hand for the pool, i.e., any tricks he may win remain in the pool, and he cannot be looed. He must declare before playing his hand or before looking at miss, whether he will play for himself or for the pool. In default of a declaration, he is deemed to be playing for himself. If all pass up to the dealer, the dealer takes the pool. *(See Division Loo, page 79.)*

Tiddle-A-Wink

This game may be played by six or eight people. Each player draws three pieces. The player holding the Double Six leads it. If this piece is not out, the next highest Double leads.

The player of a Double, either at the lead or at any other part of the game, is entitled to play again if he can—thus obtaining two turns instead of one. The game then proceeds in the ordinary way, and he who plays out first cries, "Tiddle-A-Wink", having won. In the event of the game being blocked, he who holds the lowest number of pits wins.

Domino Pool

This is a very good game for three or more players. With three, each takes six pieces; with four, five pieces; with five, four; with six, three pieces. Each player makes an agreed contribution to the pool. The right to lead is decided by one or the other of the methods already described, and the leader poses accordingly. The player to his left follows suit. If unable to do so, he passes, and the next player has the right to play. The game continues in this fashion till some player makes domino, or all are blocked. In such cases, the player making domino, or holding the smallest number of pits, clears the pool; if two players are equal, they divide.

The above is the simplest method of scoring, but sometimes the game is played to a given number, usually 100 points. A record is kept at the close of each hand of the number of pips in each player's hand, and as each player's total reaches 100 he passes out, and has no further interest in the game, the player last in being the winner. The player first out is sometimes permitted to *star;* i.e., on making a fresh payment to the pool, to have his score put back to the same number as the player next in order. With four playing, the two first out are permitted to star, as above.

The drawing principle is sometimes admitted at Domino Pool. A player who cannot follow suit is entitled to draw one piece from the stock, subject to the usual qualification that the last two pieces must not be drawn.

Mah Jong

Mah Jong is a classic Chinese game. Mah Jong means literally *Sparrows.* Chinese in the past played the game very rapidly, recognizing the various tiles by their feel. They could discard them so quickly that the playing sounded like a sparrow tapping.

A very social game, Mah Jong can be played by either three or four players, each playing individually. Usually, groups of four play this famous tile game. The game is played with dice, 136 symbolic tiles, and chips used for scoring. The object of the game is to collect as many scoring combinations as possible.

To Begin

Place the four *Winds of Heaven* buttons (the small white buttons) face down on the table. Each player selects a button and takes a seat according to its designation, East having choice of seats. The rest of the seating is as follows: South sits to the right of East; West opposite East; and North to the left of East.

East is always the *banker* for first the table. A *table* consists of four rounds, so that each player has a turn as the banker. When the last player has played East Wind for the fourth time, it is customary to total up chips and settle scores. However, any number of rounds may be played, though it is generally customary to allow each player to become and lose East Wind the same number of times.

As the banker, East distributes the chips to all the players, including himself. The value of the chips is arbitrary, but they are usually assigned values according to size; the shortest counter is consistently valued at two points.

The banker then follows this method of distribution:

2	500 point chips, totaling	1000 points
9	100 point chips, totaling	900 points
8	10 point chips, totaling	80 points
10	2 point chips, totaling	20 points

After the chips are distributed, each players rolls the dice. The highest throw is the first East Wind. The other players becoming South Wind, West Wind, and North Wind respectively, according to their seating in reference to the East Wind: South Wind to the right of East Wind, West Wind opposite, and North Wind to the left. The players can then trade their original buttons with each other to remind them of their positions.

Dealing

East Wind and West Wind place the tiles face down on the table and shuffle thoroughly, making sure to remove the extra four blank tiles. Each player then draws thirty-four tiles at random and piles them into a wall that is seventeen tiles long, and two tiles high. The interior of the Wall becomes the playing field. (See Figure 31.)

Figure 31

When building the wall, the easiest method is to use two hands. Pick three tiles with the right hand and two tiles with the left, bringing them together to form a row of five. Repeat the same operation, placing the second five on the top of the first five. Then, select three tiles with each hand, this time bringing these together to form a row of six in front of the row of five already built. Repeat, placing second six on top of first six. Finally, split this double row of six tiles, carrying three to each

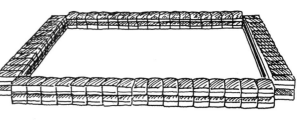

end of the five-tile wall making eleven tiles in this wall. Repeat each step until your wall is complete. This builds a wall of seventeen tiles without making it necessary to count. The completed wall is then pushed forward to position. The entire wall may be moved to any part of the table without disturbing its formation by holding the two end bottom tiles and evenly pressing on the bottom tiles inward. Do not press on the top tiles.

East Wind then throws the dice. The total number of points thrown designates the player whose wall is to be broken. Starting with himself as one, East Wind counts around the table to his right, stopping at the number of the point thrown. Figure 32 shows the various numbers that may be thrown by EAST WIND and the corresponding walls to be broken. For example, if the dice added up to seven, then West Wind's wall would be broken.

The player whose wall is to be broken throws both dice, adding the number thrown to the number previously thrown by East Wind. This

Figure 32

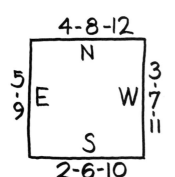

designates the point where the break will occur. If East Wind throws seven and then West Wind two, the sum of the two throws designates that the ninth tile (counting from the right) will be the point of break. (See Figure 33.)

These two tiles are known as the *loose tiles* and are placed on the top of the wall to indicate the end. If, during the progress of the game, these are drawn, the next two tiles are placed on top, and so on.

East Wind draws the first four tiles to the left of the break. South Wind, West Wind, and North Wind, (in this order) draw the succeeding four tiles. All players continue to draw four tiles at a time until each has twelve tiles. East Wind then draws the next top tile, South Wind the next bottom tile, West Wind the next top tile, and North Wind the next bottom tile, making thirteen tiles in each hand.

Figure 33

The hands are then rearranged. Each player arranges his hand according to suits, the same as in cards. (See Figure 34.)

East Wind then draws the next top tile from the wall and discards from his hand a tile, faceup on the table, calling out the number and suit, for example, "Six Bamboo" or "Red Dragon." Each player in turn draws a tile and discards one in place of this until some player completes his hand, or *mah jongs.*

Scoring

The most important feature of mah jong is scoring a host of combinations. While a player should always try to mah jong, during the progress of the game it may become evident that this will be impossible. While the player who mah jongs collects chips from all the other players and pays none out, the other players pay each other the differences between their scores. A player who does not mah jong but holds good scoring combinations may collect more points than the player who mah jongs.

For example, suppose the number of points held in each hand is as follows:

East Wind	144	points
South Wind	22	points (including mah jong)
West Wind	4	points
North Wind	6	points

Figure 34
A complete set of Mah Jong tiles

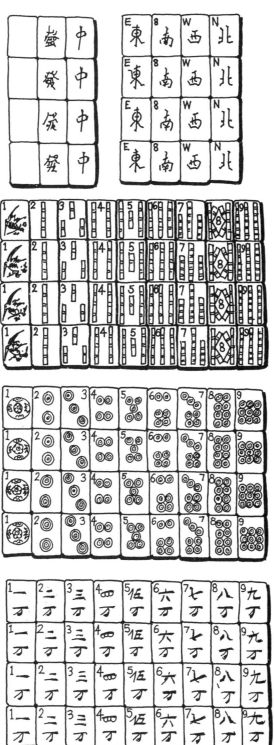

South Wind, who mah jonged, receives payment from all other players. Then, other players settle the differences between their scores.

Sequence groups have no scoring value but assist in mah jonging.

The number of points paid and received by each player would be as follows:

Figure 35

	Receives	Pays	Net Points Receives: Pays	
SOUTH WIND—has 22 points from WEST WIND " NORTH WIND " EAST WIND	22 22 44		88	
WEST WIND—has 4 points to SOUTH WIND " NORTH WIND " EAST WIND		22 2 280		304
NORTH WIND—has 6 points to SOUTH WIND " EAST WIND from WEST WIND	2	22 276		296
EAST WIND—has 144 points to SOUTH WIND from WEST WIND " NORTH WIND	280 276	44	512	

To determine the score, hands are divided into two groups:

A. *Exposed Hands.*—Groups that have been obtained by punging or chowing and exposed to the other players.

B. *Unexposed Hands*—Groups have been drawn and are unknown to the other players.

The points are tallied as follows:

A. *Exposed Groups:*

Three of a kind (except Nos. 1, 9, Winds, and Honors)   2 points
Three of a kind (only Nos. 1, 9, Winds, and Honors)   4 points

B. *Unexposed Groups:* Double the above points.

A player's own Wind or any Honor if paired: 2 points

Four of a kind, four times the amount of three of a kind.

There are certain bonuses which apply only to the player winning the Mah Jong

Mah Jong	20	points
No score in hand	10	points
No sequences in hand	10	points
Drawing winning tile	2	points
Securing only possible tile to mah jong	2	points
Drawing winning tile from loose tiles	10	points

There are other bonuses that apply to all hands. After determining the number of actual points in the hand, these points are doubled the number of times indicated, if doubling combinations are held:

Three or four of Honors	1 double
Three or four of own Wind	1 double
All tiles in one, suit with Winds and Honors	1 double
All tiles of one suit (no Winds or Honors)	3 double
All Winds and Honors	3 double

There are also several special hands, seldom held, which are valued more or less arbitrarily.

Should a hand contain more than one double, the total score is doubled for each doubling combination held. For example, a hand composed of all Honors and Winds would have three doubles, plus one double for each group of Honors or own Wind. If there were six doubles in the hand and the hand was valued at 36 points, the total value of the hand would be 2,304 points, as follows:

(1 double)	36 points doubled once	72 points
(2 double)	72 points doubled once	144 points
(3 double)	144 points doubled once	288 points
(4 double)	288 points doubled once	576 points
(5 double)	576 points doubled once	1152 points
(6 double)	1,152 points doubled once	2304 points

Paying Scores

After a player has mah jonged and the number of points in his hand has been tallied, scores are settled with the chips distributed by the Banker at the beginning of the game.

1. The player who mah jongs receives his full score from all the other players and pays no scores.
2. All other players pay each other the differences between their total scores; for example if North Wind has six points and West Wind has four points, then West Wind pays North Wind two points.

3. East Wind receives and pays double. If East Wind mah jongs, North Wind, South Wind, and West Wind must pay East Wind double the total number of points in his hand. If some other player mah jongs beside East Wind, he is paid by East Wind double his total score. Among players not mah jonging, East Wind must pay or receive double the difference between his score and each other player.

The Flowers and Seasons

After the game has been mastered, the *flowers and seasons* may be added. The addition of these tiles adds an additional element of chance to the game.

There are generally four tiles of each, numbered from 1 to 4. If your set does not include these tiles, you can assign each wind to represent a flower and season, East Wind being No. 1, South Wind No. 2, West Wind No. 3, and North Wind No. 4.

Each flower or season counts for 4 points. Holding one's flower or season (for example, East Wind holding No. 1) counts 1 double. Holding all flowers or seasons, from 1 to 4, with numerals all the same color, counts three doubles.

If your set includes the eight additional tiles of the flowers and seasons, the walls must be built eighteen tiles long instead of seventeen.

Flowers and seasons do not count in the fourteen tiles required to mah jong. They are additional tiles and exposed to view and replaced by a loose tile when drawn. Generally after drawing hands, all flowers and seasons in the hands are exposed and loose tiles drawn first to replace these, East Wind having first draw, followed by the other Winds in turn. When a flower or season is drawn during the game it is exposed and replaced by a loose tile immediately.

Cleared Hands

Many players prefer to play *all hands clear*, that is, each player must confine himself to one suit with Winds and Honors, or simply one suit, or all Winds and Honors. This makes the game somewhat more difficult but at the same time has the tendency to increase scores. There are two ways in which cleared hands are generally played:

1. The suits in which each player will undertake to mah jong are agreed upon *before* drawing hands. In this method East Wind has the choice of suits. West Wind then must choose the same suit. South Wind names his suit and then North Wind names the remaining suit.
2. Each player decides for himself the suit in which he will endeavor to mah jong *after* drawing hands. The players concentrate on the suit in which they have the largest number of tiles, taking into consideration the suits decided upon by the other players.

If cleared hands are played it is especially important to watch the discards of the other players, particularly if suits are not named before drawing. To clear a hand all Winds and Honors should be held until all but one of the three remaining suits, Circles, Bamboos, or Characters are eliminated from the hand. Every tile drawn in the suit decided upon should be held until the hand is cleared. After the hand has been reduced to one suit and Winds and Honors, the tile of least value, no matter if it is a Wind, Honor, or in the chosen suit, should then be discarded.

In choosing suits avoid, whenever possible, deciding upon the same suit as your opponent to your left. Unless you do this there is little likelihood of receiving either a chow or a pung from him, as he will hold all tiles in his chosen suit. As there are only three suits besides Winds and Honors and generally four players, two players can find themselves holding the same suit. If this case occurs, it is best for these two players sit opposite each other rather than next to each other; then they have an equal opportunity to chow the discards of the opponents whose turns precede their own.

In playing cleared hands it is not difficult to determine by a process of elimination the suits that your opponents are holding. Each player will generally discard his shortest suit. If an opponent discards Circles you can be reasonably sure he will try to concentrate on either Characters or Bamboos. Discard from either one of these suits in which you have the fewest tiles. His next discard may be a Bamboo so that you will know that his chosen suit is Characters. You can then decide on your own suit and if these discards have been made by an opponent to your left, you can choose either Circles or Bamboos yourself, depending on the number of tiles you hold in your hand.

If your opponents seem to be concentrating on the same suit, determine the suit your opponent opposite has decided upon and choose the remaining suit for yourself. You'll then have a better chance of winning in this suit. If, on the other hand, your opponents seem to be holding different suits, you should concentrate on the third remaining suit for yourself, which will in all probability be the suit chosen by the player opposite you.

Sometimes hands will be drawn in such a manner that three players will concentrate on the same suit. If you can determine that you are not one of the three, discard this suit immediately. If you should find that three players including yourself are concentrating on the same suit, do not hesitate to change to another suit even though you may have fewer tiles in that other suit than the one you had originally decided upon.

If you start out with a large number of tiles in one suit, say eight or nine, and no other player seems to be holding this suit, try to completely clear your hand. Discard all Winds and Honors each time you draw another tile in your long suit. A completely cleared hand counts three doubles, and Honors are slow to be discarded by your opponents. This is especially important in playing with the flowers and seasons for, should you draw your own flower or season, a completely cleared hand will give you four doubles. If you have only thirty-two points in your hand, doubling four times will count 512 points, more than the usual limit.

In playing cleared hands it is very difficult to hold a hand consisting of only Winds and Honors, though this can occasionally be done. Most players will hold their Winds and Honors until they have cleared their hands of all but one suit, so that unless you have completed groups of Winds and Honors, you will probably wait a long time for pungs. Remember, too, that there are only twenty-eight Winds and Honors tiles though there are thirty-six tiles in each of the other suits and also that Winds and Honors groups can only be punged.

If a hand is drawn with an equal number of tiles in two or three suits and you must play first, it may be well to discard a Wind or Honor until you get some sort of an idea of your opponents' hands. Such a discard tells them nothing, and may prevent you from discarding from a suit you might be able to build on later.

The Rules of the Game

1. *Suits.* There are five suits, as follows:

	Total Number of tiles
A. Honors	
White Dragon	4
Green Dragon	4
Red Dragon	4
B. Winds	
East Wind	4
South Wind	4
West Wind	4
North Wind	4
C. Bamboos	
Numbered from 1 to 9 (4 tiles each)	36
D. Circles	
Numbered from 1 to 9 (4 tiles each)	36
E. Characters	
Numbered from 1 to 9 (4 tiles each)	36
Total	136 tiles

The Rules of the Game

2. *Completing Hands.* The object of the game is to complete one's hand. A completed hand consists of any four groups of three tiles each and one pair, using fourteen tiles. A group is either *three of a kind* in the same suit or a *sequence* (much the same as in cards) of three tiles in the same suit (Seven, Eight, and Nine Bamboos). The grouping on the left is an example of a completed hand.

Figure 36

In some mah jong sets, the No. 1 Bamboo is represented by a bird and must not be confused with an Honor or Flower or Season. A hand may be completed by *drawing, punging,* or *chowing.*

3. *Drawing.* As explained earlier, this refers to breaking up a wall. Starting with East Wind each player may draw one tile from the wall and discard from his hand another tile. Throughout the game, each player must always hold thirteen tiles. Should some tile be drawn that is itself of no assistance in mah jonging, this may be discarded in place of a tile already in the hand.

4. *Punging.* This means securing a third tile (or fourth) to any pair (or three of a kind) already held in the hand. Any player, whether in turn or not, who holds a pair (or three of a kind) may *pung* an additional tile immediately after it is discarded by another player. When a player desires a tile just discarded he calls, "Pung!" and positions the two (or three) already in his hand faceup to his right along with the newly acquired tile.

After punging the play continues to the right; the player or players sitting to the right of the player whose discard has been punged lose their turns.

Figure 37

5. *Chowing.* This refers to securing a third tile to make a sequence group with two already held, when the third tile is discarded by the player immediately preceding on the left. When a player holding two tiles sees that he can form a sequence group with the tile just discarded by his opponent to his left, he calls, "Chow!" and places the two tiles already held, with the tile discarded, faceup to his right. A player may only chow from the player preceding him, unless he requires only one tile to mah jong. In that case he may chow from any player.

The Rules of the Game

Unless a tile is punged or chowed immediately after being discarded, it becomes dead and cannot be used later in the game. Discarded tiles are placed in the center of the table faceup, inside the wall, in any random fashion.

Should a player draw a group without punging or chowing, he does not expose these with the groups punged or chowed, but retains them in his hand. This prevents other players from learning how near he is to mah jonging.

6. *Fours of a Kind.* Any player holding a group of three of a kind in his hand may pung the fourth immediately after it is discarded. This fourth, to the group of three already held, does not count in the thirteen tiles in the hand. It is an extra tile and will increase the score.

When the fourth tile is punged it is placed faceup with the other three. However, if any player draws four of a kind during the progress of play he exposes these with the other groups punged or chowed, turning one tile over to indicate that the four tiles were drawn, as groups drawn count for more points than those punged. If the group of four of a kind drawn is not exposed in this manner before someone mah jongs, it will only be counted as a group or three of a kind. When the fourth tile is punged or drawn to a group of three of a kind, this tile does not count in the thirteen tiles held in the hand, and it must be replaced by one of the "loose tiles" on top of the wall.

Figure 38

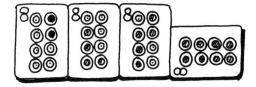

After punging a third tile to a pair held in the hand, the fourth cannot be punged if discarded by an opponent. However, if the fourth tile is drawn it may be placed with the three already exposed, and a loose tile is then drawn to replace it in the hand. When the fourth tile is drawn to a group of three of a kind obtained by punging, it is placed as shown in Figure 39.

Figure 39

The Rules of the Game

7. *Precedence.* A player who requires only one tile to mah jong has first precedence to a tile discarded whether this tile is to be used to pung, chow, or make the pair required in a completed hand. This is the only case where a chow has precedence over a pung or where a tile can be chowed from any opponent except the one immediately preceding the player chowing. If two players both desire the same tile discarded, the player who can pung has precedence. If two or three players each require the same tile to mah jong, the player having first turn after the player discarding has precedence.

8. *Draws.* Should all tiles be drawn from the wall except the last fourteen tiles including the loose tiles, all hands are declared dead and of no value. Tiles are reshuffled and a new round or *wind* is dealt. However, the players do not change their seating arrangements.

9. After all scores have been settled a "Wind" is completed. All the tiles are collected and turned face down. Another wind then begins as before.

10. East Wind retains his positions as long as he mah jongs.

11. If East Wind does not mah jong, he loses his position and East Wind passes to the player to his right—not to the player who mah jongs—and the other players becoming South Wind, West Wind, and North Wind, respectively.

12. The play continues as before. After each player has become and lost East Wind, a round is completed. Four rounds generally constitute a *table* after which the preliminaries to playing are again observed.

13. Should any player hold more or less than thirteen tiles in his hand during the progress of play and not be mah jong, his hand becomes dead. Playing continues, however, and when the Wind is finished he must pay all scores and receive nothing. No points in his hand are counted.

14. It is generally customary to set a limit on the number of points that will be paid for any hand. This is usually 300 points. East Wind may win or lose double this or 600 points from each player.

15. *Three-Handed.* This version of the game is played the same as four-handed, four walls being built as usual, the turn of the absent player being skipped

The Secrets of the Game

1. Watch the discards of the other players, especially the player to your right. Your opponent will seldom discard a tile that is paired in his hand or one which, with some other tile in his hand, will form a sequence group in case he can chow. By watching the discarding, a fair estimate of the opposing hands will be obtained that will assist in developing your own hand.

2. Too many pairs in a hand lessen the probability for mah jong. As there are only four tiles of each kind in a set, to hold two of these means that two more remain and these may be in use in other players' hands or in the wall. A sequence with *both ends open,* refers to one that can be formed into a sequence group by adding a tile to either end. For example No. 6 and 7 Bamboos can be completed by any one of eight tiles, that is, any No. 5 Bamboo or No. 8 Bamboo. Of course a sequence group can only be formed by drawing or chowing from the player preceding you, but as there are eight chances to form such a group and only two to pung to a pair, the odds favor holding such groups. Sequence groups, however, have no scoring value in themselves, so that it is well to carefully estimate one's hand before deciding how it is to be played. It will generally be

found that a hand can be arranged to take advantage of either a pung or a chow.

3. Do not be in too much of a hurry to claim four of a kind. Pung the fourth to three whenever possible, but only three of these retaining the fourth in the hand for possible use in a sequence group. Nothing can be lost in so doing unless some other player mah jongs before you have a chance. Remember, too, that if you draw the winning tile from the loose tiles you score an additional ten points more. Therefore, it will pay you to develop your hand until only one tile is required to mah jong and then add the fourth to a group of three already punged or held in the hand.

4. Always try to arrange your hand so that you will have two or more places to mah jong. Remember that there are eight chances to complete an open-end chow and only two to complete a pair. Don't let the thought that a chow is of no value in scoring, make you save for too many pungs. To gain two or four points you may lose the game.

5. The best possible hand for mah jonging is that shown in the figure that follows. It presents nine possible chances for completion, for any circle discarded will form the required number of groups.

Figure 40

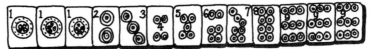

6. Mah Jong whenever possible but do not try to do so when it is evident from the other players' hands that it would be impossible. For example, let us suppose that you are East Wind and hold several groups of two or three of a kind in your hand and some other player has chowed two or three groups of sequences and is therefore probably waiting for one tile to mah jong. From the groups he has exposed you can probably estimate the number of points that he will have, should he mah jong, which is, say, 22 or 24 points. If you have, say, 40 points (including doubles) in your own hand and the other players give no indication of holding large hands, it will be to your advantage to pay the winning hand 44 or 48 points and collect probably 100 points from your other opponents.

7. Determine which is the least valuable tile when discarding; you will then increase your probabilities for mah jonging.

8. If there is a large number of Winds and Honors in your hand, hold these for a time and concentrate on one suit, Bamboos, Characters, or Circles as you can obtain a double. Concentrate on the suit you seem to have the most of, or the suit that your opponent to the left seems to be discarding. After reducing your hand to one suit with Winds and Honors, discard these as soon as more tiles of the suit decided upon are punged, chowed, or drawn. Remember that a completely cleared hand counts for three doubles. On the other hand watch the other players' discards and if they seem to be holding on to their Winds and Honors and discarding only one or two suits. In this case, do not discard the other suit to them unless necessary. In other words, you will prevent them as much as possible from clearing their hands.

9. It is generally smart to discard other players' Winds (unless you are trying to clear your hand) as soon as possible, as these are of small value to you, whereas they may double your opponents' hands.

Part Four

Bar and Basement Games

Bar and Basement Games

Pool and Billiards

Pool and Billiards are two entirely different games,
although their names are often used interchangeably.
Most people are currently playing pool games, which are
the more American and modern versions. Those games
are listed here first. The more classic games of billiards are
also included for the more adventurous. As you'll see, these
games will require different table setups, different balls, and
totally different sets of rules.

In the following instructions it is understood that the reader has some
knowledge of the necessary equipment, and its uses, for the games.

Standard Pool

The most popular version of this game, also known as *Solids and
Stripes,* is played with fifteen numbered balls and one white ball, not
numbered. The white ball is known as the *cue ball.* The cue ball is used
to hit the other balls into the pockets. The object of this game is to pocket as many balls, of all varieties, as you can.

The fifteen balls are numbered from one to fifteen respectively; the
first half are a variety of solid colors; the second half have stripes of corresponding shades. In this game the numbers on the balls are simply
used for convenience in calling the balls that the player intends to pocket, and do not in any way affect the score of the player.

Before beginning the game the fifteen balls are placed within a triangular frame on the table, and rolled so that the first ball covers one of the two spots on the felt. The highest numbered balls must be placed nearest the apex of the triangle, pointing toward head of the table.

Each and every ball pocketed counts one point for the striker, and he who first scores eight balls wins the game. Any number of players can participate in this game.

The Rules of the Game

1. The game is begun by *banking*. Each player rolls one ball across the table, directly from where he stands. The player whose ball returns closest to the starting point is the winner. The winner of the lead has the option of playing first, or passing to his opponent to play first. When a series of games is played, the players must alternate who shoots first.

2. The player who makes the opening stroke must strike the pyramid of balls with sufficient force to cause two or more balls to strike a cushion, or cause at least one ball to go into a pocket. Should the player fail to do either, he must forfeit one ball to the table from his score, and the next player plays. Should a player have no balls to his credit, the next ball he scores is replaced on the table. All balls pocketed on the opening stroke count for the player, and it is not necessary for him to call the number of the ball he intends to pocket before making the opening stroke.

3. Before making a stroke, except for the opening stroke, the player must distinctly call the number of the ball he intends to pocket (but he need not name the particular pocket into which he intends to put it). If he fails to do so the ball pocketed does not count for him, and must be placed on the spot where the pyramid of balls were first placed (called the *foot spot*), or, if that is occupied, as near below it as possible. The player loses his turn, but does not pay a forfeit, and the next player plays. Should he call more than one ball, he must pocket all the balls he calls, otherwise none of them can be counted for him. A player does not receive a scratch for failure to remove or hit a called ball, provided he hits any other ball or balls on the table.

4. After the opening stroke, each player must either pocket a ball or make contact with a ball, or strike a cushion with the cue ball, under penalty of forfeiture of one ball.

5. Should the player pocket, by the same stroke, more balls than he calls, he is entitled to all the balls he calls, and all the other balls pocketed by the stroke.

6. All strokes must be made with the point of the cue, otherwise they are foul.

7. When two players are engaged in a game, he who pockets or scores eight balls first is the winner of the game. But when more than two players are engaged, the game is ended only when the number of balls remaining on the table does not amount to enough to tie or beat the next lowest score.

The Rules of the Game

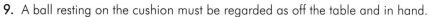

8. A ball going into a pocket and rebounding onto the table must be regarded in the same light as if it had struck a cushion, and is not counted as a pocketed ball. It remains in place where it came to rest on the table. Any ball forced off the table must be replaced on the foot spot, or, if that is occupied, as near below it as possible. If it is the cue ball, it is to be regarded as being off the table and *in hand*. The lighting over the table is not considered an object foreign to the table, and should a ball striking the fixture rebound to the table, it must retain its position on the table where it came to rest.

9. A ball resting on the cushion must be regarded as off the table and in hand.

10. When the cue ball is in *hand,* the player may play from any place behind the spot from which he started. He may shoot for any ball outside of (or across) this string. Should none of the balls be outside the string, the ball that is nearest outside is moved to the foot spot, and the player may play at it.

11. Should the striker touch the cue ball with the point of his cue, or with any other part of the cue, or with his clothing or anything else, it shall be counted a stroke.

12. If the player, before his stroke has been delivered, touch a ball with the point or any part of the cue, or with his clothing or anything else, so that the ball moves, it must be returned to its original position. The striker loses his turn for that round only.

13. A stroke is complete when all balls set in motion have come to rest.

14. A stroke made when any of the balls are in motion is foul. Should such a stroke be made, the balls are either replaced or left as they come to rest, at the option of the next player. The striker loses his turn and forfeits one ball.

15. Should a player play out of turn, his stroke is foul. The balls must be replaced in the position they occupied before the stroke, and whoever's turn it was plays. But should a player, playing out of turn, make more than one stroke before being checked, the strokes made are fair, and he is entitled to any points he may have made by such strokes, and he may continue his play until his turn is out. After his turn is out (and the player whose turn it was plays), the offending player, having had his inning, is not to play again when his regular turn comes, but must wait for his regular turn to come around the second time.

16. Should the balls on the table be accidentally disturbed by any person or cause other than the player, they are to be replaced as nearly as possible in their original position, and the player may continue.

17. Push shots are allowed; that is, it is not necessary to withdraw the point of the cue from the cue ball before the latter touches the ball. When the cue ball is in contact with another ball, the player may play directly at the ball with which it is in contact, or directly from it, and the latter play shall not be recorded as a miss, provided a cushion is struck.

18. When the striker is in hand, should he play at any ball that is within the string-line, or if, when in hand, he plays from any position not within the string-line,

The Rules of the Game

without being checked previous to the stroke being made, any score he may make from such stroke he is entitled to; but if he is checked before making the stroke, and then makes it; it does not count for him, his hand is out, and the next player plays, and all balls disturbed by the stroke must be replaced or left as they are, at the option of the next player.

19. It is a foul, and the striker forfeits one ball, if, while in the act of striking, he does not have at least one foot on the floor.

20. Should the striker, by a clear, fair stroke of the cue, pocket a ball and, after the stroke, move, touch, or foul one or more of the balls, he is entitled to the pocketed ball, and loses his hand only because of the foul, and the next player plays.

21. Should a ball that has come to a standstill move without apparent cause while the player is preparing to strike, it must be replaced. Should it move before he can stop his stroke, it and all the other balls set in motion by the stroke must be replaced, but the player shall repeat his stroke.

22. When two persons are playing, should a player incur three penalties, scratches, or forfeitures in succession, he shall forfeit every ball remaining on the table to his opponent. Should more than two persons be playing, then the offending player is automatically declared the loser of the game.

23. No player is allowed to withdraw before the game is played out; by so doing he forfeits the game.

High Low Jack Game

Any number of persons may play, the order of play being determined by banking. The fifteen ball is High; the one ball is Low; the nine ball is Jack and the highest aggregate is Game. Seven points generally constitute a game. The object of this game is to pocket as many of the numbered balls as possible. Each and every ball counts one point, and the game shall consist of any given number of points, to be mutually agreed upon.

In setting up the pyramid, the three counting balls—High, Low, and Jack—are placed in the center, with High at the head of the three named balls.

When players have each one shot left, the table is cleared and one ball is placed at the foot of the table, in direct line with the spots, and at a distance from the lower cushion equal to the diameter of a ball. This ball must be pocketed by banking it to one or more cushions. The player who pockets the ball wins the game.

Continuous Pool

Continuous Pool differs from all other games of pool. The scoring of the game is continued until all the balls in each frame have been pocketed, and the game may consist of any number of balls or points that are previously agreed upon. Each ball pocketed scores one point for the striker, and the game is usually scored upon the string of buttons over the table. Penalties are paid by deducting points from the offending player's score or string of buttons, instead of forfeiting a ball to the table.

In playing a long game of more than one night's duration, when a player shall have scored the agreed upon quota for the night, play must be continued until all the balls of the final frame have been pocketed, and each player must be credited with the ball that each shall pocket in the final frame. On the final night of a match, playing ends as soon as the leading player has scored or pocketed a sufficient number of balls to be declared winner.

The Rules of the Game

The rules for Continuous Pool are the same as those that govern Standard Pool except where they conflict with the following rules:

1. When there are only two players, and one player's score amounts to more than the total credited to the other player added to that remaining on the table, the player whose score is higher than this total wins.
2. Should the player touch a ball with the point or any part of the cue, or with his clothing or anything else, the ball so disturbed is to be replaced in its original position, or left where it rests, at the option of the next player, the offending player may also be compelled to play his stroke, but cannot score for the stroke. The striker loses his turn, and the next player plays.
3. Should a player play out of his turn, it is foul, and two points must be deducted from his score
4. Forfeiturees are counted by losing one point, instead of one ball.

Eight Ball

The object of this game is to pocket the Eight ball, but only after all of your other balls have been pocketed. The fifteen balls are divided into two categories, solids and stripes. Each player is assigned to play either solids or stripes, and then attempts to pocket only those balls that have been assigned to him. This game can be played with either two or four players—four players play as teams.

The Game

The balls are placed in the triangular frame in an alternating fashion, with one solid ball surrounded by two striped balls, or vice versa. The Eight ball is set squarely in the center of the pyramid.

The first ball pocketed, either in the initial break or by another player, determines the categories each player or team will follow. Once determined, the balls within each category may be pocketed in any random order, saving the Eight ball for last.

The Rules of the Game

The rules for Eight Ball are the same as those that govern Standard Pool except for the following:

1. A player's turn is completed if he does not pocket any ball in his category. If he pockets the opposing side's ball, the ball remains out of play, and the player forfeits his turn.
2. After all the balls in his category have been pocketed, the player must call the pocket where the Eight ball will land. If the Eight ball rolls into a different pocket or the cue ball is pocketed, the game is over, and the player automatically loses.

Fifteen-Ball Pool

The object of this game is to pocket as many balls as possible, the number on each ball being scored to the striker's credit. Therefore, the winner is not always the one who pockets the highest number of balls, but whose score yields the highest total. In this game, the ball numbered fifteen is placed in the apex of the triangular frame, pointing toward the head of the table. The rest of the balls are placed so that the highest numbers shall be nearest the apex. The game can be played by any number of players, but when two people are playing, whoever scores sixty-one points first wins of the game.

The Rules of the Game

The rules for Fifteen-Ball Pool are the same as those that govern Standard Pool, except where they conflict with the following rules:

1. Should the striker pocket the cue ball in the opening stroke, and fail to drive two or more balls against a cushion or into a pocket, he forfeits three points only for the pocketing of the cue ball. In match or tournament games the player who makes the opening stroke must play from within the string at the head of the table and must strike the pyramid of balls with such force as to drive at least two object balls to a cushion or cause at least one ball to go into a pocket. Should he fail to do either, the balls are to be set up again, he forfeits two points, and must continue to play until he drives two or more balls to a cushion, or at least one ball into a pocket. Each failure causes him to receive a scratch, i.e., pay a forfeiture of three points.
2. The player making three forfeitures in succession loses the game.
3. When two players are competing, and one player's score amounts to more than the aggregate numbers on the balls credited to the other player plus what is remaining on the table, the game is ended, and the player whose score is higher than this total wins.
4. When the striker is in hand, should he play at any ball that is within the string-line, or if, when in hand, he plays from any position not within the string-line, without being checked previous to the stroke being made, he is entitled to any score he may make from such stroke; but if he is checked before making the stroke, and then makes it, it does not count for him, his hand is out, and the next player plays.
5. It is the striker's privilege to demand the removal of obstructions from the table.
6. Rule 29 of Standard Pool does not occur in the rules of Fifteen-Ball Pool.
7. Forfeitures are counted by losing three points, instead of one ball.

Chicago Pool

This object of this game is to pocket the balls in their numerical order. The table is laid out for the game by placing the One ball against the end cushion at the first right-hand diamond sight at the foot of the table; the Two ball is placed at the center diamond sight on the same cushion; and the remaining thirteen balls are placed in the order of their numbers at the succeeding diamond sights. It is immaterial which way the numbers run in setting the balls, for they may also be set so that the One ball is placed on that diamond sight which, when standing at the head of the table and looking toward the foot or lower end, appears as the left-hand diamond sight on the end rail, with the Three ball placed at the right, etc. The three sights on the end rail at the head of the table are not occupied by any ball.

The opening stroke must be to strike the One ball. If that ball is pocketed, it is placed to the credit of the player, and he continues his turn until he fails to score. In continuing he must play each time upon the ball bearing the lowest number on the table. After playing upon that ball, however, should any other be pocketed by the same stroke, irrespective of its number, it shall be placed to the credit player pocketing it.

If the line of aim at the ball required to be hit is covered by another ball, the player may resort to a bank play, but should he fail to hit the required ball, he forfeits three points, receiving a scratch.

Should a ball be pocketed by a foul stroke, it is replaced upon the spot it occupied at the opening of the game. Should it be the eight, nine, ten, or eleven ball, and the cue ball is in hand, then the balls specified are to be placed upon the foot spot, or, should that be occupied, as near to it as is possible.

The rules of Fifteen-Ball Pool govern Chicago Pool, except where they conflict with the preceding rules.

Nine Ball

This game is similar to Chicago Pool, except it is only played with the nine solid-colored balls. The object of this game is to pocket the Nine ball, but not before pocketing the preceding balls in their numerical order, or by pocketing the Nine ball using the lowest ball on the table. This game can be played by any number of players.

The nine solid-colored balls are placed in the triangular frame in the shape of a diamond, in numerical order. The One ball is placed in the apex of the frame, followed underneath by the Two and the Three, the next layer the Four, Five, and Six, the next layer the Seven and Eight. At the base of the diamond is the Nine ball. The balls are placed with the One ball covering the foot spot, facing toward the top of the table.

The first player tries to pocket the One ball, or uses the One ball to pocket the Nine ball. The player's turn continues until he misses the lowest numbered ball on the table, or if he pockets the cue ball, or scratches. If a player pockets any other ball besides the lowest numbered ball, his turn is over, but the ball remains off the table. If a player accidentally sinks the Nine ball, the game is over, and that player is declared the loser.

The rules of Fifteen-Ball Pool govern Nine Ball, except where they conflict with the preceding rules.

Billiards

The Four-Ball Game

Arranging the Table

The following billiards games require slightly different equipment than the pool games. When not in regulation play, though, you can alter your pool table to play these games by covering the pockets and assigning the balls different values.

Most billiards games listed will require three balls. However, four are used for this game, as its name implies. In regulation play, two balls should be red and two white. One red ball is lighter than the other, and one of the white balls has a black center spot.

From the head to the lower end, the table is marked with three spots on its surface, placed on an imaginary line dividing the table lengthwise, with diamond sights on the end rails at the head and foot of the table. One spot is fixed at the head of the table and in line opposite the second diamond sight on each of the side cushion rails. This is the *light red spot,* and is known in the three-ball game as the *white ball spot.* The *dark red spot* is fixed in a similar measured position at the foot or lower end of the table. The white ball or *pool spot* is fixed five inches from the face of the lower end cushion and on a direct line with the other spots.

Playing

Any number of players can participate in this game. As in Standard Pool, the players bank the ball for the choice of balls and lead. The player who wins the choice of balls and lead must either roll his ball down toward the lower cushion, as an object for his adversary to play at, or else compel his adversary to lead off.

In leading, the player's ball must be played from within the string-line and struck with sufficient force to carry it beyond the deep-red ball on its appropriate spot at the foot of the table. But it must not pass again, after having come in contact with the lower cushion. The ball cannot touch either red ball, rest on the cushion, or jump off the table. In any of these cases, or if the cue ball is not struck with sufficient force to pass beyond the deep red ball, the adversary has the option to make the player spot his ball on the pool spot nearest the lower cushion, lead again, or take the lead himself.

No count or forfeiture can be made or incurred until two strokes have been played. Once the lead is made, neither player can withdraw from the game.

The game continues with each player playing on the white ball at the foot of the table. Should a player fail to hit the white first, or fail to hit it at all, he forfeits one point, which shall be added to his adversary's score. If a player fails to hit any of the other balls with his own, he forfeits one point, which is added to his adversary's score.

The Rules of the Game

1. The player forfeits two points when the ball rests on the cushion, or goes over the table, after having struck or been in fixed contact with the other white, no matter whether it has touched one or both of the reds.
2. The player forfeits three points when the ball that he plays with rests on the cushion, or goes over the table, after having come in contact with one or both of the reds, and not the white. The same applies if neither red nor white are struck.
3. If the player causes any ball to jump off the table, even if it is immediately returned to the table, it must still be treated as if it had fallen to the floor. If it is a red ball, it must be spotted; if a white, held in hand. Should it be the last player's ball, he forfeits two or three points.
4. If any player plays with his opponent's ball, the stroke is foul and doesn't count, unless the error is found out after a second stroke is made. Should two or more strokes have been made previous to the discovery, the progress of the game cannot be disturbed, and the player may continue his turn with the same ball, or he may have the balls changed. The same privilege is extended to the opposing player when his turn comes to play. If both players have used the wrong ball successively, whoever was first to play with the wrong ball cannot put in a claim of foul against his opponent.
5. When playing with the wrong ball, a player cannot count what points he may make, except in those cases mentioned above; he is bound to pay whatever for-

The Rules of the Game

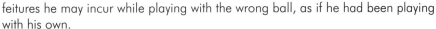

feitures he may incur while playing with the wrong ball, as if he had been playing with his own.

6. Should, however, both the white balls be off the table together, and should either player, by mistake, pick up the wrong one and play with it, the stroke must stand, and he can count whatever he has made.

7. If the player attempts to strike a ball before it is fully at rest, or while any other ball is rolling on the table, the stroke is foul.

8. If the player, when playing with the butt or side of his cue, does not withdraw the butt or side before the cue ball touches the first object ball, the stroke is foul.

9. A stroke made while a red ball is off the table, provided its spot is unoccupied, is foul.

10. A red ball that has been forced off the table shall be spotted on another spot, provided its own is occupied, and provided, also, that the nonstriker's ball is off the table at the time. The light red ball is then to be placed on the dark red spot; and if that spot is occupied, the light red is be placed on the pool spot at the foot of the table. The dark red ball is be placed on the light red spot. If both reds are off the table at the same time, and their spots are occupied by the two whites, one of the reds may be placed on the pool spot. The other must remain off the table until its proper spot is vacant.

11. If, after making a successful stroke, the player obstructs or otherwise affects the free course of any ball in motion, the stroke is foul, and he cannot score the points made.

12. A touch is a shot. And if, while the balls are at rest, a player touches or disturbs any ball on the table other than his own, it is foul. He has, however, the privilege of playing a stroke for safety, provided his own ball has not been touched, but he can make no count on the shot.

13. In playing a shot, if the cue leaves the ball and touches it again, the stroke is foul.

14. If the striker, through stretching forward or otherwise, has not at least one foot on the floor while striking, the shot is foul, and no points are earned.

15. If, when the player's ball is in hand, he does not cause it to pass outside the string before touching any of the other balls or cushion, the stroke is foul, and his opponent may choose whether he will play with the balls as they are, have them replaced in their original positions, or cause the stroke to be played over; or, should the player pocket his own ball under such circumstances, the penalty may be enforced.

16. Playing at a ball whose base or point of contact with the table is outside the string is considered playing out of the string, and the stroke is a fair one, even though the side that the cue ball strikes is hanging over, and therefore within the string.

17. Playing directly at a ball that is considered in the string is foul even though the cue ball should pass wholly beyond the string-line before coming in contact with the ball.

The Rules of the Game

18. Giving a miss inside the string when the player is in hand is foul but he may, for safety, cause his ball to go out of the string and return.

19. If a player alters the stroke he is about to make, at the suggestion of any party in the room—even if it be at the suggestion of his partner—the altered stroke is foul.

20. Placing marks of any kind whatever, either upon the cushions or table, is foul; and a player, while engaged in a game, cannot practice a particular stroke on another table.

21. When the cue ball is in contact with any other ball, the striker may effect a count, either by playing first upon some ball other than that with which his own is in contact, or by playing first against the cushion. It doesn't matter which ball the returning cue ball strikes first.

22. Should the cue ball be in contact with all the other balls on the table or if the two balls only, while the remaining ball is on the table in such a way that the player cannot play on the free ball or the cushion first, it shall be optional with him to have all the balls taken up, and the reds spotted as in the beginning of the game.

Three-Ball Carom

Three-Ball Carom is played with two white balls and one red. The billiard table has three spots on an imaginary line, dividing the table lengthwise, running from the center of the head cushion to the center of the foot cushion; one of those spots, cutting the line in two equal parts, is called the *center spot*, and the other two are situated halfway between the center spot and the head and foot cushions.

The spot at the head of the table is called the *white spot*, and the one at the foot of the table the *red spot*. The center spot is only used when a ball forced off the table finds both white and red spots occupied. Therefore, should the white ball forced off the table have its spot occupied, it would be placed on the red spot; similarly if the red ball is forced off the table, it is placed on the white spot.

In beginning the game the red ball and one white are placed on their respective spots; the other white remains in hand, and the player who plays the opening stroke can take any position within a six-inch radius, of which the spot at the head of the table is the base, but he must strike the red ball first before a count can be effected.

The Rules of the Game

1. The game is begun by banking for the lead; the player who brings his ball nearest to the cushion at the head of the table wins the choice of balls and the right to play first or compel his opponent to play. Should the striker fail to *carom,* his opponent then makes the next play, aiming at will at either ball on the table.

2. A *carom* consists of hitting both balls with the cue ball in a fair and unobjectionable way; each carom will count one for the player. A penalty of one shall also be counted against the player for every miss occurring during the game.

3. A ball forced off the table is put back on its proper spot. Should the player's ball jump off the table after counting, the count is good, the ball is spotted, and the player plays from the spot.

4. If the cue is not withdrawn from the cue ball before the cue ball comes in contact with the ball, the shot is foul, and the player loses his count and his turn.

5. If the balls are disturbed accidentally in any way other than by the player himself, they must be replaced and the player allowed to proceed.

6. If, in the act of playing, the player disturbs any ball other than his own, he cannot make a counting stroke, but he may play for safety. Should he disturb a ball after having played successfully, he loses his count on that stroke; his hand is out and the ball is placed back as near as possible in the position that it formerly occupied on the table, the other balls remaining where they stop.

7. Should a player touch his own ball prior to playing, it is foul, the player loses one ball, and cannot play for safety. It sometimes happens that the player, after having touched his ball, gives a second stroke, then the balls remain where they stop, or are replaced as near as possible in their former position, at the option of his opponent.

8. When the cue ball is very near another, the player shall not play without warning his adversary that they do not touch.

9. When the cue ball is in contact with another, the balls are spotted and the player plays with his ball in hand.

10. Playing with the wrong ball is foul. However, should the player using the wrong ball play more than one shot with it, he shall be entitled to his score just the same as if he played with his own; as soon as his turn is up, the white balls must change places, and the game proceeds as usual.

11. No player is allowed to withdraw before the game is finished, otherwise he forfeits the game.

12. Should a ball that has once come to a standstill move without apparent cause while the player is preparing to strike, it shall be replaced. Should it move before he can check his stroke, it, and all other balls set in motion by that stroke, shall be replaced, and the player shall repeat his shot.

13. It is a foul if the player shoots directly at any ball with which his own is in fixed contact, and the striker must in this instance play from balls spotted, as in the opening stroke of the game.

The Rules of the Game

14. It is a foul to place marks of any kind on the felt or cushions as a guide to play.

The rules of the Four-Ball Game govern this game also, except when they conflict with the foregoing rules.

Cushion Caroms

A cushion carom is made by the cue ball taking one or more cushions before effecting a carom, or by the cue ball making a carom, then striking one or more cushions, then either ball. When it is difficult to say whether the cue ball has struck a cushion before or after contact with the object ball, the player is given the benefit of the doubt.

Arranging the Table

The game of Cushion Caroms is played with three balls, two white and one red, using the same kind of table as in the previous two games.

In beginning the game, the red ball and one white are placed on their respective spots; the other white remains in hand, and is placed near the white spot prior to the opening stroke in the game. The player can take any position within a radius of six inches of the white spot on or within a line parallel to the head cushion, but he must strike the red ball first before a point can be made.

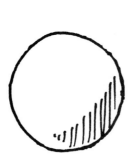

The Rules of the Game

The rules of the Three-Ball Game govern this game also, except where they conflict with the following rules.

1. The game is begun by banking for the lead. Should the player fail to score, his opponent then makes the next play, aiming at will at either ball on the table.

2. Each cushion carom counts for one point. A penalty of one point is also deducted from the player for every miss he makes during the game.

3. A ball forced off the table is put back on its proper spot. Should the player's ball jump off the table after counting, the count is good, the ball is spotted, and the player plays from the spot at either of the other balls wherever they may rest.

4. If the balls are disturbed accidentally they must be replaced, and the player allowed to proceed.

5. If the player disturbs any ball other than his own, he cannot make a counting stroke. Should he disturb a ball after having played successfully, he loses his point on that shot, his turn is over, and the ball is placed back as near as possible in the position that it formerly occupied.

6. When the cue ball is very near another, the player shall not play without warning his adversary that they do not touch.

7. When the cue ball is in contact with either or both of the object balls, it shall be optional for the player to spot the balls and play as at the opening of the game, or to play away from the ball or balls with which he is in contact, and count from a cushion.

8. When the player's ball is in contact with a cushion, the ball may be played so as to rebound from the cushion, and if by reason of this rebound it comes in contact with the two object balls, either before or after striking another cushion, the stroke is a valid cushion carom; but if the player should aim directly at the object balls when his ball is in contact with a cushion, without making the cue ball either rebound from the cushion or take another cushion before effecting the carom, it doesn't count.

9. Foul strokes are the same as in Three-Ball Carom, except for the following circumstances:

   A. If, when in hand, the striker plays at a ball that is inside or on the string-line, or if when in hand he plays from any position not within the six-inch radius.

   B. If the player touches the cue ball more than once in any way, or hinders or accelerates it in any other way than by a legitimate stroke of the cue; or if, during a stroke or after it, he in any way touches, hinders, or accelerates an object ball, except by the one stroke of the cue ball to which he is entitled.

   C. As touching any ball in any way is a stroke, a second touch is foul. Should a ball that has once come to a standstill move without apparent cause while the player is preparing to strike, it shall be replaced. Should it move before he can check his stroke, it and all other balls set in motion by that stroke shall be replaced, and the player shall repeat his shot.

The Rules of the Game

D. If any ball is disturbed, hastened, or hindered by an opponent or anyone but the player, it is a foul against the offender, whether the ball or balls are at rest while he is aiming or striking, in motion after he has struck, or at rest again after he has struck.

E. Should a player touch his own ball with the cue or otherwise previous to playing, it is foul, the player loses one, and cannot play for a sacrifice. It sometimes happens that the player, after having touched his ball, gives a second stroke; then the balls remain where they stop, or are replaced as near as possible in their former position, at the option of his opponent.

10. In order to restrict deliberate playing for a sacrifice, it shall be optional with the nonstriker, if his opponent makes a miss in each one for three successive turns, to accept the third miss or reject it, and force his antagonist to hit at least one object ball. Should two balls be hit by this stroke, there shall be no count.

Balk-Line Billiards

Arranging the Table

The bed of the table is arranged with the balk lines drawn at both eight and fourteen inches from the cushions. Spots are placed the same as are those in the Three-Ball Game.

However, in this game a solid line is drawn on the felt from end to end and from side to side of the table. The lines must be drawn, on a five-by-ten-foot table, from the face of the cushion at each of the first diamond sights, on each of the end and side rails in the four corners of the table, to the face of the cushion at each of the opposite diamond sights. Eight restricted spaces are formed, four oblong at the sides and ends of the table, and four square at the corners of the table. Caroms may be made in the large center space of the table.

The Rules of the Game

The rules of Three-Ball Carom govern this game also, except where they conflict with the following rules.

1. Standing at the head of the table, and as far apart as practicable, the two contestants shall endeavor to simultaneously play the cue balls from within the string-line against the lower cushion; the lead and the choice of balls is won by the player whose ball stops nearer to the cushion at the head of the table.
2. The first player may either require his antagonist's ball to be placed on the radius spot and take the lead himself, or he may have his own ball spotted and require his opponent to open the game. Whoever is to open the game may play from anywhere within a six-inch radius, of which the spot at the head of the table is the base, but can only score a point when his ball has hit the red before hitting the white.
3. After the opening stroke, the striker plays at either ball from any position in which he may find his own, subject to certain rules as to foul strokes.
4. One point shall be given for every fair carom, and for every failure to hit a ball the player forfeits one point to his adversary.
5. The balls shall be in balk as soon as both have stopped within any one of the restricted spaces defined by the balk lines. A ball on the line counts as if it were within it.
6. All the foul rules from the carom game are enforced, along with the following:
   A. It is foul if the striker plays directly at any ball with which his own is in fixed contract.
   B. It is foul if more than two successive shots are made on balls both of which are within any one of the eight restricted spaces. The only way in which more than that number can be made in succession within that space is by sending one or both balls out and bringing them back in again. Both balls being within the space, the striker can play once on them without sending either out; his next stroke must send at least one out; should it return and both balls be again inside, he can play one shot as before without sending either out. This process may be repeated. Should the second stroke fail to send a ball out, it does not count, the striker's turn is up and the next striker plays at the balls as he finds them.
   C. It is a foul against the nonstriker if a ball in play is lifted from the table, except in unavoidable cases in which it is provided that, because of foul or irregular stokes, the balls shall be transposed or replaced. The striker cannot make a count on the ensuing stroke.
   D. In order to restrict deliberate playing for safety, it shall be optional with the non-striker, if his opponent makes a miss in each one of three successive innings, to accept the third miss or reject it and force his antagonist to hit at least one object ball; for this purpose that antagonist's ball shall be replaced by the referee.

Darts

Originating in England, the many variations of Darts are becoming increasingly popular in the U.S., in family rooms, local bars, and in tournaments. Although the classic darts set includes a dart board with darts made of brass and feather flights, many sets are now produced for family enjoyment, with either small Velcro balls, magnets, or suction cups. No matter what your dart set looks like, all of the following games will be popular pastimes for years to come.

In the following instructions it is understood that the reader has some knowledge of the necessary equipment, and its uses, for the games. The bull's-eye of the dart board must be 5 feet 8 inches from a level ground, and the players must stand 7 feet and 9.25 inches from the board.

Cricket

The game of Cricket is a game of skill and strategy. The object of the game is to be the first player to close all of their play numbers (15-20, and the bull's-eye) and to score the most points. Any number of people can play, as long as they are divided into two equal teams.

Play begins with a single dart shot aiming for the bull's-eye, with the player closest to the bull's-eye going first. Darts must remain in the dart board to count; bounce-outs can be reshot during this initial turn. At all other times, bounce-outs are considered to be *dead shots*, and not to be reshot or scored for points.

Each player shoots three darts per turn, attempting to close his play numbers. A number is considered closed when it has been hit three times by the same player or team. All play number wedge areas count as a single score with the exception of the outer ring, which counts as a double score, and the inner ring, which counts as a triple score. The bull's-eye is divided into two sections: the inner ring (double), and the outer ring (single).

Points are scored in Cricket when the shooter has closed a play number and the opponent's play number has not yet been closed. For example, Player 1 hits the #16 wedge three times, closing that number for his team. As long as the opposition's #16 is not yet closed, any additional hits landing on 16 will score 16 points each for Player 1.

Points can be scored on any *open* play number and are worth their own face value. The bull's-eye is worth 25 points for each single and 50 points per double.

Scoring

The score is tallied on a scoreboard. The hits are recorded alongside the numbers in two columns, one for each team. The three hits are recorded as an X within a circle: one slash of the X for the first hit, the second for the second hit, and then the X is circled on the third hit. The points are recorded in two separate columns, on either side of the board.

For example, Player 2 has #16 closed and has pointed Player 1 for two additional 16's, giving the team 32 points. Player 1 has hit one #20, two #17's, and three bull's-eyes so far in this game.

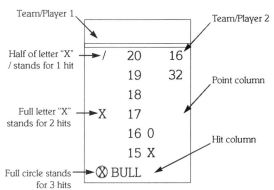

Figure 41

Team/Player 1

Team/Player 2

Half of letter "X" / stands for 1 hit

/ 20   16

19   32

18

Point column

Full letter "X" stands for 2 hits

X 17

16 0

15 X

Hit column

Full circle stands for 3 hits

⊗ BULL

Killer

Killer is a competitive game for which you need two or more players.

The object of the game is to be the only player left with points at the end of the game. You first must earn enough points to become a *killer* and then you must knock all other opponents out of the game by taking their points away.

Killer begins with a one-dart shot at the bull's-eye, but each player must use his alternate shooting hand (that is, if a player is right-handed, he must shoot the first dart with his left hand). The player closest to the bull's-eye will shoot first. Remember each shooter's play number, which corresponds to the wedge in which his first dart landed. This will be marked on the scoreboard as a point of departure.

Using his regular shooting hand, each player will try to become the killer. To become a killer you must hit your play number five times. All double and triple areas do count but you can never have more than five hits on one number at one time. For example, if Player 1 hits four 16's and he later hits a triple 16, then he would only have a total of five 16's.

Reaching killer status allows you to go after your opponents' play numbers. For every play number of your opponents' that you hit, they will lose one hit previously scored. Suppose Player 2's number is 2, and he has five points. On his turn, Player 1 hits two of Player 2's play numbers. Player 2 is no longer a killer. Player 2 then has to regain killer status in order to score more points. Once a player loses all of his points he is out of the game. The killer left is the winner.

To improve the challenge level of this game, you can make the qualifications to become a killer more difficult. For example, you can require each player to hit five triples, instead of singles, or any other combination that you can think of.

Scoring

The score is tallied on a scoreboard. Each player or team records their play number, and records their points under it.

301

The game of 301 is another popular game used in league play. With each player starting off with 301 points, the object of the game is to be the first to diminish all of your points reaching exactly the score of zero. Any number of people can play this game.

Play begins with each player shooting a single dart, with the closest to the bull's-eye going first. In order to begin scoring, each player must hit a dart into the double ring, anywhere on the board. This is called *doubling in*. On his next turn, the player shoots three darts consecutively, and the total number of points is then deducted from a 301. All darts that hit the board in either the double or triple rings are worth that multiple of the wedge.

This pattern continues until the player's score is low enough to consider *doubling out*. At this point, the player must hit another double that will bring his score to zero without going over.

For example, if a player has a score of 10 points remaining, he would have to hit a double 5 in order to win the game. The lowest score any player can have at any time is 2 points. Any score of less than 2 points is considered a *bust,* and the score is returned to the previous score before the player's last shot.

Scoring

The score is tallied on a scoreboard. Each player begins his column with a score of 301, and each score is then subtracted, moving the score closer to zero.

501

This game is nearly identical to 301, except for the following characteristics:
1. The initial score is 501 points.
2. A player can begin subtracting points immediately, including the first turn, and does not have to double in or double out at any time during the game.

Around the Clock

Not only is this a classic darts game, but it is an excellent exercise to practice with. Any number of people can play this game, playing for themselves.

Play begins with each playing shooting one dart toward the bull's-eye. The closest to the bull's-eye will shoot first. In order to begin scoring, each player must double in. The player has three tries, and needs to land one dart in each of the wedges, marked 1-20, in order. Only the darts that actually land in the correct wedges in the correct order count. Doubles and triples are included, but since there are no points in this game, they do not have extra value. The winner is the first one to complete the sequence.

Shanghai

This game is nearly identical to Around the Clock, except for the following characteristics:

1. Once a player has doubled in, the next turn is devoted solely to landing a dart in wedge #1. If he lands a dart he scores a point, and if it is in the double or triple rings, the point is multiplied accordingly. On his next turn, the player automatically begins to shoot for the #2 wedge, regardless of whether he landed a dart correctly in the previous turn.
2. *Shanghai* occurs when a player hits a single, double, and triple in the same wedge in one turn.
3. The winner of the game is the person with the most points at the end of rotation. If a player Shanghais during the game, he automatically wins.

Five's

Any number of people can play Five's, as long as they are divided into two equal teams. This is a game of concentration that also requires the greatest mathematical skills of all the darts games.

After doubling in, a player is allowed three tries per turn. The total score from his three attempts must be divisible by five in order to score. The player only scores if he succeeds, and his score is the entire amount of the throw, including doubles and triples. If one of the darts hits outside the scoring area, or bounces out of the board, then he cannot score for that round.

The winner of the game is the first player to achieve 50 points, or any other amount agreed upon by the crowd. In playing with teams, you might want to choose a higher final score for the game to last longer. Make sure the number you agree upon is divisible by five!

Part Five

Outdoor Games

Outdoor Games

Badminton

This lawn game, similar to tennis, is played with one or two players to a team. The game is played with regulation badminton rackets, net, and shuttlecocks (more often referred to as *birdies*). There is a regulation size for the court, although most people who set up badminton in their backyards play with whatever room they have.

There are three ways to score a point:

1. When the birdie lands inside the court of the nonserving team (having gone over the net).
2. When the nonserving team hits the birdie outside of the serving team's court area (or under the net).
3. If the nonserving team commits a rules violation.

Playing

To begin playing, the serving team must serve from behind their end line. The serve must be underhand. The serving team serves the birdie over the net into the court of the nonserving team. The nonserving team returns and the volley continues until one team loses the point by hitting the birdie out of the other team's area or under the net, allowing the birdie to touch the ground inside their court area, or hitting the birdie twice consecutively.

If teams are playing, the serve goes to the other side when both parties on the team have served. The players on each team rotate positions after every point.

The game is played to 15 or 20 points. Only the team serving can score a point. The nonserving team gains the serve should they win the point played, and then have the opportunity to score.

Ball Games

A variety of ball games are listed here. Many can be played in relay races, or are perfect for group activities or outdoor parties.

Preliminary Ball

This game is an organized version of an old-fashioned egg toss. Any even number of players can participate, but the best groups are between 10 and 60. You will need balls (or raw eggs) for half the number of players.

The players stand in two lines facing one another. The players of one line hold the balls. At the signal, each throws his ball to the player opposite him, who catches the ball, and throws it back. The winning team is the first to complete the entire drill without dropping the ball once.

The method of throwing and catching can be anything that you determine, but the following adds variety to the game:

Throw three times with the *right* hand, and catch with *both*
Throw three times with the *left* hand, and catch with *both*
Throw three times with the *right* hand, and catch with the *right*
Throw three times with the *left* hand, and catch with the *left*
Throw three times with the *right* hand, and catch with the *left*
Throw three times with the *left* hand, and catch with the *right*

Double Pass

Any number of players can participate, but the best groups are between ten and sixty. You will need two balls or two beanbags for this game.

The players stand in a circle, and with one taking his place in the center with the balls in his hands. Each player in the circle counts, to find out which is the fifth player at his right and which is the fifth at his left. Then the player in the center throws one ball to any player, saying at the same time, "Right! " or "Left!" The player at whom the ball has been thrown catches it, and immediately throws it to the fifth player on the correct side. This player catches the ball and returns it to the player in the center, who meanwhile has started the second ball in the same way as the first, by throwing it to any other player.

The first ball is returned to the center at about the same time the second ball is leaving, so that there is a constant passing kept up. Each player who misses the ball leaves the circle. Whoever is left with the player in the center wins.

Time Ball

Any number of players can participate, but the best groups are between ten and sixty. You will need as many balls or beanbags as there are rows of players.

The players are seated so that there are the same number of players in each row. A line is drawn about four yards from the rows of players, and another at about two yards from them.

The leader of each row takes his ball, and stands opposite his row on the far line. Then, at a given signal, the first player in each row runs toward the leader to the halfway mark. When he has reached it, the leader throws him the ball, which he catches and returns. Immediately he runs back to his seat. As soon as he is seated, the next player in the row runs to the mark, and catches the ball. So the game goes on, with the players running in turn, and each starting as soon as the previous player has seated himself.

Anyone who throws when he is not on the mark, or misses the toss from the leader makes a foul, and must repeat the play. When all have run, the leader returns to his row and seats himself with the ball in front of him. The first row that succeeds in doing this wins the game.

Bean Bags in a Circle

Any number of players can participate, but the best groups are between ten and sixty. You will need at least three beanbags for this game.

The players, standing several feet apart, form a circle. The beanbags are distributed to all players except one. Each player who holds a bag turns and tosses it to his next neighbor at the right, and instantly faces his neighbor at the left, ready to receive the next bag.

All the bags should be in motion at once. If a player fails to catch a bag, he must leave the circle. The most rapid game can be played when the number of beanbags is only one less than the number of players. The player left with the last beanbag wins.

Crisscross

Any number of players can participate, but the best groups are between four and sixty. You will need half as many beanbags as there are players for this game.

The players are divided into groups of not more than ten, and these groups each play a separate game. In each group, sides are chosen, which stand facing one another at a distance of eight or ten feet; the beanbags are given to the players of one side. The player at the right end of the beanbag row is No. 1 of that line. He begins the game by throwing his bag to the player opposite him in line, who catches it and throws it back. No. 1 of the beanbag row then throws his bag to No. 2 of the opposite line, and so on until he has come to the last player, after which he begins again with No. 1.

Meanwhile, as soon as No. 1 of the beanbag line has received his bag after his first throw, No. 2 of the same line begins throwing to No. 1 of the opposite line, and so on. In like manner, when No. 2 has received his bag after his first throw, No. 3 begins. This continues until all the players in the beanbag line are throwing, each beginning as soon as his right-hand neighbor has made his first play. Score is kept of the number of times each side drops a bag; and, when the time limit has expired, the side that has dropped the fewer bags wins.

Calling Names

Any even number of players can participate, but the best groups are between ten and sixty. You will need a beanbag and a stopwatch for this game.

The players are divided into two equal teams, standing opposite one another. One player is selected to be *It*. To begin, one player takes the beanbag, and the person who is It begins to count ten. Before It has finished counting, the player who holds the beanbag must call the name of someone on the opposite side, and throw the bag to him. The player whose name has been called catches the bag, calls the name of one of his opponents, and throws the bag back. In this way the game continues until the time limit has expired. Any player who fails to throw the bag before ten is counted, or who aims badly, or who fails to catch a bag thrown to him, must sit down. The side that has the smaller number of players seated at the end of the time limit wins the game.

Box Ball

Any number of players can participate, but the best groups are between six and twenty. You will need a box for each player; a red rubber ball, and some small stones.

The boxes are placed in a row on the floor. The players stand in a line at some distance from them, each player opposite his own box and facing it. The player at the right of the line tosses the ball into any one of the boxes. All the players scatter except the one into whose box the ball has fallen. He runs, picks up the ball, and tries to throw it so as to strike one of the other players. If he fails, he has a stone put in his box and the other players form in line as at first, and he starts the game again by tossing the ball into one of the boxes. If, however, he succeeds in hitting the player he aims at, the player who is struck is the one who receives a stone, and who starts the game again. If anyone fails in his attempt to toss the ball into a box, he also receives a stone; and the player next him in line makes the attempt. When a player has five stones in his box, he goes out of the game. The last player left is the winner.

Beanbag Target

The minimum number of players for this game is nine. You will need five beanbags for each group of nine or more players.

For every group of nine or more players three concentric circles, one, two, and three feet in diameter, are drawn on the floor; and about twenty feet from the circles a straight line is drawn to serve as the baseline. In each group a referee is appointed, and sides are chosen. The players alternate from the two sides, and each in turn stands with his toe on the baseline, and tosses the five beanbags, one after another, toward the circles. Each beanbag that falls within the inner circle counts fifteen, each within the second circle counts ten, and each within the outside circle five. The game can be made more difficult by decreasing the size of the circles or by increasing the distance between the circles and the baseline.

A board can also be substituted for the circles on the floor. The board should be about two-and-a-half by two feet, with a large hole cut near the upper left-hand corner and a small one near the lower right-hand corner. It should stand at an angle of forty-five degrees. The count, when a board is used, is fifteen for every bag thrown through the small hole, ten for every one through the large hole, and five for every bag remaining on the board at the end of the player's turn. Whichever group totals 100 points first wins.

Drop Balls

Any number of players can participate, but the best groups are between ten and sixty. You will need half a tennis ball for this game.

One player stands in the center, and the rest form a ring round him. The player in the center tosses up the ball, and calls the name of anyone of the players in the ring. The player whose name has been called tries to catch the ball before its second bounce. If he succeeds, he changes places with the player in the center. If he fails, the player in the center continues until someone does catch the ball. When a player has failed to catch the ball three times, he is out.

The game may be made more difficult by drawing a chalk circle, inside which no player may step until his name has been called. The breaking of this rule counts the same as a failure in catching the ball. Another variation is Catch Ball, where the players can run freely about the room instead of standing in a ring. The player who tosses the ball may call the name of someone who is at a considerable distance, so that great speed and alertness are required to enable the player whose name has been called to catch the ball before its second bounce.

Guess Ball

Any number of players can participate, but the best groups are between ten and twenty-five. You will need one rubber ball for this game.

All the players but one form a line. The remaining player stands several feet in front of the others, with his back toward them, and counts aloud to a number previously agreed upon. Meanwhile the ball is passed back and forth along the line.

When the given number is called, the person who then holds the ball throws it so as to strike on the back the player who stands in front. If the player is hit, he turns quickly, and tries to guess by the attitudes of the players which of them threw the ball. If he guesses correctly, the player who threw the ball changes places with him. If he does not guess correctly, he remains in front, and the game is repeated. If the player in the line fails to hit the one in front with the ball, they change places.

A variation to this game is called Ball Tag. The players are arranged in two lines facing one another, about forty feet apart. One side sends out a player who stands halfway between the lines, facing his own side. His opponents have the ball, and the game proceeds as in Guess Ball. If he guesses correctly, his side may choose a player from among the opponents to join their line; and the player in the center may continue until he fails to guess correctly, when he returns to his place, and the other side sends out a player to guess. The side having the most men at the end of the game wins.

Stool Ball

Any number of players can participate, but the best groups are between ten and thirty. You will need a tennis ball and stools, one less than the number of players participating in this game.

The stools are placed in a circle several feet from one another. A player stands in back of each stool, in any position previously agreed upon (for example, "heels together and hands on the hips"). In the center of the circle stands the bowler, who tosses the ball at any one of the players. If the player at whom the ball is tossed succeeds in batting it with his hand, all the players behind the stools change places. The bowler catches the ball or picks it up, and then throws it so as to hit any player who is out of the required position. The one who has been hit changes places with the bowler. If no one has been hit, the game is repeated with the same bowler. If, at any time, the ball is not batted back, the bowler repeats the throw until it is.

A variation may be made in the game by having the player who has been hit fall out of the game instead of having him change places with the bowler.

Target Ball

Any number of players can participate, but the best groups are between ten and twenty-five. You will need a ball for this game.

One player is chosen to be thrower. The other players are runners, and stand in a row. The thrower stands several paces distant from them toward the center of the row. At a given signal the first runner starts, runs around two sides of the room, and stops on the farther side, opposite the last player in the line of runners. During the run the thrower tries to throw the ball so as to hit the runner. If he succeeds, the one whom he has hit remains opposite the line of runners, and a second runner is called out. The game continues in this way until the thrower fails to hit the runner. The runner who has escaped then becomes thrower, and the thrower takes his place as the last runner in the line. After this the game goes on as before. When all the runners have been hit, the game ends. The thrower who has hit the greatest number of runners wins.

Dodge Ball

Any number of players can participate, but the best groups are between twenty and sixty. You will need a rubber ball for this game.

Sides A and B are chosen, and the players of A stand in a circle around those of B. The A's try to throw the ball so as to hit the B's, while the B's attempt to save themselves by running and dodging inside the circle. The A's may pass the ball among themselves as much as they choose, and leave the circle when it is necessary to regain possession of the ball; but, while they are out of the circle, they may not throw at their opponents. They must either return to the circle or throw to one of their own side. When a B has been hit, he is killed, and must stand in the circle with the A's and help them kill the remaining B's. The last B left in the circle is the winner.

Lawn Bowls

Any number of players can participate, but the best groups are between four and twenty. You will need a colored ball for each player: half the balls of one color, half of another, and a single ball of a third.

Sides are chosen, and the balls are distributed so that all the players on a side have balls of the same color. The leader of one side takes the *jack,* which is the ball of the third color, and throws it a considerable distance. The other players, alternating from the two sides, stand in turn at the place from which the leader threw, and throw their balls, trying to have them lie as near the jack as possible. When all have thrown, the side that has a ball lying nearest the jack scores.

The score is one point for each ball that lies nearer the jack than the best ball of the opposing side. Whichever team reaches 50 points first wins.

Roll Ball

Any number of players can participate, from two to twenty. You will need a ball for this game.

A line is drawn to divide the floor into two courts. On each side of this line, parallel to it, and seven or eight yards from it, is drawn a boundary line. The players divide into two teams, A and B; each team takes possession of a court, and stands behind the boundary line.

The first player of A comes forward, and takes his place on his boundary line with the ball on the line beside him. The first player from B stands opposite on his boundary line. The A player then tries to send his ball across B's boundary line by batting it with his hand or his fist. The B player tries to prevent the ball from crossing his line by running to meet it and batting it back without first catching it. If the A player fails to send the ball across the middle line, B scores a point. But, if the ball crosses the middle line and B fails to bat it back before it crosses his boundary line, A scores a point. The game continues between these two players until one of them scores a point or makes a foul. Then two other players take their places.

Fouls are (1) stopping the ball before batting it back; or (2) batting the ball so that it goes higher than the knees of the player; and (3) sending the ball so that it lodges in a piece of apparatus before it crosses the middle line. If the ball lodges in the apparatus after it has crossed that line, no foul has been made, and the player on whose side the ball is may roll it out a short distance in a direction parallel to the middle line, and from there bat it. If the ball hits the wall, it is still in play, and no foul has been made. Each foul scores one point for the opponents' side. The side that first scores thirty points wins the game.

Kick Over Ball

Any number of players can participate, but the best groups are between ten and thirty. You will need a basketball or volleyball for this game.

The players choose sides, A and B; the sides sit on the floor in two rows facing one another, with their hands on the floor behind them and their feet stretched out in front of them, leaving spaces for the ball so it can be rolled between them. A goal is marked at one end of the room, equally distant from both rows. The player who is at the farther end of the row from the goal is the scout for his side.

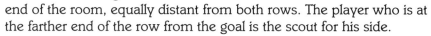

The umpire rolls the ball down the center from whichever end of the line he chooses. Each player tries, as the ball passes, to kick it so as to send it over the heads of his opponents. If a player on team A succeeds in doing this without removing his hands from the floor, the A scout runs to the goal, and then returns and sits down at the goal end of his line, in the place left vacant by the moving of the line away from the goal. Meanwhile the B scout picks up the ball, and seats himself at the goal end of his line, opposite the A scout. If the A scout is the first to get seated, his side scores two, one for the kickover and one for the goal run; but, if the B scout is the first seated, the side A scores only the one for the kickover.

Bound Ball

Any number of players can participate, but the best groups are between ten and thirty. You will need a rubber ball for this game.

A line is marked on the floor. The players divide into two equal teams, taking their positions five feet from the opposite sides of the line. The players of each team spread out, so that each individual has space to move. One player begins by throwing the ball into the midst of the players so that it will rebound from the floor as near as possible to the line. After the ball has bounced, the player who is then nearest it strikes it from above; and either he or some of the players of his side continue to strike it after each rebound, until an opportunity offers to bounce it across the line. Whoever strikes the ball when it has not rebounded from the floor, fails to strike it after the first rebound, fails to strike it from above, or permits it to roll on the ground, makes a foul. The side that first has twelve fouls scored against it loses the game.

Boundary Ball

Any number of players can participate, but the best groups are between ten and sixty. You will need a basketball for this game.

The ground or floor is marked out in a rectangle about fifteen by thirty feet, and the rectangle is divided in half by a line drawn across the center of it. Sides are chosen, and take their places in their respective fields, and stand facing one another in two rows about ten feet from the center line and parallel to it. Any player may start the game by throwing the ball into his opponents' field. His opponents catch the ball, or, if it is rolling, stop it. Their line then advances or retreats, so as to cross the spot on which the ball was caught or stopped. The catcher of the ball next throws it back to the first side, which in its turn must catch or stop it. This continues until one side succeeds in passing the ball across the outer boundary of its opponents' side, and scores a point. The winner is the team that first scores ten points.

One-Legged Football

Any number of players can participate, but the best groups are between ten and sixty. You will need a rubber ball that can be kicked easily, and a stopwatch.

At the two ends of an area are marked goal lines. The distance between them varies according to the number of players, being always large enough to allow the players to run about freely. Sides are chosen, and two captains appointed. Then the ball is put into play between the two captains. Each player stands with his right foot held in his left hand or his left foot in his right hand. With his free hand or with the foot on which he is standing, he tries to hit the ball.

The object of the game is to force the ball over the opponents' goal line. Each goal made scores one point. After the goal has been made, the ball is again put into play at the center. Whoever scores the most points in the time allotted wins.

A variation may be made in the game by having the players assume the same position as before, but hit the ball only with their free hands. Or the players may stand on both feet and run about freely, and hit the ball with either hand. The ball must in no case be thrown.

Corner Ball

Any even number of players can participate, but the best groups are between ten and thirty. You will need a basketball for this game.

A line is drawn across the center of the floor, and four goals are marked, one in each corner. The players are divided into two teams, which take their positions on opposite sides of the center line. Each team appoints two goal men, who stand in the goals on their opponents' territory, opposite their own side.

The object of the players on each team is to throw the ball to either of their own goal men. Whenever a goal man, without stepping outside his own goal, succeeds in catching a ball which has not been touched by an opponent, he scores one for his side. The opposing team tries to intercept the ball as it is thrown; if, before it is caught, they can in any way touch it without entering a goal, they score one. The players are numbered, and throw in turn, the sides alternating. A thrower must not advance beyond the middle line. A game is ended when all the players on each side have thrown. The side having the higher score wins.

Center Stride Ball

Any number of players can participate, but the best groups are between ten and sixty. You will need a large rubber ball for this game.

One player stands in the center, and the other players form a ring around him by standing with their feet apart and with each foot touching a neighbor's foot. The player in the center tries to send the ball out between the players' feet by batting it with his hand so that it will roll along the floor. The players protect themselves by batting the ball back. If any player fails to do this, and so allows the ball to pass out between his feet, he must change places with the player in the center. If the circle is large, there should be two players in the center and two balls in play.

The game may also be played with variations. The players may kick the ball instead of batting it; or they may keep the ball moving around the circle, either to the right or the left, so that the player in the center has difficulty in getting an opportunity to bat the ball out.

Medicine Ball

Any even number of players can participate, but the best groups are between six and sixty. You will need as many basketballs, medicine balls, or other large balls of uniform size and weight as there are teams for this game.

The players are divided into two or more rows, according to the number of players. The players in each row stand at equal distances from one another, and the leader of each row holds a ball. The positions of the leaders and of those the rear of the rows are marked on the floor.

At a signal each leader passes the ball between his feet to the one behind, who, in turn, passes it along between his feet to the next player, and so on to the end player, who, after making sure that the ball has touched the mark on which he stands, runs with it as quickly as possible to the leader's position in the front of the row, and immediately starts it down the line again as before.

Every time a player runs forward with the ball, the others of that row all move backward somewhat, in order to give the runner room in front and keep the spaces equal. The ball must always pass between the feet of every player in the row; and, if a crooked pass sends it out to one side, it should, as soon as possible, be brought back to the line, and started along by the player next in turn. The row that is the first to get back to its original position wins.

A variation of this game is called Arch Ball. The ball, instead of being passed between the feet, is thrown backward over the head from one player to another. Or, you can combine these two relays in the game Under and Over, where the players in each row alternate passing the ball through their legs and over their heads.

Bombardment

Any number of players can participate, but the best groups are between ten and sixty. You will need a stopwatch and half as many plastic bowling pins and medium-sized rubber balls (or beanbags) as there are players in this game.

Sides are chosen, and on each side half the players are appointed as guards and half as bowlers. A line is drawn to divide the floor into two equal fields, one for each side; and the ninepins are distributed to the guards of the two sides, who set them up in the rear of their respective battlefields. The pins should be arranged at equal distances from one another in rows in such a way that the pins of one row alternate with those of the next.

Each guard stands by his own pin to protect it, and, if it is knocked down, sets it up again. The bowlers, each armed with a ball or a beanbag, stand between the guards and the center line. The object of the game is to knock down the opponents' pins. After the play has begun, the balls may be thrown at any time until the game is ended. The bowlers are kept supplied with ammunition by the guards on their side, who pass to them all the balls that come into their territory.

Each side scores for every time that one of its opponents' pins is knocked down. No player is allowed to cross the center line. The side having the larger score when the time limit has expired is the winning side.

The game may be varied by allowing the pins to remain down when they have been knocked over. The object then would be to see which side can keep its pins from being knocked down.

Numbers

Any number of players can participate, but the best groups are between six and sixty. You will need one large rubber ball to play this game.

The players are all assigned numbers and stand together. The player who is first chosen as It throws the ball high into the air, at the same time calling one of the numbers given to the players. Thereupon all the players except the one whose number has been called run as far away from the ball as they can.

The player whose number was called tries to catch the ball as quickly as possible. As soon as he has it, he stands still, and calls out, "I got it." The rest of the players must stop running, and, without turning their heads, stand with their backs to the one who has the ball. The latter, after taking time to aim, throws the ball to hit someone on the back. The thrower can take as many steps as is his number. If he is successful at hitting someone, the one who has been struck calls out, "I was hit." The player hit then gets to throw the ball into the air and call out another number. This game continues through an allotted period of time. There are no winners or losers.

Bocce

Bocce is an Italian lawn game that is becoming very popular in the U.S. Four or more people can play. If four play, they play individually. Otherwise, the players are divided into teams of four. A playing field is created with clearly marked lines. Each team uses four bocce balls. The balls have distinctive colors and patterns so each player can identify his ball.

The Rules of the Game

1. A coin is tossed to decide which team will go first. The winner tosses the *pallino* (the smallest ball) to put it into play. The pallino must pass the midfield line and stay in bounds. If the pallino is not tossed properly by the first team, the second team tosses the pallino to put it into play.

2. The team that tosses the pallino properly then tosses their first bocce ball as close to the pallino ball as possible. The first team then steps aside and lets the second team toss their first bocce ball. Whenever a team gets their bocce ball closer to the pallino ball than the other team, they step aside and let the other team toss their bocce ball. If a team does not toss their bocce ball closer to the Pallino, then the other team continues to toss their remaining bocce balls until they get a ball closer or they have tossed all their balls. This continues until both teams have tossed all their balls.

3. Players can use their bocce ball to knock their opponent's bocce ball away from the pallino. All balls must stay in bounds at all times. If a bocce ball goes out of bounds it is removed from the game for that frame. and that frame ends. Play will resume from the opposite end of the court, with the team that originally tossed the pallino tossing it again.

4. Only one team scores in a frame. One point is given for each bocce ball that is closer to the pallino than the closest ball from the opposing team.

5. All balls must be tossed from behind the foul line. Balls may be tossed, rolled, or bounced underhanded.

6. If a player rolls the wrong color ball, simply replace it with the correct color ball when it come to rest. If a player rolls out of turn, the other team has the option to replace any moved balls to their original position or leave all balls as they are.

7. The team that reaches the agreed upon number of points for that game wins.

Croquet

Croquet is a lawn game the entire family can enjoy. An official croquet set is required, which would include eight balls, eight mallets, nine arches, and two stakes. You can also play a *half set,* consisting of four balls, four mallets, nine arches, and two stakes.

While the game can be adapted to any size lawn, the official dimensions are as follows: Length, 72 feet; width, 36 feet; corner pieces, 8 feet long; inside measurements, with a line denoting boundary of the field, 30 inches from the inside of the border. The stakes should be placed 72 feet apart; the first arch seven feet in front of the starting stake; the second, seven feet from the first; the third, fourteen feet to the right of, and one foot in advance of the second; the fourth, in line with the first and second, and twenty-two feet in advance of the second; the remaining five at the same relative distance. In the end, there will be five arches in line between the stakes, and four wing arches.

The game can be played by up to eight people, four on each side. Six or four, however, make a better game, and if there are only two players, each can use two balls.

Regardless of the number of participants, each takes a mallet and ball of the same color.

The Game

The game begins with the leader of one side placing his ball about a mallet's length in front of the starting stake, and striking it with the head of his mallet, driving it through the first arch. If he succeeds, he then tries to drive it through the next arch, and so on. As soon as he misses going through an arch his turn is over. If at his first turn he does not send his ball through the first arch, he gives his place to the next player. The leader of the other side then plays; and the others in the order of the colors on the starting stake.

The aim of each player is to drive the balls from the starting stake throughout the seven arches to the turning stake, which must be struck. This is called *pegging* or *staking*. The balls are then driven back to the starting stake.

When a player strikes his own ball so as to hit another, however lightly, he is said to *roquet* it. Having hit a ball, he can *take the Croquet*, meaning that he places his own ball against the roqueted ball so that it touches it; he then strikes it, driving one or both balls in any direction his wishes. The player can do this before proceeding further in the game, or not, at his option

As soon as the ball has gone through the first arch, the player may, with it, *croquet* (meaning to strike one's own ball when in contact with a roqueted ball) any ball that has also passed though the same arch. A player may use this opportunity to help out a fellow teammate, or derail an opponent. It is done as follows: When a ball has hit another at a distance, the player lays his own ball against the other ball so that it touches it. At this point two different methods of playing come in. One is called *tight croquet*, and the other *loose croquet*. In the former the player places his foot on his own ball, and strikes the ball with the mallet. The effect of this will be to drive the other ball in any direction the player may choose, which will be governed by whether the ball belongs to a player on his own side or not.

If the player adopts the loose croquet method, he does not place his foot on the ball, but merely places the two balls in contact and drives them both together by striking his ball. The result of this is that they fly off at different angles.

When a player has returned to the starting stake, he may either strike the peg and retire, or not strike it and be a *rover* with the privilege of traveling over the ground to assist players on his own side or damage the prospects of the opponents. Therefore, the player who reaches the turning stake first has great advantage. As soon as he begins his return journey he is able to croquet the other players, considerably impeding their progress.

The side whose balls are first driven around, and then peg the starting stake, wins the game.

The Rules of the Game

1. The players on each side are to play alternately according to the colors on the starting stake.
2. On the first play, each player may place his ball at a distance from the starting stake not exceeding the mallet handle.
3. The first stroke must be to pass the ball through the first arch
4. The ball is struck with one of the faces of the mallet head, never with its side.
5. The ball must never be pushed. A ball is considered to be well struck when the sound of the stroke is heard. A ball is pushed when the face of the mallet is allowed to rest against it, and the ball is propelled without the mallet being drawn back.
6. If a ball is struck with other than the face of the mallet, if it is pushed, or if in striking at his own ball a player hits another, it is a found stroke, and the player loses his turn; any balls disturbed shall be replaced or remain, at the option of the opposite side.
7. If, in making a stroke, a ball is driven beyond the limits of the croquet ground, it may be taken up and placed at the point where it crossed the boundary line.
8. When a ball is accidentally driven from its resting place, it is to be returned to the spot from which it was started.
9. A player can rest the head of his mallet on the ground at a distance from the ball and strike it by sharply advancing the mallet from its resting place.
10. Instead of aiming at his arch or at another ball, a player may strike his ball toward any part of the ground he pleases.
11. The balls are to pass through the course in the regular order of the arches. If a ball passes through an arch other than the arch next in its turn, or from the wrong side, it doesn't count.
12. If a ball is struck through its right arch by another ball, or is roqueted through, it is considered to have gone through its arch.
13. Any player missing the first arch takes his ball up, and when his turn comes, plays from the starting place as at the beginning of the game.

The Rules of the Game

14. A ball is considered to have passed through an arch when it passes within and beyond it to any extent, or when, if the handle of the mallet is laid across the two sides of the arch whence the ball came, the ball does not touch the handle.

15. Hitting the turning stake is equivalent in its privileges to the passing of an arch.

16. When the ball of a player hits the starting stake after he has been through all the arches, whether by his own play or by being roqueted or croqueted, he is out of the game.

17. A ball is a *rover* after going through all the arches, without hitting the starting stake.

18. A rover has liberty to croquet consecutively all the balls during anyone of his turns, but cannot croquet the same ball twice in a single turn.

19. If a person plays out of turn, and the error is discovered before the turn is completed, the ball must be placed where it stood before, as well as any balls it may have moved. If, however, the turn is completed, the player loses his next turn.

20. When a player roquets two or more balls by one stroke of the mallet, he is said to *ricochet*, and may croquet one or all, at his option.

21. As soon as a player has gone through the first arch, he is at liberty to croquet any ball that has also gone through the arch.

22. A player cannot croquet a ball that he has not roqueted.

23. A *booby* (a ball that has failed to pass though the first arch) cannot croquet another ball, nor be croqueted.

24. A player is forced to move the croqueted ball at least six inches, and cannot croquet the same ball a second time until he has passed through an arch.

25. If a player ricochets, and wishes to croquet, he must do so in the order in which the balls were roqueted, but the striker has only one additional stroke when he has croqueted.

26. If a player hits another ball that is a rover and drives it against the winning stake, he is allowed another turn, but cannot croquet the ball, as it is dead the moment it touches the stake.

27. If in tight croqueting, the ball slips from the foot and goes through the arch, or strikes the stake, the stroke does not count.

28. If, in an attempt to croquet a ball, the player's ball *flinches* (slips from beneath the player's foot), the ball on which the croquet was to be executed is free, and can be struck in its turn by its owner.

29. A player, after striking a ball, is not necessarily compelled to croquet it, but is allowed to play in any direction he pleases. He must, however, play from the place where his ball is, and not move it to another position in order to touch the ball he struck.

30. If a player croquets a ball illegally, he loses his next turn.

31. If a ball, when croqueted through its arch in a wrong direction, rolls back through the arch, it does not have to pass through the same arch in the same direction again.

The Rules of the Game

32. Should the course of a ball be interrupted by any person, the player can allow it to remain at the point where interrupted, or it can be moved to where he supposes it would have reached.

33. If a player plays with a wrong ball, he has to replace the ball and lose his turn. This is not enforced unless the error is discovered before the player's second turn.

34. If a ball is moved by a player when it should not have been touched, it must be restored to its former position.

35. The first side to have all its players pass through the arches and strike both stakes wins the game.

36. All the games shall be opened by scoring from an imaginary line through the middle wicket, and playing two balls each (not partner balls) toward the home stake. The player whose ball rests nearest the stake shall have the choice of play, using that ball.

37. A player, in each turn of play, is at liberty to roquet any ball on the ground once only before making a point.

38. A player makes a point in the game when his ball passes through an arch or hits a stake in proper play.

39. If a player makes a point, and immediately afterward roquets a ball, he must take the point and use the ball.

40. If a ball roquets another and immediately afterward makes a point, it must take the ball and reject the point.

41. A player continues to play as long as he makes a point in the game, or roquets another ball to which he is in play. A ball making two or more points at the same stroke has no additional privileges.

42. Should a player find his ball in contact with another, he may hit his own as he likes, approaching it as though the balls were separated by an inch or more.

43. A rover has the right of the roquet and consequent croquet on every ball once during each turn of play, and is subject to roquet and croquet by any ball in play. Rovers must be continued in the game until partners become rovers and go out successively. A rover that has been driven against the stake cannot be removed to make way for the next rover.

The Secrets of the Game

1. Do not play a selfish game; that is, do not be in too great a hurry to make your own arches. You may often help your side more by going back and roqueting than by running your own ball through half a dozen arches. Remember, you cannot win the game by your own ball alone.

2. Do not hesitate, either, when you can do real injury to your oppo-

nents, to abandon your own game in order to break up theirs.

3. When two or more balls are very close, it is wise to break them up before a shot is set up to defeat your play.

4. Never try a difficult stroke, however brilliant, when circumstances do not demand it. It is the safe game that wins.

Hide-and-Seek

Hide-and-Seek can be played either outdoors or indoors, depending on the number of participants, and the amount of space you have. Any number of participants can play this game.

All the players hide except for one, who is appointed as *It.* This player stands at a *home base,* turns around or closes his eyes, and counts out loud to twenty. He then opens his eyes and begins to search for the other players. If he finds a player, he chases him, and tries to tag him. The player has to run back to home base before It catches him. If he is caught he is now It and everyone else hides. If he is not caught and makes it safely back to home base, the first player is still It and must find and tag another player, and so on.

Hide the Thimble

Any number of players can participate in this indoor or outdoor game. You will need a thimble or an equally small but recognizable object to play.

All of the players are shown the thimble, or small object, at the start of the game. One of the players is chosen to hide the thimble, wherever he wants. He may either put it in some unlikely place, where it can be seen, or he may put it out of sight entirely. While he is engaged in doing this, the other players either cover their eyes or leave the room.

When the signal is given, the rest of the players begin to hunt for the thimble. The one who hid it may guide them by saying, either "Warm" when they are near the hiding place, "Warmer" as they approach it, and "Hot" when they are very near. If the players moves away from the object, the one who hid it can report, "Cool," "Cold," etc. Or, if the one who hid the thimble prefers, music may be played during the search. When anyone approaches the thimble, the music grows louder; and, as he moves away, it grows fainter.

The player who hid the object may withhold his statements altogether, but he may not purposefully mislead them. The player who first finds the thimble hides it in the next game.

Huckle Buckle Bean Stalks

In this game the thimble must be hidden where it can be seen without having to move anything, and yet where it is not likely to be noticed (for instance, on an object that is the same color). When a player sees the thimble, he must not show by his actions where it is, but must move to another part of the room as though still looking for it, and finally sit down, saying, "Huckle Buckle Bean Stalk."

The game continues until everyone is seated, when the player who first found the thimble hides it again.

Hopscotch

Figure 42

Hopscotch is a popular children's game, which only requires a few stones, a piece of chalk, and a concrete surface. While the court can be created to suit the players individual needs (and sizes) the official court is about twelve feet in length. Figure 42 shows how the court is usually drawn.

Playing

From a starting line drawn a foot or two from the beginning of the court, each player tosses a stone into box No. 1, after which the player hops on one foot into No. 1, and kicks out the stone, which is then thrown into

No. 2. The player again hops into No.1 on one foot, and then jumps and lands both feet so that one foot each is in boxes No. 1 and No. 2. The stone is kicked into No. 3, and then out, and so on, until the player fails to throw the stone into the right place, or to kick it into the right division, or lands on a line, or touches her raised foot, or steps on a line. Any of these would cause the player to lose her turn, and the next player goes. The player who can complete the board first without faltering is the winner.

In passing through boxes 4 and 5, 7 and 8, a straddle must be made, one foot being placed in each; in the others a hop only must be taken. In another popular variation, no straddling step is taken, but the player, in certain divisions, is allowed to place the stone on his foot, and so expel it from the figure at a single kick. The board can also vary in number of compartments and their arrangement.

Horseshoes

Horseshoes, or horseshoe pitching, was a very popular pastime back in the days before cars. Today, real horseshoes are pretty hard to find (originally, the stakes were made of iron, and the horseshoe was 7 1/2 inches in length, 7 inches in width, and 2 1/2 pounds in weight), you can buy a plastic or light metal set, which is easy for the entire family to play with.

Any number of participants can play this game, although only two people play against each other. More players can play together on different courts, or alternate. Each player must have two horseshoes in order to play.

The Horseshoe Court

While the court can be created to suit the players' individual needs (and sizes) the official court should cover an area of level ground at least ten feet wide and fifty feet long. The court consists of two pitchers' boxes, with a stake in the center of each. The pitcher's box is three feet square, and does not extend more than one inch above the ground level. For indoor play, the pitcher's box must not exceed six inches in height above the floor.

The pitcher's box should be filled with potter's clay or any similar substitute. The clay should be at least six inches deep at the beginning of each game, and at no time, shall surface of clay be more that one inch below the top of the box.

The stakes shall be set in the center of each pitcher's box, shall incline two inches toward each other and project ten inches above the top of the box. Where several courts are constructed, the stakes adjacent to each other shall be placed on a straight line not less than ten feet apart.

The Rules of the Game

1. No player shall make any remarks or utter any sounds within the hearing of his opponent, nor make any movement that might interfere with the opponent's playing.
2. No player shall walk across to the opposite stake and examine the position of his opponent's shoe before making his first or final pitch.
3. All players shall pitch both shoes from the pitcher's box into the opposite pitcher's box or forfeit one point to his opponent.
4. The outer edges of the pitcher's box are known as the *foul lines*.
5. In delivering the shoe into the opposite pitcher's box a player may stand anywhere inside of the foul lines. A player's toes are allowed to extend slightly over the foul line.
6. Each player, when not pitching, must remain outside and behind the pitcher's box until his opponent has finished pitching.
7. At the beginning of a game the players shall decide who has the first pitch by the toss of a shoe or a coin. The winner chooses whether or not he should go first. After the first game, the loser of the preceding game pitches first.
8. The shoe is considered pitched as soon as it leaves the player's hand.
9. A shoe pitched while the player is standing outside the foul lines is foul.
10. If a shoe first strikes outside of the foul lines or any part of the pitcher's box before entering the pitcher's box, it is considered a foul.
11. Foul shoes are removed from the pitcher's box at the request of the opponent, and are not scored or credited.
12. No player shall touch his own or his opponent's shoes after they have been pitched, until the final decision has been rendered as to its scoring value. Failure to comply with this rule shall result in both shoes of the offender being declared foul and his opponent shall be entitled to as many points as the position of his shoes at the stake should warrant.
13. A *ringer* shall be a shoe that encircles the stake far enough to permit a straight edge to touch both heels simultaneously.
14. Whenever a player knocks off his own or opponent's ringer, such knocked off ringers lose their scoring value and the player making the ringer is credited with a ringer.
15. If a player knocks on one of his own or his opponent's shoes from a nonringer position to a ringer position the changed shoe has scoring value.
16. When a thrown shoe moves a shoe already at the stake all shoes are counted in their new positions.
17. A regulation game consists of fifty points. Each game is divided into innings and each player pitching two shoes constitutes an inning.
18. All shoes shall be within six inches of the stake to score. The closest shoe to the stake scores one point. Two shoes closer than an opponent's score two points. One ringer scores three points. Two ringers score six points. One ringer and the

The Rules of the Game

closest shoe of same player, scores four points. If a player has two ringers and his opponent one, the player having two ringers scores three points. No points are scored for ties.

19. If each player has a ringer the the next closest shoe, if within six inches of the stake, shall score. If each player has a double ringer, both double ringers are canceled and no points scored. In case there is a tie of all four shoes, no score shall be recorded and the player who pitched last is entitled to pitch first on the next throw.

20. Any shoe leaning against the stake in a tilted position shall have no advantage over a shoe lying flat on the ground against the stake. All such tosses are considered ties. If a player has a shoe leaning against the stake it shall count only as the closest shoe.

21. All shoes shall be scored and announced only in their final position after all scores have been pitched.

VaRiATiONS

Three-Handed Games

In three-handed games when two of the players each have a ringer and the third player no ringer, the two players having ringers score their closest shoe, while the third player is out of this play. If all three players each have a ringer, the one having his next shoe closest to the stake scores.

Kickball

This game is an outdoor game played by two teams of at least nine players each (there can be fewer players, if necessary). Kickball is played in a manner similar to baseball, but is much easier, especially for younger players.

The Game

The players are arranged as in baseball: three in the outfield, three in the infield, one pitcher, and one catcher. The first team up bats, or kicks, the ball. The pitcher rolls the ball toward the first player, who kicks it as hard and as far as he can. He then tries to run to first base, and if he can go farther he may; if not he stays at first. At the same time the team in the field tries to catch the ball and get it to the base the player is trying to get to, and tries to tag him out. If the team succeeds in tagging him out, he has gotten an out for his team and returns to the bench. Each team gets three outs before they switch, the team that was in the field now kicks and the other team goes to the field.

The game usually has nine innings. The team with the highest score wins.

Relay Races

Relay races are popular outdoor games, and can easily be organized by children or adults. The games listed here are the classic relays of all time.

Tag the Wall Relay Race

Any number of players can participate, but the best groups are between ten and sixty participants. The instructions given are for an indoor game, but can easily be converted to outdoors, if there is a visible goal to run toward.

The players are divided into equal rows. One player give the signal, and the first player in each row runs forward to touch the wall, and immediately returns to the end of the row, and seats himself. The next player on his team does the same thing. The first row to complete the race wins.

Relay Flag Races

Any number of players can participate, but the best groups are between ten and sixty participants. You will need chalk and a variety of flags for this game. If you can find lots of different-colored flags, or U.S. state flags, that would be best.

Two long chalk lines are drawn to create a starting point and an ending point, with five to ten yards between them. The participants are divided into rows that each have the same number of players. A flag is given to the first in each row. The rows are lined up behind the starting line.

At the signal, the player holding the flag turns around, runs to the farther chalk line, turns around, and runs back to his starting point. Then the second player in his row takes the flag as quickly as possible, and runs with it, and so on. The row that finishes first wins.

The race may be varied by having the players jump or hop down the course, or by having them stop halfway and perform definite tasks, such as picking up and replacing beans or stones or performing some gymnastic exercise.

Tag

There are hundreds of versions of Tag, a universally enjoyed children's game. Some are more complicated than others. Any number can participate in any game of Tag, but the best games are between six and sixty.

In the classic version, one player is chosen to be It. He chases the other players, and tries to tag one of them. If he succeeds, the one who has been tagged becomes It.

Secret Tag

This game is played without telling who is It. All the players pretend to tag; but any player who is not It whispers to the one whom he tags, "I am not It," while the one who is It must say, "I am It."

Stoop Tag

In this game no player may be tagged while he is in a stooping position. You can create a rule and limit the number of times that a player may be allowed to stoop. After a player has stooped the allotted number of times, he can escape only by running. A further variation may be created by substituting any gymnastic position for stooping.

Goss Tag

If any player runs between the one who is It and the one who is pursued, the latter cannot be tagged, but the one who has crossed between must be chased instead. This brings cooperation into the game.

Iron Tag

A player may not be tagged when he is touching iron with his hand. The game may be varied by substituting wood or stone for iron, or by requiring that the object be touched in some special way (with the elbow, or the foot, or with four fingers at once, etc.).

Japanese Tag

The one who has been tagged must place his right hand on the spot where he has been touched, whether it is on his arm, his chest, his back, or his ankle. With his hand in that position he must chase the other players until he has tagged one of them.

Clasp Tag

The one who is It clasps his hands behind his back and keeps them there until he has tagged one of the other players with them.

Eenie Weenie Coxie Wanie

The one who is It clasps his hands in front of him, and repeats the words "Eenie, Weenie, Coxie, Wanie," and then begins to chase the other players. He can tag only with his clasped hands. The first player whom he tags he takes as his partner. With his right hand he clasps his partner's left hand, they repeat the words "Eenie, Weenie, Coxie, Wanie," and then chase the other players, and tag as many as possible with their clasped hands. Every player who is once tagged remains It for the rest of the game. After being tagged, the player must stand still and repeat the required words before he begins to pursue the other players. If he did not become a partner, he must catch a partner for himself.

Line Tag

The players stand in three or more lines, near enough together to join hands. At the beginning of the game they all face in one direction. Then, by joining hands, they make aisles between the lines. The first player in the first line runs, tags someone on the back, and continues to run between the lines. The one who has been tagged pursues. Suddenly the leader calls out, "Right face!" or "Left face!" All the players then drop hands, face in the new direction, and join hands again. This creates new aisles at right angles with the aisles previously formed, and the runners must change their course accordingly. The chase continues until the first player has been tagged or the time limit has expired. Then two more players take their places. The direction of the aisles should be changed frequently and rapidly.

Inside Tag

A circle is created in the front of the room to serve as goal. One player is chosen to be It, and stands ten feet from the goal. The other players sit on the floor. The one who is It calls the name of a player. That person tries to run, pass through the goal, and return to his spot on the floor without being tagged. The one who is It also passes through the goal, and then pursues the runner. If he succeeds in tagging him, he calls another name. If he does not, the player who has escaped becomes It.

Exchange Tag

Two children are chosen as sheriffs and stand in front of the group. The other players are seated. Two of those who are seated signal to each other to exchange seats. As they run to do so, the sheriffs try to catch them. Whoever is caught is a prisoner and sits apart from the others. Any number of players may exchange seats at the same time; but no one, even to escape being caught, may take any seat except the one for which he signaled.

Pickadill

This is a kind of tag played during the winter. A large circle is made in the snow, with paths; if there are many players, two circles are made. There is one person selected to be It for each circle, and the center of the circles is the place of safety.

Tether Ball

Each player stands on one side of the pole. The object of the game is for each player to wrap the ball around the pole by keeping the ball moving one way. The adversary tries simultaneously to block the ball and move it the other way. It does not matter whether you prefer to hit the ball in a clockwise or counterclockwise motion.

Players move the ball by hitting it with their hands. The players decide before the beginning of the game whether the ball can be hit with two hands or one. The winner of the game is the one who wraps the ball around the pole the most times during an agreed-upon period.

Volleyball

Volleyball is a popular outdoor game that can be adapted to either the beach or the backyard. Any even number of people can play, from two to eighteen. You'll need a volleyball net, a stopwatch, and a volleyball. While there are official regulations for both beach volleyball and lawn volleyball, these instructions should suffice for most amateur games.

A court is marked off seventeen by forty feet for two players, but larger if there are more. You will need about ten square feet for each player. A net is stretched to divide the court in half lengthwise. The top line of the net should be six feet six inches above the floor. If the net is stretched between poles, the poles must be at least one foot outside the foul lines.

The object of the game is to score points, by making the opposing team miss the ball and have it land on the ground. The ball must be kept in motion, back and forth above the net, by striking it with the open hand. At no time can the ball go outside the court, or touch the floor.

A member of one team starts the game by standing with one foot on the back line of the court and with the other foot behind the line, usually standing in the right corner of the court. From there the player serves the ball by tossing it lightly from one hand and batting it with the palm of the other hand. Two trials are allowed to send it into the opponents' court. If a ball in service strikes the net or fails to enter the opponents' court after two tries, the opposing sides get to serve. A player continues serving until he makes two faults in succession during service or until his side does not return the ball.

In returning, as well as in serving the ball, any number of players on the same side may strike the ball to send it across the net; but no player may strike if more than twice in succession. The volleying of the ball continues until one side fails to return it or until it touches the floor.

A ball that hits the net, if not a service ball, counts as a failure in returning. If the ball hits the net during service, it is dead, and counts as a trial serve. If any player touches the net while playing, the ball is out of play, and a point is scored for the opposite side. If any player catches or holds the ball for an instant, that also scores a point for the opposite side.

If the ball strikes any object except the floor and bounces back into the court, it is still in play. Each good service unreturned scores one point for the serving side, and the serving side also scores whenever the opponents fail to return a ball that is in play. A side only scores when serving. An inning is finished when each player has served in turn, and a game consists of any number of innings previously agreed upon.

THAT'S QUITE A RETURN HE'S GOT THERE

Part Six

Indoor Games

Indoor Games

Jacks

Jacks is a popular game of skill and coordination. It can be played alone or with any number of players. You will need a set of twelve jacks, which are small six-legged objects, usually made of either metal or plastic, and a very small rubber ball. Jacks is usually played on a smooth surface or floor. While these are the most general rules, players can vary the game by making up their own rules and creating new games.

To play, gather all of the jacks into the palm of your hand and toss them across the floor. A good toss would separate all the jacks so that they can easily be picked up one at a time. Once the jacks are on the floor, the player begins collecting them. This is done by throwing the ball up, and with the same hand scooping up one jack while the ball bounces. The ball is only allowed to bounce once, and may be caught before it bounces at all. The ball is thrown, the jack is caught, and the ball is caught all by the same hand. The captured jack is then placed in the opposite hand. This is repeated until all the jacks are picked up.

The player then tosses the jacks again. This time, he will pick up two jacks at a time. The game continues in order, each player completing a round by picking up the appropriate number of jacks. For odd numbers, the leftover jack is picked up last. A player continues from one round to the next until he loses his turn.

While the player is in the process of picking up jacks, none of the other jacks can be disturbed. A player loses his turn if he fails to catch the ball, or if he disturbs the other jacks. Once the player has lost his turn, the jacks are tossed again by the next player, and so on. The winner of the game is the first to pick up all twelve jacks in one swoop.

Marbles

ROLLIN' ROLLIN' ROLLIN'

The various marbles games have been played for centuries. There are two principle styles of play. The first consists of striking marbles out of a ring by shooting from a line; the second is played by making the tour of a series of holes, or goals, made specifically for the game. Any number of participants can play these games, unless otherwise specified.

The best method of shooting a marble is to bend the thumb at the first joint and grasp it firmly with the middle finger. Place the marble above the thumb and hold it in position with the first finger, then suddenly, having taken good aim, let go of the thumb and the marble will be shot forward.

Bounce Eye

A circle, about a foot in diameter, is drawn on the ground; every player adds a marble into the center of the circle, creating a pool.

The first player takes a marble and aims it at the center of the pool. He tries to scatter as many marbles as he can outside the ring; those that land outside the ring are then picked up and kept by the shooter. If he does not succeed in moving any marbles outside the ring, the one he shot with must remain in the pool.

When all the marbles are removed from the pool, the game is over. Whoever holds the most marbles at that time wins.

Die Shot

A marble is slightly ground down on two sides so that it will lie flat. A die is placed on top of it. A die keeper is appointed and holds extra marbles to be used as prizes.

The players, each in turn, aim at the marble from a standing position, attempting to knock the die off the top of it. If they succeed, they receive a marble from the die keeper; if they fail, they must pay him a marble. Whoever holds the most marbles after an allotted period of time wins.

Handers

A small hole is made in the ground about a foot from a wall or background of any kind. The players decide the order of play by each rolling a marble toward the hole: The player closest goes first, the next closest goes second, and so on.

The first player then takes all of the marbles and tosses them toward the hole. He claims as many as fall in; any that rebound out of the hole do not count. Then the next player takes the remaining marbles and tries to toss them into the hole, and so on. When all of the marbles have been tossed, whoever is holding the most marbles wins.

Bounce About

This game cannot be played by more than four players, each playing with only one marble.

The first player throws down his marble, and the second pitches his marble at the first. If he hits it, the first player pays the second a marble, but not the one struck on the ground.

The third player then attempts to hit either of the two marbles on the ground, collecting payment from whomever he hits. Whoever holds the most marbles after an allotted period of time wins.

Three Holes

Three holes are made in the ground, each of them being about an inch deep and two inches in diameter. They should be about a yard apart in a straight line, and clearly numbered. A starting line is fixed two yards from the nearest hole.

The first player aims for hole #1. If his marble lands in the hole, each of the other players must give him a marble. He then tries for hole #2, and so on. Each success entitles him to another shot.

If the first player fails to make the first hole, his marble must remain on the ground. On each successive turn the rest of the players are then allowed one chance to try to sink it in the correct hole using one of their marbles, as well as taking their own turn with another marble. Whoever makes the most holes wins.

One Hole

A round hole is dug into the ground, or a baseball cap is used.

Each player takes ten marbles in his hand and tries to throw all of

them into the hole or cap at the same time. He reclaims all that go in, but leaves those that fall outside where they drop.

The players throw in turn; any player who gets the whole ten marbles into the cap takes the marbles that are lying around it, and is automatically the winner. Otherwise, whoever holds the most marbles after an allotted period of time wins.

Knock Out

A lines is drawn two yards from a wall.

The first player takes a marble and rolls it against the wall, the second follows suit and so on. Any player whose marble strikes another may claim all the marbles on the ground. If a marble rolls over the line it must be replaced on the line at the point it crossed over. Whoever holds the most marbles after an allotted period of time wins.

Long Taw

This game is for two players only.

The first player places a marble on the ground. The second player places another two yards off in a line with the first marble.

The first player, standing another two yards from both marbles, then shoots a third marble at either of the first two. If he hits the marble nearest to him, he pockets it and gets to shoot at the second marble, which, if he hits, he may also pocket. Then, two more marbles are set and the second player takes a turn.

If the first player misses, the second player may aim at all three marbles on the ground. Whoever holds the most marbles after an allotted period of time wins.

Picking the Plums

Two straight lines are drawn parallel to each other, from four to eight feet apart. Each player places two or three marbles, which are called *plums*, on one of the lines, leaving about an inch between them.

The players in turn kneel at the other line and shoot at the plums, those hit being kept by the successful shooter. A second shot is not allowed until everyone has one turn. If a player fails to hit a plum, he must add one marble to the row to be shot at, but may pick up his shooting marble. Whoever holds the most marbles after an allotted period of time wins.

Ring Taw

A circle is drawn on the ground; each player puts an agreed-upon number of marbles into the circle, as close as possible but at equal distances from one another. Around this ring another is drawn, about six or seven feet away. This second circle is called the *taw line*.

The first player starts from any point on the taw line, and shoots at the marbles in the inner circle; if he knocks one out and it goes outside the larger ring, he takes it and may shoot again from the place where the marble he originally shot with stops, and may continue to shoot until he fails to knock a marble out.

When a player fails to knock a marble from the circle, his own marble must remain where it stops, unless it rolls out of the outer circle, in which case he may pick it up. The second player goes, and so on, one succeeding the other as soon as the previous player fails to knock a marble out of the ring.

The marbles that have been shot and which remain in either of the rings are treated in the same way as the marbles originally put into the small ring. The game goes on until both rings are clear. Whoever holds the most marbles at that point wins.

Pyramids

A ring, a foot in diameter, is drawn on the ground, and in the center three marbles are placed, arranged in a triangle, with a fourth on top of them, forming a pyramid.

Each player in turn tries to knock out one of these marbles from the ring, any of which become the property of the shooter, who also retains the marble he shot with, even if it remains in the ring. If his marble stops in the ring without knocking another out, it remains in the circle for the next player to retrieve. Whoever holds the most marbles after an allotted period of time wins.

Bridge Board

Figure 43

A bridge can be created from a narrow piece of board in which nine arches have been cut out. The arches should be about an inch in height and width. Numbers are placed over the arches, but not in consecutive order.

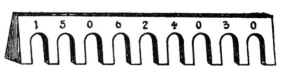

One player is appointed the bridge keeper, and the others take turns aiming at the bridge. If a marble passes under one of the arches, the player claims the number of marbles marked over it from the bridge keeper. If a player fails to shoot through an arch, one marble must be paid to the bridge keeper.

The bridge keeper should change after every round. Whoever holds the most marbles after an allotted period of time wins.

Pickup Sticks

Pickup Sticks is another classic family game. Any number of people can play this game, or it can be played alone. You will need a set of pickup sticks to play, or you can create your own set by finding a large number of identical long objects, such as pencils or pens. This game is usually played on a smooth surface or floor. While these are the most general rules, players can vary the game by making up their own rules.

The object of the game is to pick up all of the sticks, one at a time, without disturbing the rest. In this way, the game is very similar to Jacks. However, in Pickup Sticks you are allowed a tool to separate the sticks. The tool is one stick that is slightly different from the rest, either in color or weight.

On each player's turn, gather the sticks in one hand so that they are perpendicular to the playing surface. The hand is then released, causing the sticks to spread out into a larger circle, although they will be over-lapping. Then, the first player tries to pick up one stick at a time without disturbing the rest. He may pick up the sticks with one hand, or use the tool to lift the stick, and then retrieve it with his other hand. The tool can be used in any way imaginable, as long as the rest of the sticks are not disturbed. The sticks retrieved can be put aside during the turn.

A player loses his turn if he fails to pick up a stick, or disturbs the others. The players rotate turns, each time laying out the sticks for a new round. The winner of the game is the first to pick up all the sticks on one turn.

Part Seven

Party Games

Party Games

Blind Man's Buff

This version, and the variations that follow, are all favorite party games. Any number of people can participate, but the best games are with between ten and sixty players. You will need a handkerchief for this game.

One player is blindfolded and turned around three times in the center of the room. He then tries to catch one of the other players. When he has succeeded, he must guess whom he has caught. Then, the player who has been caught is blindfolded. If he does not guess correctly, he must catch another player.

French Blind Man's Buff

Any number of people can participate, but the best games are with between ten and thirty players. You will need a handkerchief for this game.

All the players are numbered, and one player is blindfolded. The others, standing some distance apart, form a ring about him. The blindfolded player calls out two numbers, and the players having these numbers change places at once. While they are changing, the blindfolded player tries to catch one of them. If he succeeds, he takes the place of the player he has caught, and that player goes in the center, and is blindfolded in turn.

French Blind Man's Buff at a Party

Any number of people can participate, but the best games are with between ten and sixty players. You will need a handkerchief for this game.

One player is blindfolded, and stands in front of the group. The rest are seated. All of the players are numbered. The one who is blindfolded calls two of their numbers; the players whose numbers have been called stand up immediately, and answer, "Here!" Two more numbers are called, and the players so designated do the same as the first two did. The one who is blindfolded then calls out, "Here I Go." At once the players who are standing change places according to the order in which they were called, the first two changing with each other, and the second two with each other. As they change, they pass by the one who is blindfolded, so he may have a chance to catch them. If he succeeds, the one who has been caught changes places with him.

Blind Man's Buff with a Wand

Any number of people can participate, but the best games are with between ten and thirty players. You will need a handkerchief and a cane for this game.

One player is blindfolded, and given the cane. The other players join hands, and dance around him until he taps three times. Immediately the other players stop. The blindfolded player points with the cane at someone in the ring. That person must take the end of the cane, and, holding it, must answer any three questions the blindfolded player asks. The player who answers may, however, disguise his voice. If the blindfolded player succeeds in guessing who is speaking, the two players change places.

A variation to this game is called Animal Blind Man's Buff. Instead of asking questions, the blind man tells the player to imitate some animal.

Bobbing for Apples

Both of these games can be played with any kind of apples, but candied or caramel apples make for more of a mess, which is always more fun!

The apples are hung by strings tied to their stems, just high enough that the players must jump to catch them with their mouths. The players' hands are tied behind their backs. The first player to eat his entire apple wins.

VaRiATiON

Diving for Apples

A tub is partly filled with water, and apples are thrown in. The object is for the players to dive in and try to retrieve the apples with their mouths, no hands allowed. Each player keeps the apple he rescues from the water.

Cat and Rat

This party game can be played by any number of players, but between ten and thirty players make for the best game.

One player is chosen to be the cat and another to be the rat. The rest of the players join hands and form a ring, with the cat on the outside and the rat in the center. The cat tries to catch the rat. The players favor the rat, and allow him to run in and out of the circle under their clasped hands; but they try to prevent the cat from catching him by lowering or raising their hands, whichever is necessary. When the rat is caught, he joins the circle; the cat becomes rat, and chooses a new cat from the players.

Cushion Dance

Cushion Dance requires six to thirty players. You will need half as many cushions (or pillows) as there are participants for this game.

The cushions are set upright in a circle on the floor, and the players join hands and form a ring around them. The circle formed by the cushions should be nearly as large as the ring formed by the players, and the cushions may be placed at a considerable distance apart. The players in the ring dance around; and each player, as he dances, tries to make his neighbors knock over the cushions while he avoids knocking over any himself. The penalty for knocking over a cushion or for letting go of hands is to go out of the game. If it is preferred, upright bowling pins may be substituted for the cushions.

A variation to this game is called Slow Poison. The cushions are placed a foot or more apart in a group, and the players join hands and form a ring around them. Instead of dancing, each player tries to pull or push his neighbors into the center of the ring, so as to make them knock down the cushions. At the same time he tries to avoid knocking down any himself. The penalty for knocking down a cushion or for letting go of hands to avoid doing so is to go out of the game. As in Cushion Dance, bowling pins may be substituted for the cushions.

Duck Duck Goose

This party game can be played by any number of players, but more than ten make for the best game.

All players sit in a circle and one player is chosen to be It. The player who is It taps every person on the head, and as he passes calls out, "Duck." He then picks one random person and taps their head and says, "Goose." That person then has to get up and chase the tapper around the circle. The person who is It has to run around the circle, and get back into the spot where he tapped the person goose. If he is successful he sits in that spot and the goose is now It. He then goes around the circle, just as before, and the game continues.

If anyone is unsuccessful in making it back to the open spot in the circle and is caught by the goose, he is sent into the middle of the circle, called the *pickle jar*. He has to sit there until someone else doesn't make it around the circle in time, at which point they trade places.

Marco Polo

This game is often played in a swimming pool, but could be played on land as well. It requires three or more players.

One person is It and he closes his eyes and walks around the pool. He then calls out, "Marco," and the people he is in pursuit of call out, "Polo." The object is for the person who is It to tag the other players as he tries to find them by the closeness of their voice, when they answer, "Polo." The player who is It must keep his eyes shut. The player who is first tagged becomes It.

Mother May I

This popular party game is best played with ten or more players.

One player is selected to be the Mother. The object of this game is to tag the Mother; once you've done this you become the Mother and everyone else tries to tag you.

The Mother stands in front of a line of players about fifty yards away. The Mother calls out one of the player's names, and he answers, "Yes, Mother." The Mother then asks them to do a specific task, for example, "Take three giant steps forward." At this time the player has to ask the Mother if he can do it by responding, "Mother, may I?" The Mother then either answers, "Yes, you may," and the task is carried out, or, "No, you may not," and the player stays where he is.

The Mother then has to keep track of all the players. Once she forgets where they are, she will surely lose her position.

Musical Chairs

This party game can be played by any number of players, but more than ten make for the best game. You will need chairs or stools (one less than the number of players), and a tape recorder or radio that can be easily turned on and off.

For a small group, the chairs are placed in a line, facing alternately right and left. For a larger group, place the chairs in a giant circle, facing out, or facing right and left. One player or supervisor is appointed to control the music.

The game begins when the music is turned on. The players march around the line of chairs. Suddenly the music stops, and the players all try to seat themselves. The one who fails to get a seat takes one chair away, and goes out of the game. The game continues until only one player is left, who is the winner.

Observation

This party game is perfect for large groups, especially from ten to sixty players. You will need twenty different small- to medium-sized objects, and enough paper and pencils for each player.

The objects are placed on the table. Each player in turn looks at them for half a minute, and then goes to a seat facing away from the table, and writes down the names of all the objects he can remember in the allotted time. The players can sit together to write down their answers, but they cannot compare notes or talk until time has run out.

The one who remembers the greatest number correctly wins the game.

Piñata

Part of the traditional Mexican birthday celebration, the piñata is a game for the birthday boy or girl to play, and all of the guests to enjoy. A piñata is always made out of papier-mâché, but the style can vary greatly. Sometimes it is made to look like an animal, or a hat, or a birthday cake. Piñatas are always beautifully decorated and stuffed with candy. Any number of players can play.

The piñata is hung, from the ceiling, about a foot out of the player's reach. The player is given a stick, blindfolded, and spun around. The player then has to figure out where the piñata is, and aim his stick in that direction. The player swings at the piñata while the rest of the crowd cheers him on, giving him directions. When he finally breaks the piñata, the candy comes out, and all of the guests rush to get their share.

Another variation of this game is to allow many players to take turns. Each player is individually blindfolded, and allowed to swing at the piñata three times. The player to break open the piñata is the winner.

Pin the Tail on the Donkey

This party game can be played by any number of players. For this game you will need Scotch tape or thumbtacks, one picture of a donkey, and several cutout tails that are either numbered or colored, one for each player.

The picture of the donkey is hung on the wall.
Each player gets one paper tail with a tack or tape attached to the top.

The player is blindfolded and spun around several times, and then faced in the direction of the donkey. The player tries to walk toward it and pin the tail closest to the donkey's behind. This is repeated by all the players. The player who gets his tail closest to where it belongs on the donkey's behind is the winner.

Red Light, Green Light

This is an outdoor party game that is best suited for ten or more players.

One player is selected to be the *traffic light*. This person stands at the front of a line about fifty yards away from the other players. The object of the game is to tag the traffic light. The person who makes the tag then becomes the traffic light for the next round.

The players are lined up and the traffic light turns with his back to the players. The traffic light begins counting out loud, at any speed that he wants, "Red light, Green light, one, two, three." After that he quickly turns around. While the traffic light is counting, the rest of the players try to run up and tag him. But as soon as he turns around, everyone has to freeze. If the traffic light catches another player moving, that player must return to the starting line.

Red Rover

This game is best suited for large groups, with no less than twenty players.

The players are divided equally into two teams. Each team stands at opposite ends of a field, holding hands to form a wall. One team begins the game by shouting, "Red Rover, Red Rover, send _____ right over," (using the name of someone on the other team).

That person must run toward the opposing team and try to break through the wall. If he succeeds in breaking through, he goes back to his team, and it is their turn to call someone over. If he does not succeed, he changes sides and is added to the team that he tried to break through, becoming a part of the wall. That team then gets another turn.

In the end, the team that captures all the players wins.

Scavenger Hunt

This game can be played by any number of participants. If there are more than ten players, they can be divided into teams of equal number.

This party game needs to be prepared for in advance; you will need several small objects that can easily be hidden, and paper and pens.

Each player or team is given a list of items. The object of the game is to find the items in the time allotted. The first team to make it back to the start with either the items, or a list of their locations, wins.

This game can be developed to varying degrees of difficulty. For younger players, the lists can be made of the exact names of the objects to find. For older players, clues can be given instead, so that each player or team has to first figure out the clue, and then find the objects. The lists can be thematic or random, depending on the party and your own creativity.

Simon Says

This classic party game is perfect for any number of players, but between ten and sixty make for the best game.

All the players stand in long lines, except for one selected player, or parent, who is chosen to be Simon. Simon will instruct the rest of the players to perform certain physical movements, and the players will follow him with that movement, until he suggests another. However, Simon must say, "Simon says," before naming the movement in order for the rest of the players to follow along. If, however, Simon omits saying "Simon says," in the command, the rest of the players do not perform the movement, even if Simon is demonstrating it.

Any player who fails to obey Simon's commands promptly, or who obeys commands that are not given by Simon, must leave the game. The last player left in the group is the winner.

Another variation of this game is called Ducks Fly. The leader of the game calls out, "Ducks fly," and raises his arms to represent flying. The rest of the players imitate him. He continues, naming any animals he chooses instead of ducks. As long as he names an animal that can fly, the players continue to imitate him; but if he names one that cannot fly, for example, he calls out, "Cats fly," the players remain motionless.

Any player who fails to obey the leader's commands promptly, or who obeys commands that are not given, must go out of the game. The last player left in the group is the winner.

Part Eight

Brain Teasers

DON'T BE AFRAID JIMMY, DADDY JUST TAKES PLAYING HANGMAN VERY SERIOUSLY

Brain Teasers

Charades

Charades is a classic game for adults and children. Charades can be altered to be difficult or simple, depending on the participants. To play, you will need some paper, a pen, and a stopwatch. Any number of people can participate, either playing alone or in teams. The object of the game is to guess specific actions that are being presented to you.

Before playing, one individual is appointed the referee. This person does not participate in the game, but is responsible for writing down a number of topics on small pieces of paper, resolving disputes, and watching the clock. The topics can be either a noun or a verb. They could be thematic, for example, a group of songs or movies, celebrities, actions, or a random mix of all of the above.

If players are playing as individuals, each player receives a piece of paper from the referee containing one idea. The game begins with the referee choosing one player to go first. That player must convey to the other players the idea that was on his paper, within the time allotted. The player acts out either the entire idea, or parts of it. At no time is he allowed to utter a word, sign specific letters, or use any physical props to get his idea across. The player who guesses what the first player is trying to convey takes the next turn. If time runs out and no one has guessed correctly, the player to the left of the first player goes, and so on. In individual play, there are no winners or losers.

If teams are playing, the referee distributes one idea to each member of every team, and the referee chooses which team shall go first. One player on each team takes a turn, and acts out his idea for the rest of his team only. If his team guesses correctly, another player on the same team takes the next turn, and so on. If the team does not guess correctly within the allotted time, the other team to the left of the first team takes the next turn. In team play, the first team in which all of the players have taken a turn is the winner.

In team play, the teams can decide among themselves specific pantomimes that can be used as clues to guess the idea. The symbols can represent a book, a movie, a song, or an action word, etc. However, once the game begins, the team cannot converse at all, especially about what the previously agreed-upon symbols mean.

VaRiATiONS

Charades for Kids

This is a great game for parties, or just for the family. Any number of players can participate. Each person can play individually, or players can divide themselves into teams, each one of no more than five players. The number of teams is not important.

One person is appointed the leader to begin the game. The leader asks the first team, "What did you see?" After a brief consultation with the team, the team answers using the mention of some physical action that the entire team can imitate. They say, for instance, "I saw a horse trotting down the street"; and then the entire team trots around the room, and back to place. The leader then asks the question of the rest of the teams, and the game is repeated each time.

If a team can't think of a response, the leader can provide one. The answers should be of as great variety and originality as possible. The following are suggested:

"I saw a butterfly flying over the flower bed."
"I saw a man walking up the street, playing a trombone."
"I saw a boy running."
"I saw a drum major leading a band."
"I saw a bird flying."
"I saw a lame chicken hopping."
"I saw a mommy caring for a baby."

Dots

Figure 44

Dots is a thinking game for between two and four people. However, it is best played with just two. For this game you will need blank paper, and as many pens as there are players. The object of the game is to connect the lines drawn to create squares; the player who has created the greatest number of squares wins the game.

To begin, a board is created on the blank paper. Draw horizontal and vertical lines of small dots, evenly spaced. A very quick game would consist of ten dots across and ten dots down. You can make the board as large or small as you would like, depending on the level of play and the number of players.

Once the board is created, each player takes a turn drawing one line at a time, connecting two dots. The dots can be connected horizontally or vertically, never diagonally. As soon as a player finishes a square, he places his initial inside the square, and gets another turn, and so on, until he can no longer create a square with the addition of one line.

Figure 45

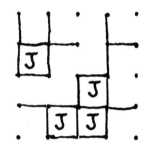

There are two strategies for Dots: The first is to block the opponents from creating a square. The second is to configure the board so that many squares can be created from the addition of one line.

Geography

Geography is the perfect family game for long drives, or quiet summer nights. Any number of people can participate in the game. The rules listed here are for the most general game, but you can add or restrict them depending on the level of play.

One player begins the game by naming a geographical reference, either a town, city, state, country, body of water, mountain range, etc. The player to the left of the first player then continues, and must name another geographical reference that begins with the last letter from the first reference. For example, if the first player says, "Oklahoma," the next player must name a state that begins with A, such as "Alabama."

The game continues with each player adding on to the last player's reference. However, no reference can be repeated: each player must keep a mental list of what has been listed. If a player cannot think of a reference, or repeats one that has already been mentioned, he is out of the game. The last player to remain in the game is the winner.

Hangman

Hangman is another popular brain teaser created especially for two players. You will need blank paper and a pen to play this game.

The first player thinks of any word imaginable. It must be a real word, and the player must know that the other player is familiar with the word and its spelling. He draws out the number of blank spaces necessary to spell out the word. Next, he draws the following diagram, which represents a gallows and a noose.

Figure 46

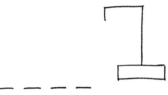

The game begins when the opponent guesses a letter that might be in the word. If it is, the first player writes it on the correct blank space. If the letter is not in the word, he writes the letter off to the side, and begins to draw in the *hangman*, by adding a circle to the noose to represent the head. The opponent continues to guess letters until he can guess the entire word. For every wrong answer, the first player adds one body part to the hangman.

Figure 47

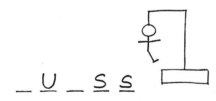

If the body is complete before the opponent can guess the word, the first player is the winner. If the opponent guesses the word correctly before the body is complete, he is the winner and it is then his turn to think of a word.

Tick-tack-toe

This classic brain teaser is also for only two players. You will need a pen and paper to play this game.

Each player chooses if he will be represented by X's or O's. The board is drawn as follows:

The player who has chosen to be X goes first. He places an X in any of the squares within the board. The next player then places an O in another square. The players continue until one player has lined up three of his symbols in a row, either horizontally, diagonally, or vertically. The first player to do this wins the game.

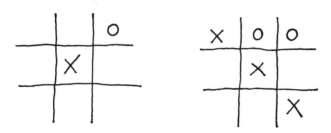

Tick-tack-toe often ends in a draw, as neither player is able to get three symbols in a row. The best games are played when the two players are of equal skill level.